W9-COY-883

THE POLITICS OF IDENTITY IN AUSTRALIA

THE POLITICS
OF IDENTITY
IN AUSTRALIA

Edited by
GEOFFREY STOKES
University of Queensland

CAMBRIDGE
UNIVERSITY PRESS

PUBLISHED BY THE PRESS SYNDICATE OF THE UNIVERSITY OF CAMBRIDGE
The Pitt Building, Trumpington Street, Cambridge CB2 1RP, United Kingdom

CAMBRIDGE UNIVERSITY PRESS
The Edinburgh Building, Cambridge CB2 2RU, United Kingdom
40 West 20th Street, New York, NY 10011–4211, USA
10 Stamford Road, Oakleigh, Melbourne 3166, Australia

First published 1997

Printed in Australia by Brown Prior Anderson

Typeset in Baskerville 10/12 pt

National Library of Australia Cataloguing in Publication data

The politics of identity in Australia.
Bibliography.
Includes index.
1. Nationalism – Australia – 20th century. 2. National
characteristics, Australian. 3. Australia – Social
conditions – 20th century. I. Stokes, Geoff (Geoffrey),
1949– .
155.8994

A catalogue record for this book is available from the British Library

ISBN 0 521 58356 X hardback

For Karen Gillen
and Barry Heath

Contents

Acknowledgements

The editor would like to acknowledge the financial support provided for research into Australian political thought by the Australian Research Council and the Department of Government in the University of Queensland. I would particularly like to thank Karen La Rocca, Rachel Little, Tony Bunney and Carla Taines for their proficiency in preparing this manuscript for publication. In addition, thanks are due to Jeremy Chenoweth for his research assistance and Karen Gillen for her invaluable comments on the project, for proofreading various versions of the manuscript and preparing the index. I must also acknowledge the good judgement and professionalism of two editors: Julia Collingwood who first encouraged me to produce the book and Phillipa McGuinness who brought it all to completion.

Contributors

DENNIS ALTMAN is professor of Politics at La Trobe University and the author of eight books, including *Homosexual: Oppression and Liberation* (rev. edn 1993); *Power and Community: Organisational and Cultural Responses to AIDS* (1994); and a novel, *The Comfort of Men* (1993).

JEFF ARCHER is a senior lecturer in the Department of Politics at the University of New England. He has published various articles and chapters on political theory, Australian and British politics.

M.D. FLETCHER is reader in Politics at the University of Queensland. He is the author of *Contemporary Political Satire: Narrative Strategies in the Postmodern Context* (1987), and editor of *Reading Rushdie: Perspectives on the Fiction of Salman Rushdie* (1994).

WAYNE HUDSON is associate professor in the School of Cultural and Historical Studies at Griffith University. He is author of *The Marxist Philosophy of Ernst Bloch* (1982) and co-editor (with Dieter Freundlieb) of *Reason and Its Other* (1993).

CAROL JOHNSON is a senior lecturer in the Politics Department at the University of Adelaide. She is the author of *The Labor Legacy* (1989) and various articles in the areas of Australian politics and political discourse.

JAMES JUPP is director of the Centre for Immigration and Multicultural Studies at the Australian National University, and Executive Director of the Academy of the Social Sciences in Australia. He edited the bicentennial encyclopedia *The Australian People* (1988), and is the author of many books, reports and articles on immigration and multiculturalism.

JOHN KANE studied politics and philosophy at the University of Bristol and obtained his PhD at the London School of Economics in 1982. After several years in the business world, he returned to academic life and now lectures in political theory at Griffith University.

MARILYN LAKE is professor of History and director of Women's Studies at La Trobe University. Her books include *The Limits of Hope* (1987) and *A Divided Society* (1975). She is also co-author (with P. Grimshaw, A. McGrath and M. Quartly) of *Creating a Nation* (1994), and has published widely on Australian feminism and women's history.

MICHAEL LEACH is a graduate student and tutorial assistant in the Department of Government, University of Queensland, and is currently writing a doctoral thesis on masculinism and Australian socialism.

GREGORY MELLEUISH is a senior lecturer in Politics at the University of Wollongong. He is the author of *Cultural Liberalism in Australia* (1995), co-editor with Peter Gathercole and Terry Irving of *Childe and Australia* (1995), and has written many articles on Australian intellectual history.

HELEN PRINGLE is a lecturer in the School of Political Science at the University of New South Wales. Her teaching and research interests are in the areas of political theory and sexual politics.

GEOFF STOKES is reader in Political Theory at the University of Queensland. He is a co-author of *Accounting for the Humanities* (1991), editor of *Australian Political Ideas* (1994), and the author of various articles and chapters on political theory and philosophy. He has also written on Australian politics and public policy.

GRAEME TURNER is professor of Cultural Studies in the Department of English at the University of Queensland. He is the author and editor of numerous books on Australian literature and popular culture, the most recent of which is *Making it National* (1994).

Introduction

Geoffrey Stokes[1]

We suffer unmistakably, though our land is so ancient, from a
most uncomfortable sense of newness. Oral legend and wonderful stories of bygone days serve to refine the imagination
of the poorer classes in the old countries and to cultivate their
hearts, but the lower classes in Victoria have no such resource.

(Guerin 1886)

This recurrent anxiety to discover and affirm what it is to be
an Australian – to define a distinctive national ethos and type
– to set up Australianity as an identifiable quality and merit
– reminds us that Australia is largely a nineteenth century
creation, and therefore congenitally diseased with nationalism, that 'doctrine invented in Europe at the beginning of the
nineteenth century' to the infinite harm and confusion of
mankind.

(McAuley 1962: 122)

Issues of identity – being clear about our identity and culture
– are an important part of how we as a nation will behave and
present ourselves in the 90s.

(Keating 1994a)

National identity develops in an organic way over time. It may
be changed by cataclysmic events like Gallipoli. But government and their social engineers should not try to manipulate
it, or to create a sense of crisis about identity. Constant debate
about identity implies that we don't already have one or,
worse, that it is somehow inadequate.

(Howard 1995a, 1995b: 3)

Australian cultural nationalists have long pursued the task of discovering, or indeed creating, a distinctive Australian character, ethos, or
tradition. It is only since the early 1970s, however, that Australian

academics have employed the term 'national identity' with regard to such projects (Inglis 1991: 14). What critics like James McAuley (1962: 123) castigated as the search for an 'essence of Australianity' we have now come to understand as a search for 'identity'. In the 1890s such cultural projects were often associated with nationalist political aspirations (see Palmer 1954), and the same may be said of those of the 1990s. Where the cultural nationalists of the 1940s and 1950s had little sympathy with political nationalism (Phillips 1988: 138), recent governmental efforts to promote Australian cultural identity have become part of a program to transform the country's national identity. Nonetheless, such programs form only one element of a multifaceted 'politics of identity' in Australia.

The political usage of the word 'identity' in English-speaking countries has only come about comparatively recently.[2] Unqualified by the adjective 'national', the term first gained popular currency during the 1950s. From its psychoanalytic origins in Erik Erikson's work (e.g. 1951, 1968) on 'identity crises' among American adolescents and American blacks, the concept of identity has risen rapidly to prominence in history and the social sciences. The word 'identity' is now deployed not only to organise our knowledge of certain kinds of contemporary political conflicts, but also to reframe and refine our knowledge of a past in which the term was never used. Such applications are evident in Australia. Since at least 1966, Aboriginal political activists have used the word 'identity' in describing their problems and political objectives (e.g. Kabarli 1966: 21). The outspoken social critics, architect Robin Boyd (1967: 55) and journalist Max Harris (1970), used the term to focus attention upon what they saw as the flaws and insecurities in Australian character and culture. The rudiments of a scholarly discourse of identity, however, are evident somewhat later in the work of the Australian sociologist Jean Martin (1972) and the historians Serle (1973), Walker (1976), and Mandle (1980). Among the historians, Manning Clark (1979) drew specific attention to a 'quest for identity' by white Australians, and Richard White (1981: viii) has called the historical enterprise 'a national obsession'.

Until the 1980s, many of the influential commentators on identity used the term in the singular. They generally assumed the existence or possibility of a single national identity. It was thought that a core of attributes, values and attitudes, albeit one that was slowly evolving, was discernible that marked things and people as authentically Australian. This belief provoked argument over which aspects of national heritage – symbols, events and public ceremonies – could legitimately be regarded as Australian. Controversy inevitably ensued over the meaning and relevance of those symbols and events (Day 1992) – the flag,

Australia Day (Blainey 1991: 37–40), the Bicentenary (Shaw 1988a: 1–15; Bennett et al. 1992) – supposed to signify the expression of an Australian identity.

For some, however, the very discussion of matters of identity and heritage merely affirmed a lack of national self-confidence (McGuinness 1993; see also Howard 1995b). Observations on the strengths or weaknesses of Australian character and national identity paralleled remarks made about the 'cultural cringe' (Phillips 1950) and its opposite, 'cultural overconfidence' (e.g. Wallace-Crabbe 1990). Yet the critics of Australian identity have seldom engaged in purely scholastic inquiries. They have frequently sought practical, remedial outcomes. That is, the 'quest' for identity has been as much about what Australians ought to be, as what they are. From the early invasion and settlement to the present, claims about social, cultural and political identity have often been used in attempts to persuade Australians to reform their ways. Journalists, novelists and historians have not only aimed to delineate the distinguishing characteristics of Australians, but also asked whether these have been adequate to the national tasks deemed important at the time (see essays in Beaumont 1993; also White 1981).

The resolutely practical dimension of this national obsession was apparent in the political rhetoric and policies of former Labor prime minister Paul Keating (1994a), who made it one of his government's explicit goals to develop a clear and coherent national identity (see also Keating 1993d; 1994b). Thus the terms of reference of an advisory committee established to plan for the centenary of Australian federation in 2001 (Department of Prime Minister and Cabinet 1994) included the statement: 'An over-riding objective will be the building of a better sense of identity for the next century.' One of the principal issues at stake was the way Australia presented itself internationally, particularly to those countries to the north with which it conducted the greatest proportion of its overseas trade. In this region Australia had, in the words of Alison Broinowski (1993: 115), an 'image problem'. Keating (quoted in Gordon 1994) explained:

> We can only play a part in it [the region] if we go to the world as one nation, as a nation united and not a nation in any way divided. That is why Australians need to be clear about their identity and proud of it. That is why you can't go hobbling to the world saying: 'Please put us in the big race, but by the way our indigenes don't have a real part of it and by the way, we are still borrowing the monarchy of another country.'

The government contended that the presentation of our national self was inadequate, and assumed that it could be corrected by creating a singular identity that reflected better the current realities. Prior to his

election as prime minister in March 1996, John Howard, the parliamentary leader of the Liberal Party of Australia, rejected Keating's
definition of the problem. Howard (1995b: 3) claimed that, although
Australians shared a common national identity, governments ought not
intervene to shape it. He also contested Keating's version of history.
Howard (1995b: 5) argued correctly that Keating's history served the
political cause of republican nationalism and marginalised Australians
who supported a constitutional monarchy. This conflict of interpretation, however, demonstrates only one narrow dimension of the
politics of identity in Australia. Increasingly, such political statements of
the problem have come under critical review.

Aims of this book

The essays in this book continue that task of criticism by rejecting many
of the assumptions underlying contemporary political debates. The
collection draws upon a range of disciplinary perspectives (political
theory, history, sociology, cultural studies), to examine the broader
political dimensions of identity discourse in Australia. Despite their
often divergent theoretical orientations, the authors would generally
reject the assumption of a singular national identity as a historical fact,
or as a political goal. Although these essays further our understanding
of Australian nationalism, their inquiries extend beyond the topic of
national identity to consider different versions of gender, racial and civic
identity. The primary focus, however, remains on the macro-politics of
identity in Australia. The essays do not consider in detail the important
micro-politics of identity associated with sexual identity, disability
or material cultural heritage. Nor do the contributors examine the
expressions of identity politics arising from allegiance to states and
regions, or those to be found within and between ethnic communities.
Worthy as these topics are, they would require another book. The aims
of this collection of essays are the modest ones of bringing to a wider
audience the variety of ways in which Australians have conceived of their
personal and collective identities, and of indicating the complexity of
identity discourse and its political function.

By attempting to shed light on the past and present political discourses about identity in Australia, the book also aims to contribute to
more enlightened public debate. The intellectual problems surrounding assertions of identity are as much bound up with how we understand
the concept as with the substantive contents of a particular identity. It
will be my task therefore to examine the concept of identity and identity
politics, and to outline the structure of identity discourse. I conclude by
reviewing the content of the different chapters and indicating their

significance for Australian debates. It must be stressed, however, that the following discussion simply sketches the main lines of selected theoretical controversies. In many respects, the account oversimplifies complex issues, and makes no claim to having provided an exhaustive analysis of the literature on identity. For various general surveys of social and political theories of identity and their critics, see Calhoun (1994b), Lash and Friedman (1992b: 1–30), and Hall (1994).[3]

Identity and its politics

At its most rudimentary, to assert an identity is to distinguish oneself or one's group in a certain way and to differentiate oneself or one's group from others.[4] Claiming a personal or group identity is a means of recognising those with whom one shares values, experiences and beliefs, as well as those who are considered to be different (Calhoun 1994b: 20). Schemes of classification and categorisation are essential to social interaction and provide the basis for establishing one's sense of personal and group identity (Lash and Friedman 1992b: 4). Peressini (1993: 16) has offered a basic anthropological account of the essential cognitive functions that identity categories perform:

> Like the concepts we use to put names to things and designate ideas, identity categories ... enable us to put names to ourselves and to others, form some idea of who we are and who other people are, and ascertain the place we occupy along with other people in the world and in society. Lastly, as a means of recognizing the members of a particular group ... identity provides the framework for interpreting, predicting or managing our behaviour or that of other people ...

All representations of collective identity (social, cultural, ethnic) comprise a substantive content which also indicates boundaries between one's own group and another. Symbols, in the form of distinctive marks, badges, insignia and flags for example, are ways of indicating both the content and the limits of group identity. To claim an identity, however, is always to construct an 'other' in more or less pernicious or benign ways.

The formation of personal and group identity is inherently a dynamic, interactive, social process, and an individual's personal identity is inextricably bound up with its relationship to a collectivity. Where there is an 'I', there is also a 'we' and a 'they', as well as various representations of those categories and the relationships between them. One way of describing this relationship is to say that we form our identities dialogically. Charles Taylor (1992: 32–3) explains this in terms that can serve as a metaphor for the process that occurs within both individuals and groups:[5]

> We define our identity always in dialogue with, sometimes in struggle against, the things our significant others want to see in us. Even after we outgrow some of these others – our parents, for instance – and they disappear from our lives, the conversation with them continues within us as long as we live.

Such dialogues may take many forms. The 'significant others' in the dialogue may be real or imagined, political leaders, historians or poets for example, who invoke a variety of collective memories, in written, oral or symbolic form. The nature and consequences of such dialogues in culture and politics provide the problems of identity that concern us here.

Conflict over definitions of identity and who should define identity is not a new phenomenon. From the more virulent manifestations of nationalist ideology and ethnic rivalry to local conflicts over heritage conservation, issues of identity politics have long been with us. Identity politics is the contest over and conflict arising from claims to or about social or group identity. It may be inspired by a sense of threat to values or material resources considered central to the very survival of a group. Such conflict may take the form of theoretical or intellectual disputes, and involves the direct exercise of, or contests over, institutional, material and symbolic power.[6] Identity politics may occur both between different groups, and within a group itself, over interpretations of key traditions, texts, and symbols, or over behaviour and possible courses of action arising from them.

At the heart of contemporary identity politics, conceived as the 'politics of recognition', is the problem of minority and/or oppressed groups, and their assertion of their legitimate interests in a polity. In largely cultural terms, Taylor explains (1992: 25) why this is important:

> our identity is partly shaped by recognition or its absence, often by the *mis*recognition of others, and so a person or group of people can suffer real damage, real distortion if the people or society around them mirror back to them a confining or demeaning or contemptible picture of themselves. Nonrecognition or misrecognition can inflict harm, can be a form of oppression, imprisoning someone in a false, distorted, and reduced mode of being.

Identity politics has its origins in the imposition of collective representations of identity and their reception or resistance by individuals and groups (see also Honneth 1995). Applying derogatory labels to indigenous peoples, gays, women and migrants in societies such as Australia still constitutes one such form of oppression.

Perhaps the most serious political problems arise when certain categories of difference harden into unbridgeable, dogmatic and apparently incommensurable oppositions; between one's own social group and

another, between superiors and inferiors, or friends and foes. The
process may be described in the modernist terminology of agency and
instrumental power. Where a dominant group defines the identity of
another (often subordinate) group in ways that are negative, and that
preclude the possibilities of redefinition or renegotiation, one may
discern what du Preez (1980: 71) has called an 'identity trap'.[7] In these
situations, the identity rhetoric invariably oversimplifies the variety in a
group, preventing recognition of shared qualities or values, and reinforces the isolation, self-absorption and intolerance of both groups.
Poststructuralists of a Foucauldian persuasion might describe the process in a different way, as involving the formation of intractable 'subject
positions' within a 'discursive formation' (Frow 1985; Mouffe 1990: 64).[8]

Where formal institutions and legal codes of conduct enforce narrow
and inflexible definitions of identity, the struggle for recognition
becomes vital. Such was the case under the policies of 'apartheid' in
South Africa and of 'protection' in Australia. These systems of domination explicitly prohibited renegotiation of black or white identity and
confined subordinate groups to a narrowly prescribed range of behaviours, social and economic activities or political options. Identity
traps give impetus to political struggles for recognition and legitimacy.
In such situations one group or the other seeks not only to redefine or
reassert its identity, but to change, reform or overthrow the system of
institutional and ideological power that maintains the identity. A central
point of struggle is that which occurs over the issue of who has the
authority to define any particular identity.

Because of the repression of other forms of political expression,
movements for transforming identity often begin with the process of
cultural revival. This may include recovering older traditions and
languages or inventing new traditions and forms of language, writing
new histories, or creating songs, plays, poems, novels in a new idiom
(see Hutchinson 1987; Smith 1991a). The new histories and literatures
of oppressed and often previously non-literate peoples that go under
the name of postcolonialism represent one such cultural project (Tiffin
1988). The significance of postcolonial critique lies in its particular
emphasis upon *identity*, its conceptualisation, formation and renewal.
This is one of During's (1985: 368) interpretations of postcolonialism
that he describes as 'the name for the products of the ex-colonies' need
for an identity granted not in terms of the colonial power but in
terms of themselves' (see also During 1992). Benedict Anderson
(1991: 205) offers an interpretation of why this occurs, especially following significant 'ruptures' with the past: 'As with modern persons, so it is
with nations. Awareness of being embedded in secular, serial time, with
all its implications of continuity, yet of "forgetting" the experience of

this continuity ... engenders the need for a narrative of "identity".' Nations (or any other community for that matter) may meet the demand for a 'narrative of identity' by creating new histories and traditions.

In liberal capitalist democracies, identity concerns have pressed activists to form political movements, of feminism, gay liberation, and indigenous self-determination. The goals have usually been to seek equal recognition in both symbolic and institutional terms, and even political autonomy. Such movements are represented as engaging in a 'politics of subjectivity', and exemplify the politics of identity. Yet, a distinction must be drawn between those movements that seek cultural recognition and autonomy within a polity and those seeking substantial forms of self-determination such as separate states (Zaretsky 1994: 199). Furthermore, movements of resistance and reform 'from below' do not exhaust the impulses to identity politics in liberal democracies. Political elites may also engage in nationalist identity rhetoric in efforts to win support or reshape the future of a country. Such a project may seek to create new types of men and women as foundations for a new vision of the polity, society or economy.

Identity discourse in politics

Identity discourse in politics usually exhibits a distinctive logic or structure of argument and evidence. From the perspective of modernist social and political theory (of either its traditional or critical varieties), the notion of identity can be understood as one component of a larger conception or theory of human nature. Neither the most abstract political theory nor the most practically engaged political ideology can do without some such conception. That is, within all political thought may be found some minimal assumptions about human needs and capacities. Such conceptions serve to indicate the limits to, or the possibilities for, political action by rulers or the ruled. Just as our conception of human nature operates as a presupposition to political argument (Berry 1986: 133), so notions of identity may perform similar functions. Linnekin and Poyer (1990b: 13) exemplify the basic logic when they write: '"Who I am" now determines what I can and cannot do, can and cannot have, can and cannot be.' As a premise within political argument a conception of identity provides a foundation for political thought and action. This is not to say that the political logic and use of evidence follow any ideal philosophical model. Discourses of identity are generally dynamic, and are reworked or reconstructed according to the political needs of the time.

The need to reform identities may also be the conclusion of a political argument articulated in terms of destiny or opportunity: 'If this is what we as a group or nation have to do, then this is what we ought to become.' In these formulations, an identity can become a source of unity and political action towards common objectives, or, depending upon the political location, a source of division and resistance. However incoherent or ambiguous, claims about group identity therefore may provide the substance of, and rationale for, nationalist political ideologies. Those who speak of the soul of a nation or the spirit of the people and claim to have divined its historic mission deploy powerful ideological resources. Adolf Hitler and national socialism are possibly the most infamous examples of this political strategy.

As we have seen, the assertion of identity inevitably requires construction of an 'other', and political struggles over identity call for the reconstruction of outside groups as 'others'. As suggested above, certain narratives of group identity, such as those of nationalist ideology, inevitably overstate commonalities within a group and exaggerate differences with others considered alien. The protagonists may tend towards 'essentialism'. That is, they may invoke the essential and ineradicable cultural traits of their group, and denounce the culture and values of the outsiders as inherently evil or dangerous.

The resources drawn upon for the construction of such identity claims are generally historical (such as stories, narratives, texts and material culture), which are deployed to establish the authenticity of the interpretation of the group. Steedman (1991: 50) has described the process as follows:

> In the project of finding an identity through the process of historical identification, the past is searched for something (someone, some group, some series of events) that confirms them as they want to be, and feel in some measure that they already are.

Hobsbawm and Ranger (1983) have demonstrated how traditions are constantly being invented or refashioned according to contemporary needs. Thus, the question of the authenticity of the traditions, the historical, literary and cultural heritage used in claiming an identity, may become a central focus of the political discourse surrounding the claim. In the construction of identities and 'narratives of identity', however, there are no definitive arbiters of historical judgement, if only because the status of arbiter is often that which is most highly contested. The recognition that identities are malleable and that identity discourse involves 'inventiveness' raises the vexed issues of the epistemological status of such inventions. The social constructivist view is that narratives of national identity and history are indeed purely inventions created to serve the political purposes of the present (see e.g. Hobsbawm and Ranger 1993). People who see themselves as members of the nation, for example, are simply part of an 'imagined community' (Anderson 1991). Anthony Smith, however, contests the more extreme relativist assumptions in these interpretations and argues that such identities and histories are never mere fictions. Not just any past can be appropriated (Smith 1991b: 359):

> Traditions, myths, history and symbols must all grow out of the existing, living memories and beliefs of the people who are to compose the nation. Their popular resonance will be greater the more continuous with the living past they are shown to be.

Pierre Bourdieu takes a similar line with reference to the efficacy of symbolic power. He argues (Bourdieu 1989: 23) that symbolic power, 'the power to make things with words', depends on the degree to which it is 'founded in reality'.[9] For such reasons it would be preferable to conceive the process of history creation as a reconstruction rather than invention. Like all cultural constructs, therefore, identities are founded upon different measures of authentic inheritance (such as ideas, material objects or geographical spaces), judicious interpretation, and unconscious selection. Another difficult question raised by postcolonial critique, but one also applicable to other movements engaging in identity politics, is whether the cultural products and political outcomes represent 'resistance' to the oppressive culture or 'incorporation' into it. Responses to such questions, however, can only be determined provisionally and by detailed investigation of the consequences for those concerned.

In summary, wherever identity is given prominence there exists a continually unfolding political project based upon unrealised ideals and aspirations (Calhoun 1994b: 28–9). The politics of identity involves political contest over the content, boundaries and practical implications of the group identity, as well as dispute over who has authority to define this identity. The public rhetoric and argument surrounding this process may be understood as a form of political thought. Such political thought offers a reinterpretation of the past from the perspective of a particular present, and articulates a vision of a future, often different in kind, and arguably better than life in the present. That future, however, may be based upon visions of community life to be found in mythical or romantic conceptions of the past. In these instrumentalist terms, a conception, discourse or theory of identity is simply another type of theoretical resource within a political ideology. Those engaged in identity politics may draw upon the universalist political discourses, such

as liberalism or socialism, or particular local claims to recognition such
as those of ethnicity or culture, or a combination of universalist and
local appeals. Drawn as they are from a variety of sources, texts, images
and symbols, such arguments will rarely exhibit the features of formal analytical political philosophy. Nonetheless, they remain of vital
importance in political life.

The chapters

The essays in this book display the interplay of the various elements of
identity discourse outlined above, and in some respects also mark out
the political identity of the writers and their fields of inquiry. The first
part offers three perspectives on the theorising of identity in Australia.
Jeff Archer introduces the categories of traditionalism, modernism,
postmodernism and postcolonialism as theoretical lenses through which
we may interpret intellectual and political debates about national
identity in Australia. From a modernist orientation he advocates the
affirmation and construction of a collective version of national identity
conceived as citizenship. He argues that this strategy will allow
Australians to build tolerant unities out of their diversities and provide
the bases for political action to solve common problems.

Carol Johnson's chapter provides an explicit comparative study
of identity politics at the national level. She examines the problem of
explaining the different versions of identity discourse in Australia and
Great Britain, with reference to British cultural studies theory and the
work of Stuart Hall. Johnson outlines the nature of appeals to personal
identity made by political leaders in Australia (Bob Hawke and Paul
Keating) and Great Britain (Margaret Thatcher and John Major). In
particular, Johnson shows how Thatcher's construction of an individual,
consumerist British identity is not comparable in content to those ideal
images of the individual represented as socially co-operative and non-
consumerist by Bob Hawke. Johnson's account demonstrates both the
utility and the limitations of transferring theory devised for one national
context to another.

Gregory Melleuish shows how advocates of national identity must
negotiate both universalist and particularist concerns and argues for a
conception of identity that entails obligations as well as rights. He
provides an account of the historical and intellectual origins of national
identity in Europe, set in terms of the struggle between what he calls
'Machiavellian nationalism' and 'Hegelian internationalism'. Melleuish
identifies similar intellectual processes at work in Australia where the
universalist collective identities of Christianity and liberalism have often
clashed with nationalist identities designed to promote particularist

national ideals. In such conflicts, Christian universalists and genuine liberal internationalists (as opposed to economic rationalists) have often been marginalised in Australian politics. Nevertheless, Melleuish claims that an ethical concern for humanity can be brought into harmony with the particularism of national identity. He argues that an allegiance to humanity does not require us to deny the obligations we owe to fellow citizens.

The second part addresses four perspectives on the role of gender and sexuality in the history and politics of Australian identities. Michael Leach explores the problem of masculine identity in early Australian socialism and reveals the existence and rhetorical function of three categories of masculinism, namely platform, androcentric and affective masculinism. Based upon an analysis of the writings of the utopian socialist William Lane, the trade unionists and Labor leaders W.G. Spence and W.M. (Billy) Hughes, as well as scrutiny of the labour journal the *Worker*, Leach indicates the contours of the struggle over masculinism and feminism in the labour movement from 1890 to 1920. Leach's central insight is that Lane sincerely attempts to shift the ruling definition of 'manly independence' along feminist lines, but that he could still only envisage autonomy for men and dependence for women. Lane's analysis remained bound to an understanding of class oppression defined primarily in relation to masculine identity.

Marilyn Lake surveys the evolution of Australian feminist thought about national identity and citizenship in the first four decades of this century and shows how Australian feminists were often caught between multiple allegiances to nation, race, and women. Lake brings to light the varieties of Australian feminist nationalism, and the contradictions that racialism and sisterhood brought to their political discourses. Early feminist nationalists, for example, conceived of their national identity in terms of racial supremacy, their political capacity as newly enfranchised citizens, and even motherhood as a national service. Eventually, Australian feminists came to reject their previous self-understanding in racialist terms and gave priority to a common or international female identity. In so doing, Australian feminists reconstructed their conception of the other, which in turn created a larger space for them to be defined by their moral difference from all men, and as the bearers of civilisation in their region.

Helen Pringle takes up the issue of the role of men and women in war and points out the sources of one conception of an Australian civic identity. It is conjectured that war is best conceived, not just as male love of violence and destruction, but as a civic romance, requiring women as an audience or chorus to its drama. According to Pringle, the memory of war plays a role in creating an Australian civic identity that involves 'a celebration of male bodies and virile death'. Drawing upon histories of ancient Greece and Rome, and her interpretation of key Australian texts, Pringle contends that war does not rest on a suppression of love among men, but requires its expression, and in so doing, male virility becomes a form of civic identity.

Dennis Altman outlines a number of the controversies about the origins and preferred forms of homosexual identity in Australian gay communities. He stresses the political significance of struggles over identity for stigmatised groups in society and points out the uneasy co-existence of social constructionists and essentialists in gay self-identification. Altman takes issue with the postmodernist challenge that 'queer theory' presents not only to gay and lesbian identities but also to the possibility of effective gay political organisation. He argues further that analysis of the social and political movements based upon homo-sexuality can provide insights into broader problems of politics and identity.

The themes of race, place and citizenship provide the focus for essays in the third part. John Kane reassesses the White Australia policy and its bearing upon past and present understandings of national identity. He takes up the issue of which values and traditions must be repudiated from the Australian past and which can be recovered with reference to the political debates about White Australia. In particular, Kane out-lines the arguments that supported a 'thick' or rich racialist concep-tion of Australian national identity, but also draws attention to early claims about a 'thin' conception of political identity. Excised from their racialist assumptions, those arguments advocating the moral equality of citizens in a democracy remain even more important for a society that conceives of itself as multicultural. Kane contends that, where cultural diversity is celebrated, the need for a civic identity, with a charter of both rights and obligations, becomes all the more pressing.

James Jupp draws attention to the important point that, by setting restrictions on immigration and criteria for granting citizenship, the national governments of Australia have consciously shaped national identity. Debates on such matters have provided the stimulus to identity politics for over two hundred years and Jupp surveys the origins and evolution of its most recent manifestation in the policy of multi-culturalism. He canvasses the range of ideological disputes over this policy and demystifies a number of the more serious criticisms made over the years. Finally, like several other contributors, Jupp questions the utility of creating a strong sense of national identity. Projecting a strong civic identity, for example, brings with it a commitment to liberty and human rights at home and abroad, whose pursuit may impede Australian trading relations with more authoritarian governments. On the other hand, promoting a clear cultural identity runs the domestic risk of suppressing awareness of the tolerant diversity that lies at the heart of multiculturalism.

Wayne Hudson and Geoffrey Stokes address current controversies about Australia's place in Asia and show the problems these raise for national identity. It is argued that advocates of strong economic and cultural engagement with Asia tend to rely upon either one of two different deterministic conceptions of place as means of influencing political agendas. The logic of the first argument is that because of our physical geography Australians ought to participate in the dramatic economic growth occurring to our Asian north. The second line of argument situates Australia in an 'Asia-Pacific' region whose economic dynamics we are urged to embrace through the Asia-Pacific Economic Co-operation (APEC) process. Hudson and Stokes suggest, however, that in both cases the arguments rely upon untheorised and relatively unsophisticated notions of place, and consequently cannot provide the required intellectual support either for economic policy or for changes in our cultural and economic identities.

Geoffrey Stokes traces the evolution of two conceptions of identity in Aboriginal political thought and demonstrates their function at the different levels of Australian politics. The first conception of Aboriginal identity, evident in many political arguments in the 1930s through to the 1950s, stressed the sameness of Aborigines to whites, in support of claims to equal citizenship rights. The second notion of Aboriginal identity retains the sense of political identity as equal citizens, but also asserts an Aboriginality based upon cultural difference, in support of claims to land, resources and even political autonomy. This chapter stresses the practical political significance of identity discourse among Aboriginal and Torres Strait Islander peoples.

The final part includes two chapters that consider different representations of Australian identities in recent Australian literature and film and discuss their political implications. Don Fletcher explores issues of identity raised by his study of two recent novels by David Malouf and Peter Carey. Drawing upon insights drawn from postcolonial critique, Fletcher departs from a traditional interpretive strategy deployed in Australian literature, which focuses upon cultural identity, to direct attention to different images and implications of political identity. In Malouf's *Remembering Babylon* can be discerned, among other things, various problems of political identification among the members of a small, isolated, rural community in nineteenth-century Queensland. Fletcher argues that Carey's novel *The Tax Inspector* demonstrates the existence of two distinct types of political identity in contemporary urban Australia. Fletcher indicates the characteristics of a 'participant' and 'subject' political culture among Carey's characters, which in turn fosters two kinds of political identity and raises larger questions about the legitimacy of liberalism. Fletcher demonstrates how both Malouf and Carey continually challenge the traditional masculinist and racist stereotypes of Australian cultural *and* political identity.

Graeme Turner's chapter reflects upon the relationship between contemporary Australian film and national identity. He explains how the Australian films produced in the 1970s, the first decade of revival, were widely considered to be part of an official exercise in nation formation. In representing Australians to themselves and to others, Australian films played a role in attempting to shape national identity, but often along the lines of the older masculinist stereotypes celebrated by the 'Australian legend'. In the second decade of revival, however, certain shifts in orientation are evident towards making films that portray a plurality or hybridity of Australian cultural identities or for which national identity is simply not an issue. Turner speculates upon the historical and ideological reasons for this change, attributing it both to a more refined understanding of nation and nationalism and to the economic evolution of the film industry itself. Turner contends that the Australian film industry has learnt to 'live with difference' and has begun to construct unifying national discourses that transcend the regressive and exclusivist images of the past.

Significance for Australian politics

Can any theoretical or practical conclusions about national identity be drawn for Australian politics from these studies? Can we discern, for example, any uniform and coherent set of characteristics that we may plausibly call an Australian identity? The brief review of theory and the Australian examples would suggest not. The essays indicate explicit political attempts to persuade us to adopt singular national identities, but they also demonstrate a diversity, fluidity and constant evolution of Australian images of identity. Australians have had access to and aspired to many different types of cultural, political and sexual identity, and they have understood and represented themselves in multiple and contested ways. These observations lead us to ask whether this fluidity and multiplicity of identities constitute a problem. Do Australians need to have a strong sense of national identity? Answers to these questions, however, will depend upon one's political and theoretical perspective, as well as historical context. A plausible theoretical response would be that we ought not promote a single identity of the old racial, ethnic and nationalist kinds, if only because there is no such identity (apart from perhaps a civic identity) to which coherent or persuasive political appeal can be made. In any case, appeals to a 'thick' sense of identity are generally exclusivist, harmful and unjust. This does not mean that in times of crisis such appeals will not, or even ought not, be made.

In Australia, committed nationalists of the conservative (Blainey 1984; Howard 1995b: 1; Mandle 1980) and labourist (Keating 1994a) kind would tend to argue for a strong sense of national identity, but may disagree on its content. Certain liberals (social and classical) and social democrats would tend to be more internationalist and universalist, placing more emphasis on our identification with humanity, or possibly even class, or the whole of creation. Nevertheless, recent arguments for replacing national identity with a notion of civic identity, have relied as much upon 'communitarian' accounts of national heritage (e.g. Kukathas 1993; Horne 1994a, 1994b) as upon universalist (liberal, democratic) principles.

Postmodernists would also reject the notion of strong nationalism, not in terms of universalism but usually in terms of its opposite, 'difference'. Those more politically astute postmodernists who retained the notion of identity would acknowledge both its ubiquity and its conventional character. They may argue for identities that were the subject of negotiation, paying due attention to the consequences of the process and its eventual product (Yeatman 1994: 105). A postmodern account oriented to justice, for example, may require the granting of public resources to those who see themselves as significantly 'different', so that they can find and express their voice in the political process, or challenge and negotiate their position in various hierarchies of oppression.

The general problem remains, however, that we are always born into a particular community and culture. We must live daily with categories of identity more finely differentiated and emotionally charged than those of 'humanity' or 'difference'. Given the intractable social reality of competing identity claims, and given that we cannot avoid categorising and differentiating ourselves from others, how best may we deal with the process? We still need to ask which 'thick' identity claims ought to be recognised and which ought to be rejected. Ought some types of identity claims be accorded a higher priority than others?

On these questions most postmodern approaches do not offer much guidance beyond possibly the rejection of unified identities, especially those founded on patriarchical and authoritarian values. Because of its refusal to engage in modernist forms of prescription, and its lack of a sophisticated normative basis, postmodernist thought cannot easily categorise those differences it would consider worth fostering and those it would consider harmful. In extreme versions (e.g. Docker 1995), the affirmation of multiplicity and indeterminacy, and the importance of micro-narratives, effectively dissolve any coherent claims to political relevance.

Even with their highly developed normative sense of value, mapped onto formal institutions of law and justice, modernists also have difficulties. Debates between liberal individualists and communitarians over the very basis of political action are also debates over the character of political identity. They are debates over whether the 'I' or the 'we' has, or ought to have, priority in political society (Strong 1992: 1–2). Such concerns provide the foundation for dispute over the propriety and viability of granting special overriding rights to a group based upon claims to a distinctive cultural identity that requires protection (see Kukathas 1992; Kymlicka 1992; Yeatman 1994: 81–2).

Few of the essays below raise the problem of the incommensurability or irreconcilability of different identity claims, and where the issue is recognised the faith in democratic accommodation in Australia remains strong. In political practice, Australian governments have begun to set clear limits and boundaries in such matters. As Jupp (this volume) shows, the more recent official meanings of multiculturalism have shifted to incorporate 'loyalty to Australia at all times and to her institutions and values and traditions'. Similarly the new oath of allegiance (1994) pledges the loyalty of new citizens to 'Australia and its people, whose democratic rights I share, whose rights and liberties I respect, and whose laws I will uphold and obey'. In these and other reforms can be seen fledgling attempts to construct a new national civic identity that has priority over ethnic, racial and religious ones. These initiatives have set not only certain kinds of identity priorities but also the boundaries for adjudication between different and competing identity claims within Australia.

A number of the studies in this book pursue a parallel path. Perhaps because of their awareness of the dangers associated with racialism and ethnic nationalism, the writers assume a need to reinforce or create some minimum sense of commonality between diverse groups living in the same country. In this regard, a number of the essayists advocate the development of a 'thin' civic identity of citizenship to which all Australians could owe allegiance. Nevertheless, the grounds for supporting this identity strategy can be either philosophical or historical or both, and they still may not solve the problems identified. Jürgen Habermas (1992: 3), for example, points out the historical evolution of a European understanding that: 'The nation of citizens does not derive its identity from some common ethnic and cultural properties, but rather from the *praxis* of citizens who actively exercise their civil rights.' Nonetheless, his advocacy of a 'post-national' civic identity imbued with 'constitutional patriotism' (Habermas 1992: 7) is largely based upon moral-philosophical grounds. Habermas' proposal recognises that a number of different 'nationalities' may be drawn together under the inclusivist umbrella of 'citizenship', and requires implementing the procedural rationality of a deliberative democracy.[10]

Although the founding arguments are somewhat different, the civic identity derived from critical theory shares much with an older liberalism. It is arguable that, for all its faults, liberal and social democratic political theory is premised upon a practical recognition of difference, and the necessity for its peaceful and rational accommodation and resolution. The rational agent that lies at the heart of classical liberal theory is the very model of a political identity that can rise above pernicious difference to recognise one's commonality with all other human beings. Political life in Karl Popper's 'open society' and Habermas' 'public sphere' requires similar virtues. Nevertheless, the character requirements of a democratic and tolerant personality, even if one could obtain precise agreement on these traits, have rarely been easy to inculcate for the mass of the population. Furthermore, if civic identity is to replace national identity, then perhaps we must ask what affective resources may be relevant to the task. What symbols and images, for example, can motivate one to a love of democracy?

Chandran Kukathas (1993: 149), among others, has argued that we would be on surer ground if we conceive of national identity not in terms of 'national character', but as 'national inheritance or a tradition'. By this he means 'a history' and 'a set of legal and political institutions'. Although he acknowledges the possibility of conflicts of interpretation, Kukathas (1993: 149) slides quickly over two hundred years of historical and political dispute to write: 'Yet insofar as a common history and common political institutions are recognised, we can speak of a political community and of a "national identity".' Kukathas is confident of both his logic and his substantive judgement about Australian history and political institutions. He may be right, but such a strategy remains well within the confines of the identity discourse outlined above. It confronts the very same difficulties of historical selection and interpretation as those claims about national character he wants to avoid.

Historical claims about citizenship identity are not unproblematic (see also Thomas 1993). Various institutions of social citizenship, involving welfare and social security rights, have figured prominently in Australian history, but their character and value have been hotly disputed. The concern for the rights of workers understood as economic citizens has been a central part of the flawed institutions of Australian arbitration and conciliation since their inception. The institutions of welfare and arbitration are founded upon those less definitive types of identity claims about Australians wanting to give people a 'fair go' (e.g. Horne 1994a). Here we must ask whether we ought to recover an actual social liberal and labourist heritage, for example, or an unfulfilled social democratic one.

Those who advocate the citizenship option, in Australia and elsewhere, are often too imprecise about what kinds of citizenship – classical liberal, social liberal, republican, or social democratic – ought to be encouraged (see Kymlicka and Norman 1994). Should we not also be concerned with inculcating the virtues required of an international citizenship identity (see Hirsch and Hirsch 1990)? It is often assumed that the minimal attributes needed for formal political citizenship in the nation state are all that is required. Such assumptions also ignore a major thrust of modern social democratic thought that has been to extend citizenship rights into the social and economic sphere. Furthermore, even at the formal, legal levels of voting and access to social security, the citizenship advocates have not confronted the range of issues about recognition and entitlement that have to be resolved. On these grounds, the ideal of constructing a unifying Australian civic identity remains just one more, albeit more defensible, identity project. Like other projects, it needs further elaboration, based upon interpretations both of abstract principles and of national heritage. It would also be subject to many of the same patterns of contest over power, resources and symbolic authority that have occurred around apparently more substantive forms of identity.

Notes

1. I am indebted to April Carter, Karen Gillen, Wayne Hudson, John Kane, Don Fletcher, Graeme Turner, Jim Walter and Martin Leet for their critical comments upon early drafts of this chapter.
2. For a general account of the older philosophical debates over 'personal identity', see Penelhum (1967).
3. For discussions of identity and difference, see Zaretsky (1994) and Grosz (1994). Further accounts may be found in Connolly (1991) and Giddens (1991).
4. This section draws upon Gillen's account (1993) on how 'heritage' is used in the construction of collective identity.
5. For two critiques of Taylor's arguments, see Rorty (1994) and Dumm (1994).
6. On symbolic power see Bourdieu (1989).
7. The philosopher Martin Hollis (1977: 106) has described an 'identity crisis' as an affliction which 'strikes when what I am no longer accounts for who I am, because what I do is no longer the acting out of what I have chosen to become. The reasons for action supplied to me no longer function as my own good reasons'. See also Erikson (1968: 295–320).

8.   Michel Foucault's early discussions of these concepts may be found in his *The Archaeology of Knowledge* (1974: 92–6, 31–9). See also During (1995) on discourse.
9.   Bourdieu (1989: 23) explains: 'It is only if it is true, that is, adequate to things, that description makes things. In this sense, *symbolic power is a power of consecration or revelation*, the power to consecrate or to reveal things that are already there.'
10. See also the critique by Matustik (1993).

Theorising Identity

CHAPTER 1

Situating Australian National Identity in Theory and Practice

Jeff Archer[1]

Australians are now confronted with a considerable choice on the menu of national identity. Some of the dishes are presented as the only authentic ones, but there is growing belief that the entire cornucopia lacks authenticity. This chapter canvasses a number of commonly used theoretical distinctions that can frame our understanding of political and historical arguments about identity. These distinctions are then deployed to illuminate both intellectual controversies over Australian identity and recent appeals to national identity in Australian politics. Contrary to the assumptions in much postmodernist thought, it is argued that recourse to collective representations of identity is essential for a politics directed towards alleviating serious social, economic and environmental problems. But contrary to much modernist identity rhetoric, it is argued that these appeals to collective identity need not reproduce the chauvinism or exclusivism of nationalist ideology. Within a careful elaboration of democratic citizenship may be developed a model of a political identity which is both tolerant and inclusive.

Before any discussion is possible about the concrete use of identity in history or national politics, we must first indicate a range of theoretical assumptions about how we may best organise our knowledge about the nature of identity. One way of examining arguments about Australian national identity is to categorise them in terms of the concepts of traditionalism, modernism, postmodernism, and postcolonialism. To use these concepts is to make a further assumption about the import-ance of ideas in human history, and the extent to which these ideas can be classified into spaces, periods or epochs which are themselves to be identified by their contrasting ways of thinking about the nature of identity. And a further implication is contained in this classi-fication. This is that we can know why some ideas become obsolete or anachronistic; that we have some vantage point from which to see the history of ideas and account for their transformations. We cannot attempt to explicate all these points in this short chapter, and we will have to paint some complex theoretical positions with rather broad brushstrokes. It would also be impossible to provide here a full account of the uses and abuses of the concept of national identity and to discuss the enormous amount of literature on Australian culture. With these provisos in mind, let us examine some of the characteristic assumptions that are involved in identity thinking, and in representative examples of thinking about Australian national identity.

Identities: Modern and traditional

The term 'modernity' is perhaps the most familiar, if also most contested, way of categorising the period of European and world history since the Enlightenment. What is signified by the term modernity is not only the distinctive character and evolution of society, economy, culture and politics, but also its modes of knowledge and assumptions about what it means to be a person or a self. In classifying this period as modern, one generally understands it to be characterised by the growth of capitalist industrial economies and large-scale technologies, the shift to a social order based upon individual merit and achievement, the spread of systems of cultural meaning based more upon material possessions or one's place of work in large public or private bureaucracies – or perhaps even the loss of meaning – and finally, the rise of liberal democracy. Central to modernity, however, are assumptions of historical progress and greater certainty in scientific and philosophical knowledge based upon instrumental forms of rationality. Modernity is also characterised by a widespread belief in the universal application of its dominant political ideas such as liberalism or socialism and their reliance upon abstract principles of individual and social rights.

The distinguishing characteristic of the identity of modern individuals is the supposition that they are 'unified' subjects who are essentially free to be the creators of their own destiny. In their ideal form, such personal identities are unbounded by the constraints of local or ethnic culture or religion. Such features allow for an increasing number of diverse demands to be made upon individuals, and to which they must respond. In the words of Lash and Friedman (1992b: 5):

> Mature modernist identity ... meant a coherent and measured acceptance and taking on of these plural demands. It also included two temporal elements. First, responsibility in the modern meant responsibility for the consequences of one's actions, a more and more difficult task in an increasingly complex society. Identity also had to do with the temporality of our existence.

As in all identity discourses, these images of the modern identity gain their meaning from a sense of the other, in this case that which has been lost from the premodern periods of history, or what have been called 'traditional' or tribal forms of society. The usual images of the premodern identities are those that are essentially local, founded in complex systems of religious or spiritual meaning. Those persons who inhabit a premodern world are thought to understand themselves primarily in terms of their close bonds to their community. Such bonds and personal identities are formed by their immediate face to face interactions, and individual destiny is inherently bound to that of the group, clan or tribe into which they were born. Lash and Friedman's (1992b: 4) description is again apt:

> Thus pre-modern identity can be very generally understood as externally (or in Kant's sense 'heteronomously') determined. In 'tribal' societies it is kinship-ordered cosmologies that define identity in terms of deciding *who* one someone is. In the archaic civilizations of the world religions, it is a transcendent godhead or pantheon or hierarchy of deities which take on these nominating powers, though the secular realm is clearly on the rise.

Nevertheless, such conceptions of traditional identities can also be understood as arguments about an idealised past which can be used to legitimate a modernist program (Gunnell 1978). In effect, traditionalism is a modernist claim on history. It is not the same as a premodern identity. It may be ventured that modernist identities are nostalgic but self-referential attempts to compensate for the loss of premodernist belonging. William Connolly (1988: 1) depicts the conventional account of this loss and its replacements:

> Modernity has lost a world of rich tradition, a secure place in the order of being, a well-grounded morality, a spiritual sensibility, an appreciation of hierarchy, an attunement to nature; and these vacant places have been filled by bureaucracy, nationalism, rampant subjectivism, an all-consuming state, a consumer society, a commercialized world or perhaps a disciplinary society.

Yet a different and more positive interpretation of the difference between modernity and traditionalism is possible. For example, Karl Popper (1966) has represented the political tensions between democratic modernity (which includes its ancient philosophical precursors) and authoritarian traditionalism as a struggle between the 'open society' and the 'closed society'. As Popper recognised, the task of forming tolerant individuals capable of free and critical judgement, essentially modern liberal rationalist identities, confronts constant pressures to retreat to the safety and security of traditionalism (Stokes 1995).

Among the many competitors for political identity, nationalist ideologies provide perhaps the most powerful and paradoxical attractions. In their quest for national power and unity, and the formation of a distinctive national identity, nationalists rely upon appeals to tradition and may advocate the suppression of alternative identities, either ethnic or intellectual, which would enable criticism of the nationalist project. The sub-variety of exclusivist ethnic nationalism is the basis for much violent conflict around the world, exemplified in the aftermath of the regime changes in Eastern Europe and the Soviet Empire in the late 1980s. At times of rapid and often violent change, exclusivist nationalism may offer the security of identity and defined place in a larger group.

Identities: Postmodern and postcolonial

Since the 1960s, many commentators have identified the onset of a new period of history accompanied by a new philosophical and aesthetic outlook, both of which have implications for how we understand identity. The terms used to describe these shifts, postmodernism and postmodernity, are widely used, but there is little agreement about their usage. Nevertheless, it is worthwhile to distinguish here between *postmodernity*, which is a sociological description of aspects of contemporary culture and economy, possibly most evident in North America (see Harvey 1990a; Jameson 1991), and *postmodernism*, an intellectual movement which rejects what it takes to be a series of ideas about freedom, reason and progress inherited from the European Enlightenment (Lyotard 1984). Conceived as a new era of history, postmodernity encompasses such diverse sociological and economic tendencies as the rise of mass society, the growth of new electronic information technology, deindustrialisation, and the onset of late capitalism.

As a philosophy, postmodernism incorporates arguments about the loss of legitimacy and failure of Enlightenment ideals, the collapse of the moral and aesthetic bases of modernism, and the deconstruction of the 'meta-narratives' or ideologies of modernity. Even concepts such as nature and the future can no longer be taken for granted (Rose 1991). Postmodernist thinkers influenced by poststructuralists such as Michel Foucault also query the modernist assumptions about the links between personal identity, the self, reason and power (see Rabinow 1984; O'Sullivan 1993). For Foucault (1974: 116–17), there were no subjects, agents or discrete personal identities in the modernist sense, only 'subject positions' formed by a 'discourse' or a series of statements in a wider 'discursive formation'. In such discourses there is no truth, only discursive regimes of truth or political struggles over truth (see Foucault in Rabinow 1984: 72–5).

Other postmodernist thinkers, influenced by the French philosopher Jacques Derrida (see 1978), have taken up the notion of 'difference' (originally the neologism *différance*) as an attempt to overcome the alleged exclusive and oppressive antagonism to those 'others' which lie outside a given identity. Those deploying the notion of difference recognise that a national identity, for example, is constructed on an animosity to other nations, or ethnic groups within a nation. It is argued further that invocations of national identity also work to disempower and exclude a range of different people from the practical working of the nation as a democratic community (Young 1990a). Typically, these 'others' include women, homosexuals, the elderly, the disabled, migrants, ethnic and racial minorities and the indigenous population, as well as all foreigners. Nevertheless, the notion of 'difference' operates as a postmodern version of identity (Connolly 1991), albeit one which seeks to dispense with binary oppositions.

These postmodern versions of identity offer new images of substantive content founded upon different theorisations of the nature of history, society and the individual, as well as greater pessimism about the possibilities of progress in knowledge. In terms of content, individuals living in the postmodern world are seen as having a multiplicity of potential identities and being able to make a range of identity choices or experiments. Such choices, however, may be based on many criteria – aesthetic, political or psychological – but debate occurs over the extent of personal choice or social control involved (see Lash and Friedman 1992b: 6–7).

While there are many attractions to the political practices of avoiding scapegoats, challenging oppressive authority, and questioning the limits to our senses of self with irony and playful humour (Connolly 1991: 67), postmodernism brings with it the danger of a slide into cynicism, meaninglessness and political disempowerment. When reality and truth lose meaning, when there is only difference constructed through discourse, and when no communal ethic can be appealed to, there are few grounds for normative choice and for determining which differences ought to be fostered and which ought to be repressed. It is therefore difficult to avoid a retreat into either political quietism or purely individual resistance.

As an intellectual orientation, much postmodernist thought questions the idea of a unified and legitimate political community; a polity with a set of common ethical objectives. Just as it denies the certainties of meaning in modernist ideological thought (Eagleton 1980), a postmodern appeal to the indeterminate and discursive readings of textuality also undermines any notion of political theory as a guide to political action. It is wrong, however, to see the intellectual movement of postmodernism as a unified world view, just as it would be a mistake not to expect major disagreements among modernist thinkers (see Frow 1991). For example, according to Christopher Norris (1992), Derrida, if not all his disciples, subscribes to a version of reality that is not relativistic, and this is to be contrasted with writers such as Baudrillard for whom there are no longer any reliable standards for confirming our claims about reality and truth.

Anna Yeatman is one theorist aware of both the deficiencies and the political promise of postmodernism. Yeatman seeks to establish a postmodern critical theory that will transform or deconstruct modernist emancipatory politics. The aim is to open up a space for contestation, debate and dialogue that does not presuppose a 'regulative, sovereign normative authority' (Yeatman 1994: x) or a unified self or subject (see also Yeatman 1995). Yeatman's (1994: 7) postmodern politics of difference, however, still assumes the possibility of a type of agency that provides some minimal commonality between divergent and incommensurable political projects. Yet Yeatman (1994: 7) does not claim any strong or final universal meaning for emancipation, seeing it as 'always relative to an established, discursive order which is already of the past'.

Related to postmodernism in its attack on Eurocentric rationality, and also to much anti-Enlightenment feminist thought, is the concept of postcolonialism, particularly in the way it is used in cultural studies. In this discourse-based series of arguments, the formerly marginalised and colonised peoples of the world make a bid for discursive power through deconstructing the knowledge found in the texts (documents, histories and literature) of their colonial oppressors and of those indigenous elites who have retained colonialist values and culture (Spivak 1990). Many exercises in postcolonialism have a somewhat different political agenda from those of much postmodernism, and also retain a stronger sense of the possibility of human agency and human 'subjectivity' (see Mishra and Hodge 1993). A central task of postcolonialism is to reclaim (there is an element of traditionalism here) distinctive identities (or differences) in national ideology or culture.

On one interpretation of postcolonialism, Australian writings also can be put alongside those formerly disempowered writings of Africa and Asia, and contribute to a new inversion of values (Tiffin 1991). That is, the former ruling values, assumptions and culture of the colonial power can be rejected or transformed and that which had previously been viewed in a negative light can be celebrated. This process is supposed to lead to new powerful versions of national identity that avoid the problems of Eurocentric rationality and power. Such an approach has some advantages for critics discussing Australian national identity. It conveniently allows us to abandon the ideological stereotypes and assumptions left in old arguments about the tyranny of distance and the cultural cringe. But, like the further shores of postmodernism, post-colonial arguments for inversion are likely to be at the expense of any shared ethical position. Political theory becomes impossible and, for all its apparent radical political criticism, this position on identity does not allow any basis for concerted political action. These arguments operate primarily at the level of culture and do not impinge directly upon problems of institutional or economic power.

National identity in Australian history and culture

Many of the theoretical orientations towards national identity may be found in the mass of literature and public commentary about what it means to be an Australian. At its most basic, this amounts to no more than a series of competing modernist claims to an exclusive and combative version of Australian national identity. A typical example of this was evident in the exchange between John Singleton and Phillip Adams on the television program, *A Current Affair*, as reported in the *Sydney Morning Herald* on 11 September 1992. Here Singleton questioned Adams' Australianness because Adams didn't drink, smoke, watch football or go to the races. Singleton's celebration of the ocker stereotype as a badge of the fair dinkum Aussie has proved a powerful ingredient in some slick advertising campaigns, but it excludes millions of Australian citizens from this uniform version of the authentic Australian nation.

The same problem of stereotypical, exclusivist authenticity can be found in some of the academic literature on Australian national identity (Archer 1990). Russel Ward's (1966) account of the typical Australian is possibly the epitome of the modernist approach to national identity. From his research into popular writings, poems, ballads and bush songs, Ward draws a number of conclusions about the nature of a distinctive national mystique. The typical Australian is represented as a bushman, who is, among other things, practical, courageous, taciturn, sceptical and independent, yet loyal to his mates. Such qualities, Ward argues, were to be found in the itinerant shearers and drovers of the Australian outback in the nineteenth century and in the various literary representations of them. He is explicit that such features are mythical but that they also have a basis in historical and social reality (Ward 1966: 1). In his attempt to portray the origins of national identity in the outlook of ordinary Australian workers, he is insufficiently aware of other sources on national identity, which might have allowed a different and more

complex story (see Magarey et al. 1993). Nor is he critical of the social
function of such images and consequently fails to see how it excludes
women and Aborigines.

Much debate has occurred over unifying themes in historical myths
such as the bush legend or the image of the colonial child's growth to
maturity. Part of this industry consists of demythologising such visions
by appeal to alternative historical and sociological facts. This is evident, for example, in the attempts by John Carroll (1982; 1992) and
others to demythologise Ward's conclusions, which then lead to a
revised mythology of authenticity, this time incorporating the conservative values of the would-be demythologisers. For example, John
Hirst's (1992) account of the 'pioneer legend' focuses upon the values
and experiences of those who settled and worked the land and is
explicitly conservative. The Australian virtues Hirst portrays are those of
the pastoralists and farmers who owned or leased their own land and
property. The 'others' in this version are largely based upon place. Hirst
writes: 'Their enemies are drought, flood, fire, sometimes Aborigines;
never low prices, middle-men, lack of capital or other pioneers.' Other
conservatives are concerned to portray nationalism in a positive light as
an important unifying force (e.g. Mandle 1980) and offer different
sources of national character. Geoffrey Partington (1994), for example,
thinks it vital to remind us of the shared Britishness which he regards as
central to early Australian conceptions of themselves and their polity.

Some of those on the radical left would share Ward's focus upon
ordinary Australian people, but point out their diversity and a range of
other cultural qualities based upon the widespread suffering of
oppression and the experience of inequality. In their 'people's history',
for example, Burgmann and Lee (1988a: xv) aim to reject simplistic
unifying appeals to the 'national interest' and emphasise the potential
agency of oppressed Australians. Thus, although the term 'identity' is
not used, these writers retain a primarily modernist conception of
unified subjects among the diversity of Australian identities.

For those of a more liberal persuasion, the Australian identity and its
heritage is represented in resolutely modernist terms but characterised
primarily by intellectual values. John Passmore (1992) sees its origins in
the great historical events and universalist philosophies of ancient and
modern Europe. Eugene Kamenka (1993) notes the toleration of
Australians, but sees the lower forms of nationalist culture as mostly a
'copy'. He points out that what was distinctive for him, growing up in
Sydney after emigrating from Europe as a child, was the Australian
propensity to engage in rigorous criticism, and the attachment to
universalist cultural and intellectual values. For Kamenka (1993: 27)
what was significantly Australian was the lack of nationalism of 'race and

place', and a schooling in which 'Australia was not the be-all and end-all or even the focal point of education or of our lives as lives of the mind'.

From a postmodern perspective, studies in popular culture aim to avoid the problems of exclusivity. Among the best historical work in this area is that of Richard White (1981: viii–x), who argues that all images of national identity are inventions. 'When we look at ideas about national identity', White (1981: viii) says, 'we need to ask, not whether they are true or false, but what their function is, whose creation they are, and whose interests they serve.' He demonstrates a range of changing and partial explanatory mythologies, and relates these to wider historical and cultural arguments in Australia. The broader political problem in cultural studies is that writers in this tradition tend to accept every icon as of equal importance, and slide into that postmodernist cultural relativism that is situated, almost randomly it sometimes seems, in the space signified by the name Australia. A related difficulty is that postmodernist versions of identities can become a matter of taste only, to be ignored, reproduced, discarded, relished or whatever we choose to do with them.

National identity in Australian politics

Let us now examine some familiar modernist usages of national identity in Australian politics. First we may consider the politician, the public servant, the commentator, the theorist (sometimes an international relations realist) who claim to have defined or divined that most dangerous of political weapons, the national interest. Behind all such claims lies a conscious or unconscious ideological certainty in which one geopolitical or metaphysical or mythological construction of the national tradition is held to be the only authentic version of a national identity. From Hitler's *ein volk* to the Australian electoral slogans in March 1993, those of the Australian Labor Party's *One Nation* or the Liberal Party's *Fightback!*, we can detect attempts to present one partisan program under the legitimating banner of national interest. Such ideological certainties are clear examples of modernist types of national identity. They often appear in the conventional wisdom of a ruling elite, where the power to set political agendas serves to narrow the boundaries of political choice.

The economic orthodoxy dominant in current Australian politics is a good example of such a restricted political vision. Politicians from all major political parties, most of the leading political and economic media commentators, senior public servants, business leaders, representatives of producer group peak bodies and leading public sector administrators all agree that the market is a necessary good in itself.

This is despite the compelling evidence of the failure of markets to solve human problems in even the comparatively simple business of food distribution within and between countries (Wells 1990). Political imagination is generally restricted to the registering of raw indicators of economic growth or recession.

One view of economics, neoclassical economic theory, with all its ideological assumptions about the primacy of individual choice and the virtues of self-interest, is taken to be the description of the actual and the only possible political landscape. In this world view, the personal identities public policy aims to foster are essentially those of discrete individuals who are defined by their capacities to possess, produce and consume commodities. To question the role of the market or the benefits of its associated philosophy of managerialism is to invite ridicule by the rulers and their apologists. The charge of economic illiteracy is to be expected by anyone rash enough to rock the boat of national interest.

A link can be established between such economic rationalist ideologies and cultural arguments about the Australian national interest. For example, certain views of a unified or single national interest can also appear in the context of official speeches or discussion papers on Australia's cultural diversity, such as in a keynote address to the Royal Australian Institute of Public Administration entitled, 'Multi-culturalism as Public Administration: Myths, Challenges and Opportunities'. This paper, delivered by Sandy Hollway (1992), former acting secretary, Department of the Prime Minister and Cabinet, makes much of the success the government has had in managing cultural diversity through the use of the principles of access and equity. The problems of language education are significant in a land where one-tenth of the population was born in a country in which English is not the first language, and where other problems emerge from providing services to the one-fifth of the population born overseas.

In this discussion of diversity, there are several references to unity, to what might be called identity with difference. First, there are identity claims linked to the economy, where microeconomic reform and the reduction of tariff barriers are compared with harnessing the untapped economic potential of migrants and the freeing up of discriminatory migration policy in order to make Australia more open and competitive in the global economy. In the same paper, reference is made to some cultural values that allegedly unite Australians. Multiculturalism, it is argued (Hollway 1992: 249), 'is underpinned by an overriding and unifying commitment to Australia, to its interests and to its fundamental liberal democratic values'. And in the course of an argument that multiculturalism is not merely propaganda which tells Australians what to think, authentic Australian society is depicted as healthily sceptical. In this way, liberal notions of tolerance and diversity become part of the rhetoric of national interest. A modernist argument about the certain ends that constitute the national interest has appropriated both difference arguments and an older argument from political theory about the means whereby political association is possible. This appeal to a common citizenship, however, is a very different idea from that of national interest, and I shall return to this theme.

Similar points were made in a speech by Paul Keating (1992) to the Federation of Ethnic Community Councils. Here multicultural policies are portrayed as the creative force behind our rich, diverse and tolerant society. In the course of praising the contribution of ethnic migrants, and in condemning his political opponents for their lack of multi-cultural tolerance, Keating stresses the migrant knowledge of overseas markets. Trade is the main game and, like the port cities of old Asia and Europe, Australia is urged to achieve greatness from the wealth and ideas that flow at the 'crossroads of cultures'. Close rhetorical links can be made between this multicultural debate and the current partisan arguments about the symbolism of the monarch and the Australian flag, and the extent to which Australia can be considered as part of the Asian region. These arguments often include a notion of national identity with postcolonial overtones. In time, they may lead to a removal of the Union Jack from the Australian flag, but there is some distance to be covered before we find a suitable replacement for the European place-name of the 'Far East' when referring to those states to the north with which Australia now has major trading relations.

In all these current Australian political debates, partisan political struggles, particularly those promoting a universalist economic ideology based upon the inescapable constraints of markets, are embedded in arguments for difference and diversity. The argument for national independence within a republican framework can be inserted in the contradictory argument that it is a mark of economic maturity that we open up our economy to global competition, even when this involves widespread foreign ownership of Australian land and business (Atkinson 1993). Thus the contradictions within modernist economic certainty confront a relativistic version of identity of a postmodernist kind.

Arguments about Australian national identity are traditionalist when constructing golden ages for current use. These may be the rugged mateship of the bush, the egalitarian utopia of the socially progressive early twentieth-century Australian state, the Aboriginal success in sustainable land-use and primitive communism, or even a nostalgic view of Anglo-Celtic suburbia at a time when the world was safe for children. All such views use a version of tradition to attack some perceived current

problem or to defend some current policy or institution. Overall, however, no simple theoretical categorisation of arguments about Australian
national identity is possible; their rhetoric combines various theoretical
strategies and assumptions – traditional, modernist, postmodernist, and
even postcolonialist.

Political theory and citizenship: Towards an Australian civic identity

Given the account above, we must ask whether national identities are
merely ammunition for rival ideological certainties, or utopian quests
for authenticity, or webs of postmodern and postcolonial textual
interpretation. If any of these characterisations are true, then we can
trust no version of national or cultural unity. Everything in Australia
connects, but only at the level of interpretative diversity. There are
considerable dangers involved if we accept this conclusion of despair.
Notions of human worth and the power of humans to affect political
change of any kind rest on the premise that we can imagine, in
association with others, how the world is and how it might be, and can
act on this imagination (Wolin 1960). This is the perspective of an
enduring and influential conception of political theory. It is a view of
human association that is not the creation of modernism; it existed in
theories of citizenship in ancient Greece, for example. It is a view that
has undergone massive transformations since premodern times. Various
modern philosophers have attempted to appropriate it, and versions of
postmodernism and postcolonialism have tried to undermine it.

During the past two centuries the typical unit of association for such
joint imagining has been the nation-state. By its deconstruction of the
nation, the state and universalist political ideology, the postmodernist
project threatens to incapacitate virtually all associations and arguments
that allow the unity in diversity of political life. Nevertheless, without
some shared belief, some shared identity, there is little possibility that
humans can respond to the international market forces, the global
revolution in communications, or the great problems of poverty, oppression and environmental destruction.

Citizenship is an ethical and political concept that allows us to consider the agreed means to achieve our disparate ends within the same
political association. In practice many people will be excluded or
overlooked from full participation in political life, and notions such as
difference may be enlisted to minimise this, but this does not mean that
citizenship is merely a mask for oppression. There are great dangers in
allowing postmodern and postcolonial arguments to discount the
desirability (or even the possibility) of citizenship. As Pocock (1992: 55)
has argued:

When a world of persons, actions, and things becomes a world of persons, actions, and linguistic and electronic constructs that have no authors, it clearly becomes much easier for the things – grown much more powerful because they are no longer real – to multiply and take charge...

Another way of looking at Pocock's defence of citizenship in a postmodern world is to say that, unless we construct some unity that allows for diversity, we are collectively at the mercy of those unities that do not allow for diversity. Postmodernity may not be avoided, but we should not rush to embrace postmodernist ideas so enthusiastically that we allow ourselves no defences against the still remaining modernist, oppressive ideologies. This does not necessarily mean that we have to maintain a unity with diversity at the level of the nation-state; there are other alternatives at international and sub-national levels. But it does mean that the Australian state is one arena where the possibility of unity with diversity can be explored. If some understandings of Australian national identity promote the possibility of a common citizenship with communitarian and tolerant values, these should not be discarded lightly.

Many interpretations of Australian political institutions do none of these things. Some writers portray the Australian state as an avenue for the imposition of oppressive racist, sexist or class values (see the essays in Muetzelfeldt 1992 and Watson 1990), as an arena for soulless utilitarian or economic rationalist policies (see e.g. Horne 1992; Carroll and Manne 1992), or even as a lawyer-dominated descendant of a penal colony where the people are subjects but never citizens (Davidson 1991). In these disparate interpretations, the Australian nation state is identified with one unity only, and it discriminates against a range of possible diversities. According to these values, the Australian state should be abolished or reformed radically to allow a diversity to flourish. The liberal democratic interpretations of the Australian nation-state see these reforms as now largely in place. The liberal democratic ethos is here seen as an accurate description of a tolerant diverse polity, united by an active and powerful citizenry who share the same associational values. It is this version of Australian national identity which is implied in Paul Keating's argument about unity with diversity in relation to multicultural policy, discussed above. This citizenship argument is obscured in Keating's text, however, because his speech also attacks his political opponents and presents a discussion of Australian trade in terms of a modernist conception of national interest. These narrow partisan messages obscure the general argument about how, as citizens of Australia, in a shared polity, we make an agreement about the way we disagree.

Conclusion

My general argument about citizenship will, of course, be denied by
those who see this as an attempt to legitimise and give priority to one
particular liberal, or possibly social democratic, ideology at the expense
of all others. According to this argument, the advocates of citizenship
claim a position beyond ideology which is merely a mask for particularistic ideological dominations. In terms of the argument of this chapter,
liberal democratic views of citizenship may be rejected by postmodernist
critics because they present a mythological narrative of modernist or
traditionalist authenticity. Once we accept the need to overcome current forms of domination, we must find some basis for association.
Questions of interpretation may divide us, but political problems can be
overcome only if we attempt to construct tolerant unities in our
diversities. National identity conceived as citizenship is an important
item, whether it is something that already exists or something to be
constructed in the future by our collective political imagination. Part of
this imagining has already begun in Australia (see Horne 1994a; 1994b).

To construct some acceptable version of national identity is no easy
task in a world divided between the multiple identities of postmodernism, postcolonialism and the meta-narrative-based certainties of
modernist identities. Reference to the plasticity of the construct 'Serb'
would not help us when faced with a committed ethnic cleanser in
Bosnia, for example. And the range of meanings of 'Australian' makes it
difficult to hold on to the citizenship version, or to give it any ascendancy over the other versions of identity. The publicity of citizenship
should not become the propaganda of the politician or an image to sell
a beer, although, of course, it cannot avoid such appropriation entirely.
The search for an Australian national identity linked to citizenship is an
integral part of the wider task for political theory to find how political
power can be legitimated so that it is deserving of respect and support
(Dunn 1985). This is a particularly complex problem in the context of
postcolonial national identity in Australia. Of course, a tolerant version
of our national identity is not a sufficient response to all our current
problems. Without such a collective identity, however, it is unlikely that
the problems of modernism, postmodernism and postcolonialism can
be addressed at all.

Notes

1. This chapter is a much revised version of an earlier paper (Archer 1993)
    presented to the Symposium on Assimilation, Pluralism and Multi-
    culturalism, University of New England, October 1992. I am grateful to
    Geoff Stokes for his suggestions for revision.

CHAPTER 2

'Other Times': Thatcher, Hawke, Keating, and the Politics of Identity

Carol Johnson[1]

Australian analyses of mainstream economic and political discourse during the Labor period of office 1983–96 have tended to pay relatively little attention to the codes, images, meanings and concepts of personal identity evoked by Australian Labor rhetoric. That is, they have not examined the leaders' own projections of personal identity, or the (often related) forms of personal identity they appealed to among the electorate (see e.g. Maddox 1989 and Jaensch 1989). Yet, this is an important area if one wishes to understand some of the ways in which individuals can relate to, and identify with, public political discourse.

It is a sphere in which everyday life meets the discourse of party politics; where people can find that government rhetoric melds with personal experience; where both agreement and resistance can be generated.[2] It is a crucial aspect of political legitimation. Australian work, arising from the field of cultural studies, provides useful analyses of political images and meanings during this period but generally overlooks issues of personal identity. For example, Meaghan Morris' insightful *Ecstasy and Economics* centres around (the then) Treasurer Paul Keating's use of economic discourse (Morris 1992). Another example is the work of Graeme Turner, which also draws on cultural studies frameworks to analyse images and meanings in the context of national identity but tends to neglect issues of personal identity (Turner 1994).

By contrast, there is a rich British literature, frequently coming out of cultural studies, which attempts to analyse the codes, meanings and images associated with both the Conservative governments and the British Labour Party. That tradition draws on a combination of feminist, neo-Gramscian, Baudrillardian, poststructuralist and postmodernist insights into constructions of identity. It includes contributors such as

37

Stuart Hall (in his later, more postmodernist incarnation), other contributors to the *New Times* debate, and a number of commentators who
have engaged critically with their work, including feminists such as
McNeil (1991a, 1991b) and Stacey (1991). It is a unique tradition in its
attempts to relate influential theoretical insights regarding consumer
identity, fragmentation, multiple subjectivities and the complexities of
constructing gender identities to the analysis of political leadership and
political regimes. The bodies of theory on which such analyses draw are
frequently claimed to have a broad, international application for conditions of modernity and/or postmodernity.[3] It will be argued here that
these British analyses can contribute useful insights for Australian
commentators by drawing attention to a series of issues regarding the
politics of identity which Australian political commentators have failed
to address.

Nevertheless, despite a frequently assumed international applicability
by commentators such as Hall, the differences the British analyses
highlight are often just as significant as the similarities. In other words,
attempting to apply British theorisations of political identity to the
Australian context not only raises useful insights but also draws
attention to the geographic and historical specificity of some key
arguments regarding political identity and therefore highlights the
need to develop specifically Australian insights. It is especially
appropriate to undertake comparative analyses using British material
given that Keating frequently attempted to distance Australian Labor
from what was claimed to be the Liberal Party of Australia's Thatcherite
agenda (Keating 1993b: 2; 1995: 6) and given that Tony Blair, the British
Labour leader, has expressed interest in learning from the Australian
Labor experience because of the similarities between the two labour
parties (*Australian* 13 July 1995). Indeed, I have argued elsewhere that
British cultural studies approaches have also been most useful for
analysing Liberal discourse in documents such as *Fightback!* (Johnson
1993).

In particular, it will be argued here that the British work draws
attention to the importance of Australian Labor's appeals to a broad
cross-spectrum of political and social identities. The British work also
draws attention to the importance that gender identity plays in the
construction of a political leader's image and in attempts to gain
political legitimation. Some other aspects of the British work, however,
have proved to be far less relevant to the Australian experience, particularly arguments around consumer identity or the analyses of leaders'
own personae in terms of fragmented subjectivities. Consumer identity
frequently took a back seat to Australia's balance of payment problems
as the Hawke government attempted to dampen economic demand.

Hawke and Keating's personae tend to be characterised by considerable cohesion rather than playing with multiple identities. Similarly, their economic and social policies tend to emphasise consensus and co-operation between various social groups rather than celebrating difference and fragmentation.

Some of the insights that can be gained by comparing and contrasting the British and Australian experiences can be seen when one examines Hall's analysis of the deficiencies of the British Labour Party's response to Thatcherism. In Hall's view, the party not only appealed to outdated personal identifications, for example to a male, blue-collar working class (Hall 1988a: 263–6), but also lacked a vision of what a future socialist society, and future everyday life, would be like.

> In its profound empiricism, [Labour] ... has mistaken adaption to the present as progress towards the future. In fact, realistically, Labour can never adapt enough to become the 'natural inheritor' of capitalism (Hall 1988a: 209).

The Australian experience suggests that Hall may be mistaken. The Hawke government enjoyed considerable electoral success while depicting itself as a government that had both adapted to the present and was a 'natural inheritor' of capitalism. The Hawke government expounded a vision of a future built on temporary restraint: a technologically superior, twenty-first century Australia where, by dint of hard work, flexibility and brains, the 'lucky country' would become the 'clever country' with a high standard of living.

Similarly, Labor saw itself as addressing new personal identifications. Australian Labor has often been accused of betraying traditional voters (e.g. Maddox 1989) or of trying to appeal to somewhat contradictory class identifications (Fiske et al. 1987: 166–7). In many respects Labor, along with influential sections of the Australian Council of Trade Unions (Manning 1992), wished to provide a new image for workers to identify with – the flexible, smart, multi-skilled, post-Fordist worker of the 'clever country'. This worker could also be a multicultural, female worker (Johnson 1990b). According to Hawke (Australia 1991: 3776), the worker would be on good terms with his or her employer, co-operating to increase productivity and benefiting from the employer's productive activity. One might well wish to argue that the Hawke vision had flawed underpinnings and that the actual outcomes were very different from those predicted (see e.g. Johnson 1989, 1990a, 1990b; Watts 1990; Stilwell 1993). Nevertheless, feminist and left critiques do not change the fact that the appeal of the ALP government was a very broad, if somewhat economistic, one. There were niches here for everyone working in the public and private sectors to identify with, including traditional male workers, female workers, Asian workers and efficient, productive businesspeople.[4] Although Hawke was the key architect of consensus policies, Keating (1987: 175) endorsed Hawke's broad direction, arguing that 'the major achievements of the Australian Labor Party ... have always come when Labor most effectively identified with the objectives and aspirations of the Australian people as a whole'.

As well as depicting itself as the defender of ordinary Australians against the party of privilege, in Hawke's view (Australia 1991: 3777), Australian Labor was also seen as a natural inheritor of capitalism. These two strands were not seen as contradictory given that Labor governments, while prepared to be critical of some sections of capital, were not fundamentally opposed to capitalists or capitalism per se (Johnson 1989: 9). The policy of narrowly targeting welfare benefits enabled the government to claim that it was genuinely helping the under-privileged while it also gave support for right-wing policies of 'economic rationalism'. Rather than advocating extensive welfare provision, Australian Labor deregulated markets and increasingly reduced the welfare sector (Johnson 1990a).

Australian Labor had worked out a response to the dilemma which Hall believed faced British Labour when the Keynesian, welfare state consensus that had been shared to some extent by both parties collapsed (Hall 1988a: 185). It was this post-Keynesian world that Hall argues Thatcherism occupied brilliantly. Hall, however, did not allow adequately for the possibility that labour governments could also formulate post-Keynesian strategies that involved a substantial move to the right rather than a reformulation of a left-wing labour agenda. The Hawke government was attempting to integrate a Labor agenda with some elements of watered-down New Right economic policies characterised by support for selective privatisation, deregulation, corporatisation, real wage cuts and narrowly targeted welfare policies. But Australian Labor governments were selling these policies using strategies, codes and imagery that were frequently very different from those used by Thatcher to sell her tougher, and even more right-wing, policies. A major difference in the images and meanings evoked to sell pro-market policies lies in the emphasis on individualism. Thatcher has continued to stress the sense of 'individuality' and initiative as a key feature of the British national character (*Guardian* 22 April 1992: 19). There were very similar statements in the right-wing Liberal Party's *Fightback!* document as they tried to redefine Australian character (Liberal Party of Australia 1991: 25, 27; Johnson 1993). The Hawke government placed much more emphasis than did Thatcherism on people being members of social groups that were working together, on a co-operative capitalism rather than an individualistic enterprise culture. Whereas Thatcher attacked unions, Hawke sought union co-operation with business. In short, Hawke appealed to a form of group identity, Thatcher to a conception of individual identity. Partly because of his contentious belief that New Right Thatcherite economics could be 'dismantled in a moment' (Hall 1988b: 59, 63), Hall has been highly critical of 'rational' accounts of political ideology, in which individuals are 'interpellated' (to use an Althusserian term) into a rational calculus and framework of identity (cited Franklin et al. 1991: 24). Nonetheless, one of the features of Australian Labor's program was precisely its attempt to win support for a form of 'economic rationalism' based on the argument that if all groups in society co-operated together, they would all eventually benefit from market-oriented policies and short-term sacrifices.

The emphasis on group, rather than individual, identity was only one of the relevant differences in the identity politics of the governments. Particularly in later works where he engages with postmodernist thought, revealing some Baudrillardian influences, Hall argues that Thatcherism managed to make huge inroads into popular culture partly because, unlike Labour, it appealed to people's identity as consumers.[5] He suggests that the crucial role of consumption in determining political identity is an international feature and that consumption was designated as a crucial space where individuals could exercise their sense of freedom and self-expression.

> The fact is that greater and greater numbers of people (men *and* women) – with however little money – play the game of using things to signify who they are. Everybody, including people in very poor societies whom we in the West frequently speak about as if they inhabit a world *outside* of culture, knows that today's 'goods' double up as social signs and produce meanings as well as energy. (1989: 131)

While not wishing to dispute that issues related to consumption can play a significant role in displaying aspects of identity, they need not play such a central role in party political discourse. Indeed, Joel Krieger (1991) has disputed whether consumption issues played such a major role in the British electoral context. Certainly, in the case of the Hawke government, consumption was viewed as a very problematic aspect of identity. First, the most crucial form of consumption was seen to be consumption by foreigners who would buy Australian exports. Second, given the balance of trade problems, ordinary Australians were meant to be restraining their own consumption until Australia was once again able to stand proudly in the international economy, hence the emphasis on both wage restraint and cutting consumption of imports. Note also that it was an issue of national identity rather than individual identity that was being stressed in respect to consumption within the context of economic globalisation. One cannot assume that particular features are universal.

One therefore needs to have a more complex conception of the interrelationship between the 'cultural' and wider economic and political relations than Hall's theoretical insights suggest. Such interrelationships might throw light on why there has been a general move to the right internationally; why that move to the right can take significantly different forms and how that move can be 'sold' by, or in spite of, mobilising significantly different images and meanings. This is not to deny that other questions, which Hall contentiously depicts as 'irrational', such as emotional identification and style, are also important aspects of mainstream political identity. Indeed, one of Hall's (1988a: 261) major theoretical contributions is seen to be his analysis of subjectivity. For example, Franklin et al. (1991: 23) note that:

> Hall argues for a more complex model of subjectivity which allows for simultaneously contradictory identifications, lack of closure or linearity in the stories told and of our positioning as subjects (or objects) within them. Indeed, he suggests that one of the strengths of Thatcherism was precisely its ability to offer multiple, adverse and contradictory identifications, thus successfully including within its discourse and narratives many different, even opposed, sets of interests.

What is interesting about the Hawke period, however, is the way in which it can offer a quite coherent and logically consistent narrative about a healthy capitalist economy in which numerous groups in society have shared interests and a positive (non-contradictory) role to identify with.

At the same time, there are more personal (but not necessarily less rational) narratives being told that go far beyond the narrowly economistic conceptions of identity favoured by the Hawke government. A useful way of uncovering some of the private, rather than public, identities being invoked is to analyse the gender implications and positionings of the political discourse. Although Hall (1989: 132) argues for the need to attend to how gendered identities are formed, he has been criticised for neglecting exactly this point (Franklin et al. 1991: 25). Maureen McNeil (1991a, 1991b) has pointed out that gender identities were very important within Thatcherism. Some of these were negative, as in the Thatcher government's attacks on the welfare state as the 'nanny state' and other attacks on female-dominated professions such as social workers (McNeil 1991b: 14–16). Nevertheless, Thatcher's image also appealed to complex conceptions of femininity as she cooked for her cabinet and compared the national economy to a housewife's budget (Franklin et al. 1991: 34–5). Marina Warner (1985: 51) points out that Thatcher often called upon distinctively British female images from the past. Her persona combined 'Britannia's resoluteness, Boadicea's courage with a proper housewifely demeanor'. Beatrix Campbell (1991: 23) argues that Thatcher's 'mutations were among the keys to her modernity, she was a multiple personality, the housewife in a flak jacket, a manager, a wife and a warrior . . .'[6]

Although Hall neglects this important gender component when discussing the appeal of Thatcherism, he did criticise Labour's attempt to distance itself from gender and racial issues in the 1987 election by embracing the image of the traditional, male, trade unionist, Labour voter. Neil Kinnock, the leader of the Labour Party, 'appeared as a manly "likely lad" who owed everything to the welfare state. His "familial" image carried not a single echo or trace of feminist struggles over two decades' (Hall 1988a: 263). Hall (1988a: 259–67) argued that such an image was not the one with which to counter Thatcherism ideologically but that Labour needed to appeal to the personal, political identifications of women, Asian and Afro-Caribbean people, as well as the prosperous 'new' working class.

Hall's analysis does offer some useful pointers for a discussion of the Hawke government. It has already been noted that the Hawke government attempted to appeal to new forms of working-class identifications that went beyond traditional blue-collar work by constructing an image of the flexible, multi-skilled worker of the future. While the Hawke government still tended to work from a model that privileged male workers, it at least tried to incorporate women into this model as honorary male workers, albeit often in part-time jobs (Johnson 1990b). The government was attempting to appeal to a multicultural and gender inclusive working class as well as to sections of business. Nonetheless, the experience of the Hawke government also reveals the need to go beyond the limitations of Hall's analysis of political identities. In order to understand some crucial features of Hawke's own image, one needs to analyse the gender politics of Hawke's image, particularly the important role played by appeals to masculinity.

Hawke's personal image went far beyond the somewhat economistic and workerist conceptions of identity purveyed by government policy, although his image was much more coherent than Thatcher's. Perhaps Thatcher's 'multiple personalities' owed more to her juggling of gender stereotypes than to postmodern fragmentation. As a male prime minister, Hawke had far more conventional and consistent gender stereotypes to appeal to. Hawke's image drew on a particular version of masculine identity: the sports-loving bloke with a soft heart; the man's man who could cry.[7] His multiple prime ministerial personalities were historically consecutive rather than simultaneous: the former alcoholic philanderer who embraced sobriety, monogamy and Pritikin. He was a suitable role model for a country that was meant to be transforming itself. Women did feature in Hawke's personal imagery but as objects of either male sexual desire or of husbandly respect, or both. Part of the Hawke persona was a narrative about heterosexual romance.[8] Hawke (cited in *Australian* 20 December 1991: 16) shed tears during a March 1989 interview with Clive Robertson when discussing his past as a womaniser, saying, 'I was unfaithful to my wife ... She understood it was part of a pretty volatile, exuberant character and she knew my love for her had never changed'. Hawke's confession appeared to have little effect on his prime ministerial popularity. Indeed, it may have fed into a well-known romance narrative in which Hazel Hawke featured as a capable woman who won back her erring, drunken husband through her constancy, and contributes to his success. Hazel Hawke was typically depicted as a loyal woman in the media. Her profile in the *Australian* (20 December 1991: 11) on Hawke's defeat was headlined 'Popular Hazel – ally, friend and foil'. Bob and Hazel were meant to be a couple that ordinary Australians could identify with.[9] Bob liked women so much, he even supported some policies on affirmative action.

At the same time, while Hawke depicted himself as a caring man who could cry over his marital infidelities, his daughter's drug problems and the massacre at Tiananmen Square, he also displayed some very conventional aspects of Australian masculinity. First, Hawke was closely associated with images of male sporting prowess because of his regular attendances at major sporting events as well as his own participation in golf, tennis and cricket. His quintessential 'ockerism' is exemplified by his statement when Australian won the America's Cup in 1983: 'There's no need to declare a national holiday. We are going to be a nation of zombies anyway. Any boss who sacks anybody for not turning up today is a bum' (cited in *Australian* 20 December 1991: 16). In his statement when stepping down as Prime Minister, he hoped that the Australian people would 'remember me as ... the larrikin trade union official who perhaps had sufficient sense and intelligence to tone down his larrikinism to some extent ... but who in the end is essentially a dinki-di Australian' (*Australian* 20 December 1991: 2). Larrikins are not only likeable rascals, they also engage in behaviour that tends to be identified with a version of working-class masculinity. As part of Hawke's populist image, he wished to be remembered as, 'a bloke who loved his country ... and who was not essentially changed by high office' (*Australian* 20 December 1991: 2). In the latter respect, it is interesting that even his association with rich businessmen was initially frequently depicted not as his being corrupted by high office but as his having a wide circle of mates. Photographs of Hawke with big business mates were common (McEachern 1991: 3). Here, as elsewhere, Hawke's personal image appears to be relatively coherent rather than fragmented – the reformed larrikin whose charm could bring Australians together for the common good, the facilitator and negotiator, the real man who could care for both his business and labour mates. His personal style complemented his government's wider economic discourse. What is noticeable is the relative coherence and logical consistency of the identities in question, a feature that appears to contrast with Thatcher's multiple images. Nevertheless, what is also significant, as the feminist analyses of Thatcherism have pointed out, is the importance of the *gendered* identities and narratives being evoked.

Identity politics is also an area that is fraught with pitfalls for party leaders. As charismatic political figures such as Thatcher and Hawke come to symbolise the governments which bear their name, there is always the probability that their parties will see it as expedient to drop them once their governments lose favour, particularly if their government's vision of the future has been undermined by the harsh realities of the present, for example by a serious recession. In this respect, the identification of a government with an individual figure is itself an ideological construct, frequently concealing essential continuities in political regime.

This is certainly true in the Australian case. As one would expect given Keating's crucial role as Hawke's treasurer, there are important continuities between the Hawke and Keating regimes. Keating's emphasis on co-operation which featured particularly prominently in his 1993 election speech was largely a further development of Hawke's emphasis on consensus and national reconciliation. Both ideas were extensions of Labor's long-time emphasis on social harmony (Johnson 1989). Hawke had also set the scene for a central part of Keating's electoral strategy in the final speech he made as leader of the Labor Party. In that speech, Hawke emphasised the divisive and troglodyte nature of the Opposition while depicting Labor as the party of co-operation, fairness and equity (Australia 1991). His sentiments were very similar to those expressed by Keating (1993b: 2) at the beginning of his 1993 election speech when he argued that Australians faced a choice 'between the Australian traditions of fairness and equity, and the economic and social jungle of Reaganism and Thatcherism which other countries have just abandoned'.

Despite their similarities, the images and meanings appealed to under the Hawke and Keating governments differed in two areas. A major difference lay in the ways in which Keating utilised explicit appeals to national identity while Hawke's appeals tended to be more implicit.

The difference was not just in intellectual commitment, speechwriters such as Don Watson, or political commitment, but in style. Hawke (*Advertiser* 8 July 1992: 8) stated that he did not want to get his 'knickers in a knot' over the issue of republicanism. Indeed, he hardly needed to since his appeal to conceptions of Australian identity lay partly in his own persona as a reformed larrikin and mate. Paul Keating, the stand-offish, severe, ex-treasurer who wore hand-sewn Italian suits and collected antique French clocks, had to appeal to conceptions of national identity much more directly. Both appeals were also influenced by different emphases in their economic conceptions of the world. Hawke's consensual economics was the economics of mates co-operating together in hard economic times. Paul Keating's co-operative economics still evoked conceptions of Bankstown residents pulling together (Keating 1993b: 7), but also involved transforming Australian economic identity in order to survive globalisation and develop closer links with Asia (Keating 1993b: 3).

There is another important difference related to the ways in which both men attempted to make appeals to conceptions of identity. Meaghan Morris (1992: 50) argues that during his period as treasurer, Keating's use of language produced an identification with an enunciative practice that eroticised economics, rather than an identification with Keating himself or 'an immanent communal identity'. The 'popular refusal to *identify* with Keating was a constitutive feature of his media image' (Morris 1992: 32). While Morris (1992: 51–4) makes some fascinating points about codes, images and meanings (for example, regarding Keating's vision of plenitude and the eroticisation of his economic appeal), she says relatively little regarding a key issue discussed here, namely the broader concepts of identity evoked by the Hawke and Keating governments. She argues that the economically 'educated' citizenry was to play an almost passive role in endorsing 'the modernising actions taken by the state on our behalf' (1992: 76). Consequently, Morris misses the important fact that the Hawke and Keating governments' economic policies appealed to 'identities' which promoted conceptions of a 'general' interest and provided roles for most sections of the population to play in economic restructuring. Nonetheless, Morris is correct that Keating did not ask us to identify with him personally to anything like the same extent that Hawke did. Hawke asked us to identify with his personal foibles and failings in a way that was unthinkable for Keating.

There were also significant differences in the forms of masculine identity to which Hawke and Keating appealed. Keating made several statements suggesting that some images of Australian masculine identity, such as yobs around the barbie, need to be transformed in order for us to succeed in the world market and become an international tourist destination (*Weekend Australian* 4–5 July 1992: 1). Hawke's appeal partly lay in his former yobbish characteristics. The contrasts were also present elsewhere; for example, Hawke was a former cricketer who constantly attended sporting functions, Keating argued that we needed to export ballet troupes as well as manufactured goods (*Weekend Australian* 11–12 July 1992: 3). Keating played faithful husband to Hawke's image of reformed philanderer. Both appealed to different conceptions of Australian masculinity, Keating as a cultured government 'executive', Hawke as the perennial good bloke who was a bit of a softie underneath. Both, however, were appealing to particular masculine stereotypes.

Underneath the different images and meanings that were being appealed to, there was an important degree of continuity that went beyond the shared emphasis on co-operation. Keating claimed to be somewhat less market-oriented after becoming prime minister, largely as a result of what were seen to be policy failures in the light of the recession. Nonetheless, while Keating's landmark economic statements such as *Investing in the Nation* reflected the need for some increase in government assistance to industry and government expenditure on welfare during high levels of unemployment, they still stressed the importance of the private sector and saw welfare largely as a safety net (Keating 1993a: 40; 1993c). The market remained an important part of Keating's vision of social democracy. He argued that Australia's energy 'flows from the genius and ambition of our people which the combination of liberal democracy and free markets alone can deliver' (Keating 1993b: 4).

Keating drew on the imagery and meaning of the Hawke period, adapting them to fit his own, rather different, political style. One could argue that Australia has seen a somewhat more successful transition than that exhibited in Britain. There were significant disjunctions between the personae of Thatcher and Major. Hall argues that Major's accession to power has forced him to reassess his previous belief that Thatcherism was not Thatcher. He now recognises that

> there is a kind of 'fit' between the public figure and the private persona, between what appear to be privately held values and a public philosophy. This fit is very important in securing identification, which is one of the things about Thatcherism that is most significant. (Hall 1993b: 14)

One could argue that it is precisely that lack of 'fit' that has bedevilled Major's attempt to resurrect some of the popularity of Thatcherism by returning to 'back to basics' on issues such as crime, social disintegration and family breakdown. It is not just that Major suffers from a singular lack of charisma himself. He has been beset by scandal as his government attacks single mothers only to find that cabinet members have fathered illegitimate children, or supports sexual 'normality' only to find a leading Tory politician dead in women's clothing with a plastic bag over his head. As Hall (1993b: 14) points out, Major attempted to present a 'kind of alternative to Thatcherism – Thatcherism with a human face'. One could add that the face has proven to be only too human. Unlike Keating, Major has not been able to use public appeals to national identity to try to overcome the deficiencies in his own persona. While Keating could draw on continuities in images of Australians co-operating together, there were disjunctions between Major's attempts to project a dampish 'human' face and Thatcher's conceptions of national identity. Certainly, Thatcher has implied that there was a contradiction between her own emphasis on the 'British' values of individualism and self-reliance and Major's purported attempts to forge a consensus between 'wet' and 'dry' conservatives. She argues that 'consensus is the absence of principle and the presence of expediency' (*Guardian* 22 April 1992: 19). The contrasts with the Australian situation, in terms of emphasis on both co-operation and conceptions of national identity are clear.

Conclusion

This chapter draws attention to the problems involved in assuming that simple cross-national generalisations can be made about the politics of identity. When a commentator such as Hall raises questions about multiple identities, rationality and consumption, he is being influenced by a combination of poststructuralist and postmodernist perspectives; a tradition from Foucault to Baudrillard that has tempered his original neo-Gramscian perspectives. The material in this chapter has raised questions about how relevant some of those theoretical tools are for analysing Australian government discourse. This should not come as a surprise to those poststructuralists and postmodernists who take their arguments against universalising and totalising theories seriously. It may be a timely reminder, however, for some commentators who wish to use poststructuralist and postmodernist insights to develop a new set of universalising categories around concepts such as identity, rationality and consumption.

Nonetheless, this chapter has drawn on insights from British work in cultural studies to draw attention to the useful contribution that analyses of the politics of identity can make for our understanding of political regimes. Governments, political parties and political leaders do utilise appeals to popular conceptions of identity in order to increase their electoral appeal. Those conceptions of identity are not only the more obviously public ones such as appeals to nationalism but also, as this chapter has endeavoured to show, intensely personal ones. Indeed, the latter may play an essential role in enabling people to mediate between the somewhat abstract nature of government policies and the politics of everyday life. As Stuart Hall (1988a: 261) has pointed out, how people vote partly depends on how they 'see themselves', and how they 'imagine their future' within particular political scenarios. That is undoubtedly one reason why appeals to personal identifications are so prevalent in party political discourse. It must be said, however, that whereas such appeals may contribute to electoral success, they offer no simple formulae for winning government.

Notes

1. My thanks to Jean Duruz for her comments on this work.
2. This study concentrates more on how governments and political leaders have depicted themselves than on the issue of how those depictions might have been received and/or resisted. I have analysed Keating's appeals to a broad range of social groups in more depth in Johnson (1995, 1996).
3. For an overview of some key debates regarding conceptions of identity, including a variety of modernist, postmodernist and poststructuralist positions, see Lash and Friedman (1992b).
4. I have not yet come across an analysis of the racial assumptions underlying the Hawke government's general economic and social policy documents but suspect that the male workers they privilege (Johnson 1990b) are white and anglo-celtic.
5. Interestingly, Hall's work on racial identity places less emphasis on consumption than is the case in his writings on Thatcherism (Hall 1987, 1990); this trend has continued in his most recent post-Thatcherite writings on personal identity (Hall 1996; Hall and Chen 1996). For useful discussions of the relationship between consumption and identity see Nava (1992, chapters 8, 9, 10); Tomlinson (1990) and Featherstone (1991). For an insightful critique of *New Times*, see Clarke (1991).
6. Thatcher's multiple personalities could produce perceived contradictions as when her use of the royal 'we' seemed inconsistent with her position as self-made grocer's daughter. My thanks to Kate Bowles for drawing my attention to this point.
7. For possible psychological roots, see Anson (1991).
8. For a discussion of Thatcherism's promotion of heterosexuality, see Stacey (1991).
9. Bob and Hazel finally separated in November 1994, and divorced in 1995.

CHAPTER 3

Universal Obligations: Liberalism,
Religion and National Identity

Gregory Melleuish

'From humanity, via nationality to bestiality' – thus the Austrian poet Grillparzer is quoted in Joseph Roth's tale 'The Bust of the Emperor' (1986: 164). Roth then explores the sources of national sentiment and finds them in the envy and discontent of those who believed that their true worth had not been recognised in bourgeois society. The supporters of nationalism were 'discontented teachers in primary schools who would have liked to teach in secondary schools, apothecaries' assistants who wanted to be doctors, tooth pullers who could not become dentists, junior employees in the Post Office and railways'. This idea that nationalism was the refuge of the disappointed and unsuccessful is given further credence by Ernest Gellner's fable (1983: 58–62) of Megalomania and Ruritania in which he notes that Ruritanian intellectuals had far greater chances of gaining posts in an independent Ruritania than in the competitive environment of the Megalomanian metropolis. It seems confirmed in the Australian case when it is noted that major advocates of Australian nationalism, including Vance Palmer, P.R. Stephensen and Manning Clark, had each been less than successful in the metropolis.

Are therefore the advocates of a stronger national identity in Australia the arch enemies of humanity, leading us a further step down the road to bestiality and barbarism? Writing in 1860, John West (*Sydney Morning Herald* 5 July 1860) claimed that the common interests of mankind always took precedence over those of nationality because national feeling was only 'sentiment'. West believed that the progress of civilisation would detach men and women from their feelings of clanship, arguing that there were no essential racial differences (see also Melleuish 1993). His contemporary Charles Harpur (Mitchell 1973: 79), attacked 'that blood-drinking Juggernaut – National Glory'. A little more than a generation later, Australians, including their intellectuals, were exalting the claims of nationality and denying the importance of humanity. This change parallels the developments in Europe described by Gellner, and the introduction of such policies as White Australia would seem to confirm the truth of Grillparzer's statement.

My task in this chapter is to explore the relationship between strong conceptions of national identity and the ideas of those who have continued to plead the cause of humanity in a century when the voice of humanity has too often been reduced to a whisper. Before we can begin this task, I believe that we must explore some of the implications of the idea of identity and the history of struggles over identity in Europe. Identity is concerned with our connections with those with whom we identify. Those connections can be weak or strong; they can be close and personal or distant and somewhat abstract. Every individual carries a number of identities that range from the immediate and particular to the universal. These identities include those of family, school, religion, occupation and workplace, political party, city, nation, ethnicity and humanity – perhaps even the whole of creation.

Identity in history and theory

Identity is not just a matter of identifiable connection to others. It may also supply the foundation for asserting rights or requiring obligations. Here I would like to explore the issue of obligation. A sense of identity may encourage us to feel some sense of obligation to those with whom we identify, because we are able to feel a sympathy towards those with whom we share something. We do things for our family members that we would not do for other people, we give money to local charities that we would not give to foreign ones, and so on. In this sense our obligations to those who are closest to us are much more direct and concrete as compared to what we owe to humanity in general. A tension also exists between our particular and our universal identities and obligations in that there is a tendency for individuals to limit their sympathies to a limited circle.

Until the formation of the European Community, the development of modern Europe had seen the range of forms of primary political association and allegiance narrow down to one – the nation-state. For several hundred years before the nineteenth century, other political forms flourished along with the nation-state, including the city-state and the empire (Tilly 1992). Moreover, there was a range of possible identities and obligations including strong local identities, kinship ties, religious identifications and loyalty to one's local city. Writing in mid-nineteenth century Australia, John West (*Sydney Morning Herald* 5 May 1854) did not believe that the future belonged to the nation-state, and advocated federalism in Australia as a way of combining the strengths of the city-state and the empire. Only at the end of the nineteenth century did the 'inevitability' of the nation-state become apparent. In Australia it was C.H. Pearson (1894) who recognised that in the modern world it would be the state that would claim the primary loyalty of the individuals living within its borders.

The primacy of the nation-state as a political form led governments to encourage individuals to identify themselves primarily as a member of that nation-state. Such an identification follows from the claim of the state to a monopoly of the legitimate use of violence within its borders. For example, the state claimed the right to punish rather than allowing the family of the victim to exact revenge. In assuming the primary identity of its members, the nation-state had to deal with those other identifications, both particular and universal. One solution was that proposed by Hegel under which the particular identities of family and civil society are absorbed and transcended by that of the state, which thereby incorporates and transcends these lesser identities. For Hegel (1991), the nation-state was the ultimate and universal expression of our nature because it expressed our identity as ethical beings. This happy conjunction of universality and nation-state is not as apparent as Hegel believed.

Rousseau (1973: 113), following Machiavelli, emphasised the incompatibility of the otherworldly and universal message of Christianity and the type of religion required by the state to bind its citizens together. He advocated that the state have a civil religion to which individuals must adhere if they are to be good and true citizens. This conflict between the universal pretensions of Catholic Christianity and the claims of the state came to a head during the French Revolution. In drawing up the Civil Constitution of the Clergy, the French state assumed full sovereignty over the church. The result was a divided church that was increasingly persecuted because it was not viewed as completely loyal to the French state. The logical extension of this process was to create a new social ethos that would play the role in the French republic of civil religion. Although it recognised some sort of supreme being, this religion was essentially pagan and patriotic in nature (see McLeod 1981).

France paid a considerable price for opening up this conflict between church and nation. Deep fissures in the French national identity were created: one was *either* a secular republican *or* a Catholic royalist. This was symbolised in the struggle, at the village level, between the schoolteacher and the priest. Which of the two represented the true France? America was more successful in combining the universal claims of religion and the particularist aspirations of the nation-state. The Lockean tradition of natural rights guaranteed by God enabled Americans to conceive of their republic as an expression of God's will. In America the civil religion of the nation-state did not stand in opposition to the universal principles of Christianity and liberalism – instead, it embodied those very principles.

The distinctive experiences of France and America indicate that the relationship between the universal identities required by Christianity and liberalism and the more particularistic identity of the nation-state will vary according to circumstances. How any individual state deals with the problem depends on the circumstances under which that state came into being. It is by no means certain that the claims of the state and those of humanity will be reconciled, nor that the members of a nation-state will want to bring them into harmony. Similar problems may be observed in Australia.

The problem of universalism and particularity

Those who seek to bring humanity into harmony with national identity are usually those heirs of a doctrine of social sympathy under which individuals rise from a particularistic concern with self to a universal sympathy with the whole of humanity. In a way this is just Hegel taken a step further so that humanity rather than the nation-state becomes the ethical goal of humanity. In Australia this ideal was first expressed by the founding principal of the University of Sydney, John Woolley (1862), who argued that an individual discovered his true self through the development of his capacity for universal sympathy. Only in that way could an individual develop his or her full moral potential. As we shall see, this has been a consistent liberal position and one that cannot be reconciled with the limitations that restricting identity to the nation-state places on human sympathy. On this account, nationality as ultimate goal can only stunt humanity's capacity for moral development.

The heirs of Machiavelli and Rousseau are happy to restrict their sympathy to the boundaries of the state. Mutual obligation only extends to people who are similar in terms of ethnic origin or shared cultural traditions. Outside this group, there are those who threaten the continued existence of the nation as an entity capable of expressing its particular virtues and values. Hence the nation-state has the right to deny entry to those who would weaken its moral fibre and to develop policies that build up the virtue of its citizens. In this sense the 'Australian Settlement' (Kelly 1992) of the early twentieth century is no more than a logical extension of the political ideas of Machiavelli (1970), and its supporters his, largely unconscious, heirs.

This chapter argues that there has been a conflict in Australia between the universalist identities contained in Christianity and liberalism and those identities developed to express national ideals. (A similar argument could be mounted for international socialism.) Unlike their American cousins, Australians generally have been unable to unify their national and their universal obligations, instead preferring to invest in their nationality at the expense of their humanity. Various conceptions of Australian national identity have absorbed those elements of liberalism and Christianity which could be made to conform with nationalism, and restricted to the margins those elements that could not. Until recently, the universalist obligations of religion and political philosophy have been down-played. The dominant images of Australian national identity have often been those associated with distinctive features of place, such as the outback, and various military variations upon them. Over the last decade, however, the universalist rhetoric of international free trade *has* been combined successfully with the rhetoric of national economic development. And opposition to what has been called economic rationalism has come from religious as well as secular political quarters.

The source of this dichotomy between universal and particular lies in the peculiar circumstances of Australian social development. Neither liberalism nor Christianity has been able to present itself as truly universal but instead has been stigmatised as being partial in nature. In effect, liberalism has been presented as a class doctrine, and Christianity has been dogged by sectarianism. Nineteenth-century free trade liberalism conceived of itself as founded on a set of universal principles that would eventually raise humanity to a higher stage of moral and commercial development (Melleuish 1985). Its advocates argued that the spread of the values of civilisation and science through the intercourse of nations was a spur to human progress and the prelude to the creation of the brotherhood of humanity. As such it was not opposed to a doctrine of human rights that transcended race and nationality. Its opponents successfully stigmatised it as the ideology of the commercial upper classes seeking to undermine the position of good, honest British workers, and to favour the interests of less civilised and racially different foreigners. In other words, free trade was portrayed as an attack on the obligations that the employers owed to members of their own community. It became a matter of irreconcilable demands – one supported either the principles of liberalism or the rights of free-born Englishmen. As Pearson (1894) argued, the former were seen to be attained only at the expense of the latter; and in a democratic community, this could only mean that liberalism's universal pretensions would be submerged by a doctrine of national interest.

The liberalism of Thomas Hill Green played a key role in justifying this tendency in Australia. Green upheld a doctrine of social rights in which the ultimate source of rights was not God but the society of which the individual was a member, because 'every right is derived from some social relation' (Green 1941: 146). Our rights grow out of our membership of families and other forms of association up to and including the state. This doctrine of social rights could be absorbed by the men who helped to create the Australian settlement because it created a form of national identity emphasising social solidarity and the mutual obligations existing among the members of the Australian Commonwealth. It helped to create the belief that Australia constituted a moral community. But was it to be a moral community asserting itself against the rest of the world or one that found its fulfilment in that wider set of obligations that constituted humanity?

We are back in the dispute between the heirs of Hegel and the heirs of Machiavelli. Greenian liberalism, like Hegel but unlike Machiavelli, could be extended beyond the nation-state to encompass humanity, and this did in fact happen among a number of Australians who claimed the Greenian heritage, namely Francis Anderson and his students. It could also, however, be assimilated to a doctrine of national efficiency whereby the social solidarity created by the sense of moral identity is intended to create a more powerful and productive nation in the commercial battle against other nations. The national identity created in this way becomes an emblem of the *virtu* of the nation, an expression of its capacity to exert itself. More recently, Francis Fukuyama (1992) has written of *thymos*, or the need for individuals to feel self-worth. It is this need for self-worth or self-assertion that characterises this particular understanding of national identity.

The dominant political conceptions of Australian national identity have been able to absorb a modified version of liberalism that was willing to recognise the moral primacy of the nation-state. Rowse (1978: 42) has argued that this form of liberalism sits easily with utilitarianism because it accepts as its goal an efficient nation-state that fulfils the needs of its members and realises their moral potential. One consequence of this situation is that many of the specifically liberal elements are washed out of the discourses about Australian national identity. In part, this is because they are opposed to the insistence that the nation-state remain the ultimate boundary of social sympathy and hence social obligation. Nevertheless, liberals in Australia can be divided up into two camps which may be described as 'Machiavellian nationalists' and 'Hegelian internationalists'.

'Machiavellian nationalism'

Machiavellian nationalist liberalism has been concerned primarily with ensuring the strength of Australia so that it can become a competitive player in the international arena. This tradition can be traced back to the writings of Clarence Northcott (1918) and W.K. Hancock (1930). Both Northcott and Hancock believed that the primary problem facing Australia was finding a way to reconcile Australians' desire for justice and the imperative of efficiency. The context was an international order composed of nation-states, each seeking to fulfil its vision of a just social order and to create prosperity for its people. But there is no real standard of international justice. Hancock accepts that other countries have their own conception of a 'fair price' and if attaining that fair price means the ruin of Australia, there is no court of appeal.

According to this liberal vision, Australians, in their pursuit of justice, have developed character traits that destroy the efficiency of the Australian economy, thereby sapping the strength of the nation. In their quest for virtue Australians had lost their *virtu*. Indeed this loss of *virtu* became the defining characteristic of the Australian national identity for a whole generation of journalists and writers as they bemoaned the laziness, self-interestedness and hostility to ideas of the inhabitants of the 'lucky country'. The crucial point for Hancock was that without an efficient economy producing a certain level of prosperity, the quest for a just social order would be seriously undermined. There had to be a reconciliation between justice and efficiency, virtue and *virtu*, or else the rest of the world would leave Australia far behind.

This form of Machiavellian national liberalism re-emerged with a vengeance during the 1980s. Again Australia was perceived to be falling behind in the great race of nations because it was pursuing policies that were undermining its national strength. If it was to avoid the fate of becoming the 'poor white trash of Asia', it needed a strong dose of efficiency to restore its *virtu*. The means for achieving this goal was to open up the economy to international and domestic market pressures. Hence the former Secretary of the Treasury, John Stone (1985), proclaimed the need to 'de-regulate or perish'. Great emphasis was placed on the 'discipline' of the market. Economic rationalism was not put forward as a policy that would dissolve Australia into the great cauldron of international capitalism, but as a means of rebuilding Australia's national vigour. John Stone (nd), for example, is a genuine Australian patriot.

Nor did economic rationalism necessarily involve the abandonment of the pursuit of justice. Rather it placed the virtue/*virtu* split within Australian national identity back on the agenda. There were those who believed that the pursuit of virtue could be absorbed into the pursuit of *virtu*. The Liberal Party (1991), with its *Fightback!* policy document, came close to asserting this position, and it could be argued that this contributed to their failure to regain office. There can be no doubt that in the 1980s and early 1990s the Labor Party was much more successful in balancing the imperatives of economic rationalism as the foundation of a new national *virtu* with the traditional Australian ethos of the 'fair go'. Perhaps it could be argued that Labor felt more comfortable with recent developments because it had always been the party of national efficiency and so could accommodate itself to what has been largely a change in the means adopted to attain that goal. If protection no longer delivers the goods, then a good dose of deregulation may do the trick. What has not changed is the belief that obligation stops at the boundary of the nation-state, and that humanity is to be subordinated to the interests of nationality. International free trade is not considered an end in itself, the establishment of a peaceful and co-operative international order, but a means to be manipulated in the name of the nation-state for the purpose of increasing the strength of that state. Australian advocates of free trade acknowledge the possible flow-on benefits to global trade and other countries, but this is not their prime objective.

'Hegelian internationalism'

Hegelian internationalist liberalism views the creation of just such a co-operative international order as the final product of the spinning of a web of social sympathy that begins with the individual and his or her search for self-realisation. The individual moves in ever increasing circles from family to school to state and finally to humanity. Individual fulfilment comes through an expansion of one's sympathy as one encounters each new level of human association. Eventually the individual is capable of expressing his or her fully developed nature as someone capable of understanding and expressing their responsibilities towards humanity. To allow one's development to stop short of humanity is to fail to realise one's potential as a human being.

This view of human nature emphasises the positive benefits to be gained through the enlargement of one's sympathy and the consequences of allowing it to remain at a level below humanity. Such individuals become stunted in their approach to the world, the victims of their petty fears and jealousies. This variety of liberalism also emphasises the co-operative side of human nature. The expansion of human powers involves the development of the capacity of human beings for co-operation. At a social level, international co-operation is the outcome of the fulfilment of the principles of humanity.

Although much of this sounds somewhat idealistic, it has had a long and distinguished history in Australia from John Woolley to Ernest Burgmann and beyond. It has been effectively confined to the margins of Australian political life because it was not willing to sacrifice humanity to nationality. It was not opposed to the idea of the nation as a form of social organisation within which justice could be pursued. But it insisted that the achievement of co-operative principles within the nation-state was only the prelude to their attainment at an international level. Nation-states were not competitive entities always seeking their own advantage, but steps on the road to the establishment of a fully co-operative humanity. Consequently, adherents of this form of liberalism supported free trade as a form of international co-operation. Protection was a product of the competition between nation-states. Equally nationalism was to be abhorred when it prevented the growth of the mutual bonds of humanity. None of this makes much sense either to a Machiavellian or to the ordinary citizen of a nation-state.

The significance of Hegelian internationalist liberalism is not that it has had a major impact on conceptions of Australian national identity. Rather it is that it has survived as a minority outlook in a society largely hostile to its tenets. Despite the rhetoric, the revival of free trade in the 1980s owed very little to the ideals of this form of liberalism. As we have seen, that revival is fully explainable within a Machiavellian framework. And yet it does survive in such works as Charles Birch's *On Purpose* (1990) as a framework from within which a critique of the shortcomings of Machiavellian national liberalism can be launched. Humanity has not yet been expelled from the vocabulary of Australian politics.

Moreover, there are good reasons to believe that a healthy national identity will be in harmony with the ideals of humanity. Ernest Burgmann (1944) argued, in a similar way to Simone Weil (1978), that individuals have a genuine need for roots that will provide them with that security within which their individuality can flourish. A people that is secure in its roots will be able to deal with the wider world with confidence and self-assurance, seeing other peoples not as com-petitors but as possible partners. After all, Machiavelli's political doctrines developed within the context of a highly unstable and in-secure Italian political situation where changes of government were the rule rather than the exception. Following Weil one could argue that Australians, like the ancient Romans, are an insecure people driven to dispossess others because they, themselves, were dispossessed. Their exclusive vision of themselves and the national identity that followed from it was the consequence of that insecurity and root-lessness. Hancock argued a similar position in 1930 (see also Melleuish 1995).

The liberal desire to harmonise the national and the universal identities of people can be seen as no idle dream. There is no reason why the two cannot be seen as complementary. Instead, it is arguable that the Machiavellian form of liberalism is the abnormal or perverse variety, at odds with the true interests of both humanity and the need for individuals to possess a secure identity.

There is yet another problem with the operation of Machiavellian national liberalism in Australia. As we have seen, identity implies obligation. In Australia there has been a strong historical tendency to exclude Aborigines from images of national identity, and to define them as the 'other', outside those images. One consequence of this development is the recent growth of the belief that European Australians have different obligations to Aborigines than they have to each other (see Brunton 1993). Even when this idea is cast in a positive light, it faces profound difficulties that can be resolved only through the adoption of an identity that recognises humanity as the ultimate source of obligation. A commitment to humanity must recognise that obligation transcends particularity, without wanting to abolish particularity as the soil in which the roots of identity grow.

Christian and liberal identities

Christianity has long been excluded from discussions of national identity. Hancock's *Australia* does not even mention religion at all, nor do the many books that took up his themes. This is curious when one considers just how important religion was in helping most Australians to define their identity. The great divide between Protestants and Catholics cast its shadow on many aspects of Australian life from education to politics, to sport, to the public service and to the police force (see Hogan 1987). There were even Protestant and Catholic department stores in most of the capital cities, as for example in Sydney's Horden's and Mark Foys. The essential problem was that while Christianity claimed universality it practised division. In cultural terms, it was long the major source of division within Australian society. On this basis it appeared safer to exclude religion altogether from popular images of national identity because there was no common ground between Catholics and Protestants.

And yet religion was not banished completely. The problem was largely viewed as one of doctrine or dogma; the solution appeared to be to strip Christianity of its doctrinal elements so that what was left was universal spiritual truths and morality. Nevertheless, this program was only ever attractive to Protestants, usually of the liberal or secular variety. George Shaw (1988b) has argued that the Judeo-Christian ethic entered into the school system as a form of moral education designed to prevent the inheritors of a vice-ridden society from straying from the straight and narrow path. As such, Christianity may be said to have entered into the Australian national identity as a series of 'thou shalt nots' learnt either dogmatically at a Catholic school or non-dogmatically at a state school. Although it has long been a subject of fun, it remains true that wowserism is an important element of liberal and conservative images of Australian national identity.

Many intellectuals sought a solution to the religious problem by searching for a more spiritual religion that satisfied their longings for universality. In the late nineteenth and early twentieth century, many liberal Australian intellectuals chased after theosophy and spiritualism, including Alfred Deakin and Christopher Brennan (see Gabay 1992 and Roe 1986). These religions particularly appealed to those liberals attracted to Hegelian internationalist liberalism. They were very much a minority, limited to what was then the educated minority of Australian society. Nevertheless, the more recent emergence of New Age religions in Australia demonstrates that they were not alone in their eccentricity.

Conclusion

Those seeking a universalist religious identity in Australia have often been placed in a similar position to universalist liberals. To leave the solid ground of particularist identity, be it national or religious, and to go in search of a more universal identity meant to leave the mainstream of Australian life and to risk being regarded as at best somewhat eccentric. For a long time this has meant that Australians, with few notable exceptions, have remained locked within the confines of their particularistic identities, generally satisfied with the limits that were thereby placed on their capacity to develop their humanity. One tendency in Australia, however, was to make essentially secular acts, like heroism in war, into sacred ones, and to imbue them with the spiritual qualities and respect previously reserved for religion.

And yet the universalistic ideals of both liberalism and formal religion have remained within the fabric of Australian culture. It could be argued that the demise of the 'Australian Settlement' during the 1980s, combined with changes in the international order, including the end of the Cold War and the process of globalisation, has created an environment within which the universal values of liberalism with its emphasis on international co-operation may yet flourish. Nevertheless, as we have also seen, many of the changes that have occurred in Australia during this period indicate the residual strength of Machiavellian nationalist liberalism. The nation-state is by no means about to disappear. Perhaps the best that can be hoped for is that with the disappearance of the 'Australian Settlement' the old restrictive form of nationalism will slowly be replaced by a more positive variety which recognises that adherence to humanity does not entail the denial of those obligations we owe to our fellow citizens, but rather extends and completes them.

Gender and Sexuality

CHAPTER 4

'Manly, True and White': Masculine Identity and Australian Socialism

Michael Leach[1]

As feminist historians and theorists of 'men's studies' have argued, masculinity is a relational construct which can only be understood in the context of gender relations (Scott 1988; Roper and Tosh 1991). More important, however, the relationship of masculinity to femininity is one of power: the changing forms of masculinity are always represented as more valuable, and generally as more powerful than those of femininity. As Roper and Tosh (1991: 2–4) argue, masculinity is crucially shaped in relation to men's social power. Consequently, representations of masculine identity not only reflect men's social power over women, but are also integral to power struggles between men. The feminist historian Joan Scott (1988: 6) has argued that the meanings of sexual difference are invoked and contested across a range of power struggles. Similarly, other theorists have stressed the importance of power relations between men in understanding gender relations and constructions of masculinity (Saunders and Evans 1992: xix; Carrigan et al. 1985). Some of the most interesting theoretical work on gender focuses on the role of gender as an organising principle for social structures, exploring the ways in which the meanings of class and race are partly established through contested understandings of gender identity and sexual difference (Scott 1988; Roper and Tosh 1991; Grimshaw 1993).

Conceptions of masculine identity have only recently been recognised as important themes in Australian cultural history. In her pioneering article on the topic, Marilyn Lake (1986a: 116) argued that men in Australian history have been treated as 'sex-less' universal subjects, rather than as pursuing particular 'masculinist' gender interests, along with the divergent concerns of class and race. Lake's primary contention is that 'gender-blind' historiography has ignored masculinity as a social and political construction requiring historical explanation.

As a consequence, historically defined gender identities appear in analyses of Australian political culture as natural, static and unproblematic 'sex roles'. Any history of *male* domination and power remains concealed by the presumption that power and interests inhere solely in the categories of class and race.

A number of articles, focusing on the operation of 'masculinism' in Australian history and political thought, have highlighted its importance and analytical utility (Lake 1986b; Allen 1987; Saunders and Evans 1992; Gilding 1992; Magarey et al. 1993). Lake's own work (1986a) examined the role of masculinism in the radical nationalist school, exemplified by the *Bulletin*, and (1986b) in the writings of the influential Australian socialist William Lane. In her discussion of Lane, Lake argued that the platforms and representations of Australian socialism were informed by a particular conception of masculinity and a working-class male anxiety over gender status. My aim here is to expand upon these themes and examine the nature and importance of ideas of masculine identity to Australian socialist writers. In general, the analysis confirms that the ideological discourse and strategies of early Australian socialism need to be acknowledged as, among other things, expressions of a 'masculinist' politics.

Australian socialist thinkers aimed at forging a positive working-class identity from a constellation of powerful contemporary discourses apart from those of socialism. These included ideologies of nationalism, national character, racial unity, social Darwinism and, importantly, gender identity. Often derived from powerful discourses of 'Empire', some of these themes were incorporated uncritically into Australian socialist thought. Most, however, were reframed to add ideological strength to the movement. These elements did not exist separately but formed an interdependent cluster of values constructing a socialist and unionist identity for Australian (male) workers. Ideas of masculinity and manhood were central to this identity. In reaching this conclusion, I argue that we must refine our conception of masculinism. Second, I contend that important socialist feminist challenges to the dominant 'masculinism', such as those offered by William Lane, were undermined by a largely uncontested version of class analysis which was defined primarily in relation to masculine identity.

Contesting and conceptualising masculinism

Lake's work on masculinism has stimulated much debate among historians (McConville 1987; Scates 1990; Docker 1993). The debate between Lake and Scates is particularly interesting as it focuses on the work of William Lane, one of the leading figures in 1890s Australian socialism, author of the influential labour novel *The Workingman's Paradise*, and, I would submit, clearly a socialist feminist. Lake (1986b) argues that notions of manhood and masculinity were central to early Australian socialists' analyses of capitalism and class relations. For socialist writers like Lane, working-class oppression was not only a question of economic exploitation, but one of masculine degradation (Lake 1986b: 55). Capitalism was portrayed as emasculating, robbing men of their independence through the institution of wage labour, which not only denied men the value of their labour, but forced them to work on another man's terms (1986b: 54–6). Through unionism, and under socialism, male workers could 'retrieve their status as men' (1986b: 54). Lake claims that while Lane saw men and women as equal, the dichotomy between manliness and womanliness remains central to his analysis (1986b: 60). More generally, she argues that Australian labour movements were characterised by their adoption of Chartist strategies: manhood suffrage, the male living wage, and the exclusion of non-white and female labour (1986b: 56). In this sense, the institution of the family wage in 1907 may partially be viewed as an achievement of a masculinist politics (1986b: 62). In a reply to Lake's argument, Bruce Scates (1990: 45–6) identifies Lane as a socialist feminist, arguing that he was not solely preoccupied with masculinity, but with challenging the gender order, particularly the sexual division of labour and the sexual domination of women by men. A discussion of the concept of masculinism may shed light on what is at issue in this debate.

Masculinism may be generally defined as the political expression of specifically male gender interests and practices, analogous with, but diametrically opposed to, feminism (Magarey et al. 1993: xviii; Allen 1987: 618). The term 'masculinism', however, can be seen as comprising three distinctive but interdependent categories. The first category may be labelled *platform* masculinism, and refers to explicit policies – such as the male 'living wage', manhood suffrage, workplace exclusion of women, and so on – which advantage men over women. This form of masculinism has been readily identifiable as outright sexism. The second category is *androcentric* masculinism, which is more implicitly masculinist in the sense that it presumes that the male is the primary subject of political or historical analysis. This form of masculinism can be seen in both primary and secondary texts of the labour movement. In treating the masculine as a universal norm, it also presumes that men unproblematically represent the interests of women from a similar class and race. Similarly, androcentric masculinism may conflate ideals of masculinity with broader notions of national tradition or identity (Lake 1986a: 117).

The third category, related to the second, might be described as *affective* masculinism. I use this term to refer to direct appeals to masculine *identity* as a device for the political mobilisation of men. Whereas androcentric masculinism generally affirms the public sphere and politics as an unproblematically or naturally male domain, affective masculinism specifically exhorts the male subject to act in one of the variety of contested ways a man should act. Affective masculinism takes the form of an appeal to a sense of masculine identity, and commonly seeks to construct a particular identity with reference to a set of political goals. In this sense, the principal function of affective masculinism is to convey the meaning of a political position with reference to masculine identity. The meanings of such representations are conveyed through processes of differentiation and exclusion. Masculine identity is constructed and sustained by its contrast with the 'other', such as 'womanliness'.

On this analysis, therefore, both Lake *and* Scates may be correct. Lane, I would suggest, is demonstrably pro-feminist, owing more to the visionary egalitarianism of Edward Bellamy and William Morris than many of his Australian contemporaries. Lane does not share, but rather contests, the *platform* masculinism of the labour movement. He is, however, as Lake demonstrates, preoccupied with masculinity. To the extent that Lane's egalitarianism is derived from essentially masculine values, presented as universal, then his work may be considered to be a form of *androcentric* masculinism. Yet what characterises Lane's socialism is the centrality of *affective* masculinism, the use of appeals to masculine identity to convey the meaning of class oppression and relations. In the following pages I will explore a number of the key components and tensions within platform masculinism and affective masculinism in the early writings on Australian socialism.

Platform masculinism

An examination of the explicit policies of the labour movement towards the 'woman question' is a useful starting point, not simply because of their importance to definitions of gender, but because they can be seen as specific outcomes of a broader concern with the nature of masculine identity.

For male writers in the early labour movement, issues surrounding women's 'proper sphere' were, albeit to varying degrees, considered sufficiently important to warrant serious attention. For some, like Lane, the questions of women's labour were central to both the critique of capitalism and the strategies of the union movement. For others, these subjects could be conceived of as secondary, but could rarely be ignored. The content of debates concerning women's oppression and their place in the labour movement focused primarily on two questions: women's involvement in the paid workforce, and the sexual division of labour. The discourses of 'platform' masculinism were constructed in various ways with issues of sexuality and reproduction, significantly, receiving less attention. Other concerns included the status of marriage, the family, and women's suffrage.

In her study of the Victorian socialist weekly *Tocsin*, Patricia Grimshaw (1993: 100) argues that men's responses to these issues were informed by a gendered sense of their own identity, though the hegemony of the dominant masculinist positions was occasionally contested. This pattern is reflected across the key primary texts of Lane (1980), Spence (1909), Hughes (1970) and Jensen (1909), and in the Queensland socialist journal, the *Worker*. Political positions on the 'woman question' ranged from the Darwinist misogyny of Jensen to the socialist feminism of Lane. Somewhere in between these extremes the dominant expression of socialist masculinism alternated between the active support of women's civil emancipation and the protection of male wage levels and their status as breadwinner.

The official platforms of the nascent labour movements in the early 1890s reflected a tradition of radicalism attributable in part to British Chartism. Provisions demanding manhood suffrage and minimum wages for men were the norm, though the Queensland branch, under the influence of Lane, advocated adult suffrage as early as 1890. By the middle of the next decade, however, most of the various state and federal platforms supported adult suffrage, civic equality and equal pay for women. Some, like New South Wales, supported 'equal work rights' for men and women. These later provisions revealed the extent of the influence of first-wave feminism and, probably, that of socialist feminists within the movement itself. Moreover, it reflected the important and active commitment of the labour movement on issues of civil and political equality for women. Very early in the history of the organised labour movement, Lane urged his comrades not to accept franchise proposals that excluded women (*Worker* 13 June 1891: 5). On the other hand, Jensen (1909: 20) could argue that women's participation in the socialist state could lead to corruption as they had not yet been educated politically. While the mainstream of the socialist movement was committed to women's enfranchisement by the late 1890s, it was far more equivocal and was occasionally hostile to questions of women's paid labour and economic equality (cf. Grimshaw 1993: 112–13).

On the whole, the labour movement viewed women's waged labour, like non-white labour, as a threat to men's wages and conditions.

Significantly, competition from cheaper female labour was understood in gendered terms as a threat not only to economic solidarity as workers, but to men as men. Strong conceptions of masculine identity are evident throughout the varying responses to questions of women's paid labour. Male labour was considered primary, indeed superior. While labour produced all wealth, masculine endeavour was clearly regarded as more productive and hence worthy of higher wages. Cheaper female labour undermined not only wage levels, but other foundations of masculine identity: the ability to afford marriage, to avoid unemployment, to pro-vide for dependants. As Grimshaw (1993: 109) argues, strategies on the issue of women's paid labour fluctuated between unionisation and exclusion. Both strategies, however, reflected a primary concern with protecting male wage levels. The *Worker* from its inception consistently supported the unionisation of female labour. Lane argued very early on that the refusal to organise women workers was anti-socialist, a view which apparently attracted much opposition (*Worker* 1 April 1890: 1). Nevertheless, part of his argument reveals the masculinist concerns informing the debate. Organising women, he noted, was 'the only way to effectively prevent the competition of women' (*Worker* 1 April 1890: 2).

Generally, those supporting unionisation fell into two camps. On the one hand, Lane's call for unionisation was complemented by strident criticisms of the existing sexual division of labour (Lane 1980: 74–7; *Worker* 1 March 1890: 15). Women should be free to 'choose their own sphere', and unionisation would provide protection for women as well as preventing the undercutting of men's wages. By contrast, the dominant position of the labour movement was premised on the exclusion of women from long-term participation in waged labour. For these writers, unionisation of single women was essential primarily to reduce competition from cheaper female labour. Male wages could then be sustained at a level sufficient to make marriage economically viable, thus removing women to their 'proper sphere' as wife and mother, and freeing up jobs for other men to provide for families (*Worker* 17 August 1895: 7). Thus women could expect equal pay, but not equal par-ticipation. As one later commentator candidly put it (*Worker* 8 January 1920), the equal pay axiom was founded on the view that:

> [F]ew women would be the professional and industrial equals of men, and that consequently, when employers were called upon to make a choice between paying high rates to men or women for work of a similar character, they preferably would pay it to men, thus acknowledging the men as superior workers. The other idea underlying this Labor motto was to ensure that cheap female labour should not take the place of dearer male labour. Both ideas intended and expressed justice to women ... It may be accepted as

certain that the intention was for exceptional women to have equal chances
with able men ...

Beneath the egalitarian rhetoric of Labor's electoral platform
commitments to equal pay and even 'equal work rights', intense debate
and general insecurity about the workforce participation of women
continued. Moreover, the separate planks in the platforms were given
different priorities. These platforms were often compromised in
negotiations with the state, and undermined by union practice.
Significantly, such provisions were often accompanied by demands for
state 'subsidies to maternity'. While these demands were progressive
and, indeed, in line with some feminist calls, in another sense they
betray by implication a somewhat different attitude to the existing
sexual division of labour. One contemporary critic (St Ledger 1909:
153), an anti-socialist but sympathetic to the union movement, believed
maternity subsidy provisions arose from debates over the Harvester case,
and the settlement of the living wage at the standard suitable for
married rather than single men. St Ledger (1909: ix) approved of the
family wage decision, remarking that charges that labour sought to
weaken the marriage tie were 'foolish and unwarrantable'. Certainly
Lane had been conscious of these possibilities and their implications
when writing *The Workingman's Paradise*. Nellie, the socialist feminist
heroine of the novel, in debate with another socialist, strikes out at her
masculinist counterpart: 'you would leave the present relationship of
women to Society unchanged, except that you would serve her out free
rations' (Lane 1980: 72).

Chapter seven of *The Workingman's Paradise*, 'A medley of conversation', is, as well as being the primary vehicle for Lane's socialist
feminism, a fascinating chronicle of competing masculinist ideologies
within the socialist movement. Nellie, Ford and Geisner are found to be
advocating 'perfect equality between women and men' and women's
freedom to 'find their own sphere' (1980: 71). Stratton, on the other
hand, believes women are in their 'proper sphere' as wife and mother:
'Full-breasted and broad-hipped, fit to have children! ... and none of
them should work except for those they loved and of their own free will'
(Lane 1980: 71–2). Lane clearly endorses the former position, though
the means by which Nellie clinches the argument is revealing: 'you can't
raise free men from slave women' (1980: 73). Nevertheless, Lane's
conception of socialism was one that conceptualised the 'recognition of
women's equality' as an arena of struggle distinct but equally important
to 'the reorganisation of industry' (1980: 123). Lane's problematisation
of sexual politics also extended, though to a lesser degree, to questions
of reproduction (1980: 75) and domestic violence (1980: 20).

The marginalisation of socialist feminism and its replacement by a more strident platform masculinism is documented in the history of the *Worker*. Lane, under the pseudonym 'Lucinda Sharpe', wrote a regular column which provided socialist feminist perspectives on a range of issues. From 1890 to 1893, 'Lucinda' was a stern critic of the sexual division of labour (*Worker* 1 April 1890: 15):

> Most women put in 17 hours out of the twenty-four and get nothing for it whatever but board and clothes. The men wonder why the women don't make home happy and why, in the name of all saints, they don't keep young and smiling and plump and generally grateful to the lordly being who does so much for them.

By 1895, after Lane's departure to Paraguay, 'Lucinda' became a contented housewife, railing against women who take men's jobs, arguing that the solution to the problem of women's competition is marriage. 'Lucinda' even goes so far as to question the need for women's franchise, as when in her natural sphere 'she has only an enquiring curiosity for what happens outside' (*Worker* 17 August 1895: 7). By 1905 'Lucinda' had disappeared altogether from the pages of the *Worker*, along with general debate over 'women's sphere' and sexual politics. Platform masculinism had achieved ascendancy within the labour movement. The *Worker*'s coverage of women's issues from this time was incorporated more rigidly within the frameworks of class analysis, as the column 'In a woman's mind' demonstrated by its dominant focus on unionisation of female labour. For these writers, women had 'issues' if they were paid workers, but if they were in the home, which was considered their place, their interests were inseparable from those of husband and family.

Though the platform masculinism of the labour movement did not go unchallenged from within, it had emerged as dominant well before the Harvester judgment enshrined the male breadwinner as the primary subject of the federal Arbitration Court. Reactions to the 'woman question' were structured by a conception of masculine identity as public, productive, and fundamentally different from feminine identity. Importantly, understandings of masculine identity not only structured approaches to gender politics, but were central to the analysis of capitalism and class relations (see Grimshaw 1993: 100). As Saunders and Evans (1992: xix) note, understandings of gender are constructed in 'a multiplicity of ways and locations, not simply at those cutting edges where the genders meet'. Ironically, the use of masculine identity as a reference point for the meanings of oppression and class relations was one of the defining features of Lane's socialism.

Affective masculinism

For the researcher interested in the role gender identity plays in structuring political debate, the amount of information available can be eye-opening. The secondary texts of Australian labour history hardly serve as adequate preparation for the sheer extent and prevalence of notions of gender identity in the 'primary' sources. Indeed, the absence of a recognition of masculine identity as a prominent theme in Australian political thought is prima facie evidence supporting Lake's charge of androcentrism: there is no lack of material for those who are looking. Certainly, for the theorists and activists of the early labour movement, masculinity was neither irrelevant nor secondary.

Concepts of manhood had a number of important functions in socialist thought. Firstly, the notion of manhood posits a prior political order from which a claim to rights can be made and legitimated. Claims to manhood ground 'ideological' debates in the realm of the 'natural' truths of biology, or at least in the widely accepted truths of gender. It thus serves as a 'neutral' benchmark for establishing the worth of a position. Conservatives, liberals and socialists alike could ask, 'What are the consequence for manhood?', even as they affirmed its own ideological nature by contesting its definition.[2] Understandings of masculine identity filtered through most important political debates, conveying the meanings of positions on class relations, oppression, racial competition and nationalism, among others. Moreover, this appeal to masculine identity, 'affective masculinism', seeks to secure the political commitment and mobilisation of men by embedding political positions in the 'deeper' certainties or, indeed, anxieties (Lake 1986b: 54) of gender identity.

For the 'utopian' and reformist socialists of nineteenth-century Australia, finding a political identity for workers was not simply an economic question of their relationship to the means of production. Socialist or unionist identities were assembled from the broader 'Empire' discourses of race, nation, civilisation and gender identity, partially reconstituted to bolster the radical platforms of the labour movement. Although the ways in which concepts of race and nation structured the understanding of class have been explored (e.g. McQueen 1970), the significance of gender identity remains somewhat neglected. In pursuing this line of inquiry, of course, it should not be forgotten that claiming 'rights as men' is one way of asserting *human* rights in response to manifest oppression. But these important questions are not neglected themes in Australian history. As Scott (1988: 88) argued in her studies of British and French socialist movements, the use of sexual difference and gender identity in constructing and naturalising the meanings of class requires attention. In adopting this

approach, it can be argued that the platform masculinism of the
Australian labour movement was ultimately the corollary of an understanding of oppression and class identity defined in primary relation to
masculine identity.

William Spence's (1909: 54) tribute to the men of the labour
movement succinctly captures a widely held stance on the nature and
importance of a socialist and unionist identity that extends beyond the
economics of class membership: 'Rough and unpopular many of them
may be, but manly, true and "white" all the time, and the movement
owes them much.' Throughout the nineteenth and early twentieth
century, the notion of manliness had currency across the ideological
spectrum, and through it an extensive range of political arenas were
fissured with understandings of masculine identity. As noted earlier, one
of these arenas was the workplace. Jensen (1909: 46), for instance, could
argue that the employment of women 'ought to be a good thing if not
overdone' in that it 'tends to make women more strong minded and
independent', in effect more masculine. Just as the definition of paid
labour as a sphere of masculine endeavour influenced responses to
questions of women's participation, concepts of manhood underwrote
analyses of relations between capital and labour.

For while the sphere of paid labour was defined as masculine, under
capitalism it was the realm where manhood would be lost or won. This
is one of the enduring images permeating the socialist analysis of class
society. As Lake (1986b: 55) notes, working-class exploitation was commonly cast in terms of masculine degradation, defined by the loss of
'manly independence'. The term 'manly independence' and its particular meaning were undoubtedly inherited from the iconography of
British Chartism (Lake 1986b: 56). McClelland (1991: 82) explains that
the term 'independence' had a distinctly masculine form and meaning
in British Chartism, in that it was defined by the ability to maintain
dependants within the home. Reflecting its artisan basis, 'independence' also implied some freedom in the sale of labour power and in
the regulation of their particular trades. Above all, independence meant
not being a wage slave. For Chartists, maintaining this conception of
'independence' was the primary function of collective organisation
(McClelland 1991: 83).

The influence of these ideas on the Australian labour movement is
apparent in the approaches of its major writers. Spence (1909: 16)
attributes part of the strength of the early labour movement to the
'hundreds of artisans' who were trade unionists before emigration.
Moreover, the credo of independence was an inherent feature of
Australian identity (Spence 1909: 17):

> Though forced to earn a living by working for another man, the Australian
> worker never lost his independence of spirit. He would not cringe to anyone.
> The employer was to him nothing more than a man – certainly no better than
> himself.

The theme of working for 'another man' recurs consistently in
Australian socialist thought as the ultimate injustice of capitalist social
relations. For Spence, Hughes and particularly Lane, the 'degradation'
of manly independence is a primary vehicle for transmitting the
meaning of working class oppression. Indeed, it is a central theme of
The Workingman's Paradise. Capitalism 'crushes the manhood out of
men' (*Worker* 1 August 1890), reducing them to brutes 'consciousless of
the dignity of manhood' (Lane 1980: 36–7). Through unionism, men
can defend 'that which is dearer to them than property – their
manhood' (*Worker* 1 July 1890: 2). But unionism is ultimately not
enough: 'The evil is in having to ask another man for work at all ... The
whole wage system must be utterly done away with' (Lane 1980: 108). To
be a man again, the worker must organise and co-operate to secure his
independence 'until men live like mates and pay nothing to any man for
leave to work' (1980: 117).

To replace 'another man' with 'employer' in these passages is to
significantly alter that part of the meaning that resides in the rhetorical
appeal to a masculine self-image. Affective masculinism seeks, in this
way, to mobilise men politically through the emotive appeal to a sense of
masculine identity. The rational claims of politics are given meaning
and force by emotion: anxiety, revulsion, anger, pity, belonging. As
Lane's protagonist acknowledges upon his conversion to socialism
(1980: 113): 'Mates! Do you know that's a word I like?' said Ned. 'It
makes you feel good, just the sound of it.'

The primary consequence of affective masculinism, however, is that
of inscribing the movement and, arguably, even the definition of class
itself with masculine meanings and priorities. As Lane demonstrates,
'masculine' does not necessarily translate into 'male'. Nevertheless,
where the understanding of oppression is conveyed with primary
reference to masculine identity, and the struggle is coded as the 'getting
of manhood', women's participation becomes problematic to say the
least. Their position becomes secondary, and often consists in
encouraging men to be manly (see Lane 1980: 3, 213; Spence 1909: 53).
Masculine identity assumes a primacy, both as the subject of oppression
and as the agent of change. Moreover, the claims to justice made by
early Australian socialists are similarly structured by their use of the
prior political order of gender. In one sense, they are strengthened:
capitalism violates the *natural* order of gender in which men have

independence. As Scott argues, gender naturalises particular meanings of class.[3] In another sense, they are structured along masculinist lines. For 'manly independence' is a political condition established not only in relation to an owning class, but necessarily in relation to working class women, who must remain dependent.

The tension between Lane's socialist feminism and his use of affective masculinism is evident in his vision of a new society as expressed by one of the female characters (Lane 1980: 12): 'there would be such a doing and such an upsetting and such a righting of things that ever after every man would be his own master and every woman would only work eight hours and get well paid for it.' The contradiction in Lane's socialist vision lies in his attempt to include women in a movement that is defined, even by himself, with primary reference to masculine identity. Socialism will reclaim manhood by delivering independence to working men, for women it will provide work and decent conditions. The highest ethics of socialism offer autonomy and self-mastery to men, for there is no need for women to be 'their own masters', indeed there is no word for it.

Lane's analysis of oppression under capitalism is deeply gendered. Men become 'brutes' and lose the dignity of independence and manhood. Women become hard, defeminised and above all 'wearied' and 'weary' (1980: 5, 36, 37). Nonetheless, that which men have lost becomes the theme of the struggle for a socialist society: 'Neither ballots nor bullets will avail unless we strive of ourselves to be men' (1980: 225). Lane's important challenge to the platform masculinism of the labour movement was substantial yet ultimately partial, undermined not only by the wider opposition and indifference to socialist feminism, but by his own understanding of class relations which affirmed a pre-dominantly masculine identity for the socialist movement (see Lake 1991: 116).

Conceptions of masculine identity were also used to communicate the meanings of other ideological positions integral to Australian socialist thought. In effect, most discourses utilised by Australian socialism were brought into sharper focus through the 'affective' use of gendered representations. Ruling class and Chinese men are depicted in ways that are an affront to 'true, white' masculinity. They both leer covetously at white working class women (Lane 1980: 9, 25), the implied threat of rape and subjugation playing upon chivalrous and proprietal notions. Ruling class men are 'round-bellied' (Hughes 1970: 10), 'loudly jewelled' and unmanly (Lane 1980: 25). But there are exceptions. Lane's depiction of Strong, a squatter, outlines the ultimate priority of notions of masculine character and race, rather than class. Ruling class men are not condemned, in the final analysis, by their ownership of the means of production, but by their decadence, disloyalty to race and their unmanliness. The manly and white among them will be redeemed by socialism and will have their place in the progress of humanity and civilisation (Lane 1980: 27):

> Those fat men are only good to put in museums, but these lean men are all right so long as you keep them in their place. They are our worst enemies when they're against us, but our best friends when they're for us. They say Mr. Strong isn't like most of the swell set. He is straight to his wife and good to his children ... Only he sees everything from the other side and doesn't understand that all men have got the same coloured blood.

This was a view widely held within the labour movement. Capitalism divides white men, setting them at war with each other to the detriment of the race and civilisation (see Spence 1909: 52; Lane 1980: 204–6). According to Jensen (1909: 131), class society destroys manhood, putting the race at risk of becoming 'weak and effeminate' in the struggle for survival.

This notion of a prior unity defined by race and masculinity was an important basis of the socialist critique of capitalism. The strength of race and nation lie in its 'crop of men' (Hughes 1970: 10), its 'vigorous young manhood' (Spence 1909: 369). This strength is squandered by capitalism but will be reclaimed by socialism. Just as British Chartists demanded justice on the basis of their status as 'free-born Englishmen' (McClelland 1991: 82), Australian socialists looked to the powerful imperial discourses of race and manhood to support their radical platforms. But they also turned to the distinctly Australian understandings of masculine identity: mateship and the 'Australian legend'.

Socialism, but mainly unionism, was represented as a political commitment which came easily to the Australian man. Socialism is mateship (*Hummer* 16 January 1892 in Clark 1955: 587–90), but proscribed by the ties of race and masculinity. As Spence argues (1909: 78): 'Unionism came to the Australian bushman as a religion ... It had in it that feeling of mateship which he understood already, and which had always characterised the action of one "white man" to another.' Socialist thinkers adopted the perceived strengths and peculiarities of the Australian national character, as it was expressed in the imagery of the radical nationalist 'Australian legend'. They saw socialism as an inherent ethic among Australian men, but one which needed to be organised and politicised. Other virtues of Australian bush masculinity were appropriated, particularly co-operation, generosity and pragmatism. Spence, for instance, invokes the image of the 'practical man' to demonstrate the superiority of the unionist to both the effete ruling class (1909: 377) and revolutionary socialists (1909: 381): 'No practical man can conceive it possible. It is not a healthy way of doing things.'

Lane, however, is critical of the bushman legend. Part of his project is to reconstruct a socialist mateship without the politically unhelpful and, indeed, often misogynist larrikinism. Mateship for him is not only a social ethic, but also an economic one, defined by material co-operation and sharing (1980: 17–18). Mateship is real, forged in the bush; but larrikinism is a fiction: 'We're not all built to one pattern any more than folks in town', declares Ned, who, in keeping with Lane's socialist feminism, doesn't drink, smoke, gamble or 'womanise' (1980: 60). As Scates argues (1990: 45), Lane's male characters deliver important challenges to contemporary understandings of manliness. While Lane enshrines 'manly independence', he also shifts the definition of 'manly' along pro-feminist lines. Nevertheless, it is masculine identity that remains primary to defining and explaining the aspirations of Lane's socialism.

Conclusion

It has been argued here that certain conceptions of masculine identity were integral to early Australian socialist constructions of a working-class political identity. Understandings of masculine identity as public, productive and 'other than' feminine identity structured the dominant political discourses of the labour movement on the many issues sur-rounding the 'woman question'. Nevertheless, the socialist approach to such issues was not uniform and may be understood better by reference to three different conceptions of masculinism, namely 'androcentric', 'affective' and 'platform' masculinism. In that Australian socialists generally assumed masculine values provided the standards for society, their masculinist ideas may be categorised as androcentric. When such assumptions are rendered into practical policies, the result may be called platform masculinism. Rhetorical attempts to mobilise working-class men, as men, to implement such policies represent various forms of affective masculinism.

Willam Lane offered significant challenge to that dominant form of platform masculinism that sought to affirm and institutionalise masculine values by means of policies such as manhood suffrage, the living wage, and exclusion of women from the workplace. Lane's androcentrism was qualified by a strong commitment to equality between working men and women. Argued in egalitarian terms, Lane's political thought represents a type of socialist feminism which was eventually marginalised within the labour movement of the early twentieth century.

Ironically, analysis of Lane's 'affective' discourse demonstrates that the potential scope of his challenge was undermined by an under-standing of class oppression defined primarily in relation to masculine identity. The emotive appeal of socialism as a means of overthrowing class oppression offered the possibility of realising 'manly' values such as those of 'independence'. Significantly, such values are inconceivable, or not considered appropriate, for most women. For the fictional heroine Nellie, autonomy is only possible by rejecting the life options of being married and having a family. Women's independence is only attainable by relinquishing what would have been central to the dominant ideal of adult female identity of the time.

Notes

1. I would like to thank Geoff Stokes for his valuable comments on this chapter.
2. The currency of notions of manhood in ideological debate is evident in Hughes' ironic retort to an unnamed conservative critic (1970: 142): 'If private enterprise cannot sell fresh milk and cheap fresh fish, what in the name of all that is manly and independent can it do?'
3. Another example of this can be found in Hughes' *The Case for Labour* (1970: 67). He defends the notion of a binding caucus solidarity against conservative charges that Labor MPs 'are not their own masters' by likening it to other 'normal' arrangements such as the marriage vow. Similarly, Hughes demonstrates the superiority of reformist socialism using the analogy of manhood coming to a boy. Socialism, like manhood, cannot be immediately instituted but must develop gradually (1970: 85-9).

CHAPTER 5

'Stirring Tales': Australian Feminism and National Identity, 1900–40

Marilyn Lake

> Children of a foreign soil – daughters of a different race, but sisters in a common cause we have assembled here in the capital of a great country. Let all of us remember these days with pleasure (Friedland 1902).[1]

In 1924 leading Australian feminist Bessie Rischbieth (1924) wrote to Carrie Chapman Catt, president of the International Women's Suffrage Alliance: 'Australia offers such tremendous possibilities: it is the youngest of the great continents in developement [sic] and a comparatively small population makes it possible to sow the seed now of the sort of civilisation women of all countries dream about'. 'Feminist campaigns', Maggie Humm (1992: 7) has observed, 'are inevitably shaped by national priorities and national politics'. Feminist ideology and practice have also been shaped, as Vron Ware (1992: 119) has argued, by the 'social, economic and political forces of imperialism' within which much nation-making has taken place.

Feminist aspirations, as Bessie Rischbieth's early identification made clear, have often been complicit with nationalist agendas and conceits (see also Humm 1992: 6). But feminism as a movement concerned with the rights and status of women across cultures, as a 'radical movement that can unite women across existing divisions of class, race and culture' (Ware 1992: xvii) is also, as the opening tribute by Sofja Livorna Friedland suggests, an internationalist force, comprising an alliance and perspective capable of disrupting and challenging racial barriers and nationalist exclusions. Moreover, insofar as nationalist movements incorporate a masculinist politics, asserting the rights and status of an injured colonial manhood, they risk womanly indifference, the alienation of feminists, the possibilities of hostile critique and the mobilisation of a dissident feminist politics.[2] As Hall et al. (1993) note, collaboration between nationalism and feminism was full of contradictory possibilities and these multiple possibilities were borne out in Australia. The articulations of feminism and nationalism were various, ambiguous and shifting. 'Australia was a new country, a nation forged by the pioneering spirit', Bessie Rischbieth told an audience in London in 1935. Unfortunately, however, 'the men of the New World forgot the women standing by their side. They drew up a Constitution for their New Colonies giving citizenship to one sex only. Consequently Australian women had a long struggle for Enfranchisement' (Rischbieth 1935). Feminism could be simultaneously at one with, but at odds with, nationalism. This chapter demonstrates the shifting identifications between nationalist and internationalist tendencies in Australian feminism.

Australian feminist nationalism

Feminism is a version of identity politics reifying the gendered identity of the homogeneous 'woman'. But women are heterogeneous. As Homi Bhabha (1994) has written, the singular identity is split the very moment it is articulated by the collective body.[3] As there are none who live purely as women, so there is no pure feminism existing outside relations of nationality, ethnicity, class, race, sexuality and religion. In this chapter, I wish to explore the contradictions of Australian feminism's national identity in the first decades of 'nation-building', pointing to feminism's simultaneous identification with and challenge to dominant nationalist narratives, policies and priorities. Nationalism, for example, encouraged an identification with the racial conception of national interest enshrined in White Australia; feminism pointed to the imperative of an anti-racist politics of sisterhood. Thus did Vida Goldstein inform a meeting of the Australian Federation of Women Voters that our 'Eastern neighbours' resented 'Australia's arrogant discrimination against them'. Goldstein (1930) continued: 'It is not too late for Australian women, while upholding a White Australia as a present economic and social necessity, to keep before the people the moral necessity of friendliness towards all races'. Nationalism encouraged a proud identification with the white man as heroic pioneer and an understanding of women's influence as a crucial dimension of this pioneering and civilising process; feminism also suggested an understanding of the white man as brutal sexual predator and civilisation as source of contamination and force of destruction. Thus could Mary Bennett (1934) despair at the imminent demise of 'white supremacy in the Pacific', while also lamenting (1933a) that 'the terrible plight of "civilised" Aborigines is the logical conclusion of our own dealings with them'.

While nationalist discourse cast motherhood as a national service and accorded child-bearing high status and economic support, feminists like Rose Scott (*Woman Voter* 5 July 1913) sometimes perceived in these inducements to fecundity only an excuse for male sexual licence, and they demanded instead a 'purer patriotism' enshrining sexual restraint and eugenic motherhood (quality not quantity).[4] Nationalist conceptions of Australia as a social laboratory and state action as a progressive force for reform encouraged feminists to look to the state to secure women's freedom from conjugal authority. Thus, while nationalists advocated child endowment to safeguard and nurture future citizens, feminists also urged the introduction of motherhood endowment to end the 'sex slavery of married women' (Lake 1993).

Feminism was enmeshed in imperialist, racist and nationalist politics. It produced and was produced by historically specific conceptions of white Australian womanhood, forged in simultaneous opposition to and identification with the Old World values and the 'kinsmen' of Britain. Feminist identities were also defined in opposition to and identification with their 'native sisters' in Australia and 'Asian sisters' in China, Japan and India. White Australian feminists negotiated the complications, ambiguities and tensions inherent in their multifaceted identities. Their racial consciousness and nationalist commitments shaped and gave authority to their feminism; their feminist goals qualified and disrupted their nationalism.

In the beginning, Australian feminists identified proudly with their new national state, 'this Land of Promise', 'the land of the Southern Cross' (Rischbieth 1926), and claimed (Goldstein 1902a: 218): 'Australia now leads the way in the suffrage movement.' Enfranchised and rendered eligible to stand for national political office by the first Commonwealth parliament, white Australian women were pleased to define an identity of interest between themselves and the new nation. In 1903, the 707 founding members of the Victorian Women's Political Association (WPA 1903) dedicated a 'memorial of gratitude' to the ministry in the first Australian parliament that placed Australia in the 'proud position of being the first nation to recognise that women are justly entitled to the inalienable right of self-government'. Commenting on her historic 1903 candidacy for the Senate, Vida Goldstein insisted that 'there was no danger of a woman candidate being insulted or ill-treated by an Australian audience' (Goldstein 1904). Around 1910, a letter was sent by Australian women's groups offering support to the beleaguered suffragettes in Britain in their militant campaign to free women from 'a legal and industrial slavery': 'We, the Enfranchised Women of Australia offer our reverent appreciation of the Spiritual Insight and Fidelity to Principle that are enabling you to speedily overcome the opportunist and materialist forces arrayed against you' (Enfranchised Women of Australia 1910). Thus did such women proudly proclaim their national identity and identification.

A kinship of blood and race

The legislation that enfranchised white Australian women had simultaneously disqualified Aboriginal women (and men) and other non-whites from full citizenship rights: the identity of the 'enfranchised women of Australia' was, thus, also constituted explicitly in terms of racial difference in a nation-state founded on racial imperialism. Their racial identity was also crucial to these white women's sense of themselves. Feminists represented themselves, at home and abroad, self-consciously, as the new citizens of the New World. They became, like white men before them, pioneers in a triumphal nationalist narrative, pioneering a new world of liberty. They were cutting a 'new path through the tangled woods of conventionalism' and casting 'a bridge over the stagnant waters of custom' (Scott 1903).

'A new land is for new ideas', wrote Vida Goldstein in the Boston *Christian Science Monitor* (28 November 1918),

> and the active, energetic Englishmen, Scotsmen and Irishmen who came here quickly reflected the big, broad ideas developed by pioneering work in a vast continent, whose strange native inhabitants, fauna and flora, seemed literally to transport them to a new world of thought.

'Australia's great heritage', affirmed Bessie Rischbieth (1935), 'is the Pioneer Spirit – it is natural for our people to look ahead because we are a new country'. Her hope was that the 'annihilation of space' made possible by 'modern advancing communications' would not 'hopelessly involve the New World in the mistakes of the Old World' so there was 'no chance left for social experiment' (Rischbieth 1935).

These nationalist narratives confirmed feminists' sense of racial identity with British and American women. All were 'kinsmen' [*sic*] derived from the same 'familiar' stock. 'We feel proud to remember', the letter of the Enfranchised Women of Australia (1910) told the 'Women of England', 'that we are of your blood and race'. And in her 'Open Letter to the Women of the United States' in 1902, Vida Goldstein (1902a) identified 'the constant influx of ignorant aliens' into America as one of the obstacles to suffrage there and observed 'because we women in the land of the Southern Cross are reaping what England and America have sown, we are all the more eager to help our English sisters and American cousins in their struggle for freedom'.

The terms of Goldstein's reception in the United States in 1902, when she attended and was appointed secretary to the International Women's Suffrage Conference, must have confirmed her sense of racial kinship (despite her own mixed descent) with women of British heritage. Entries in her autograph book penned by English and American women paid tribute to their common 'ancestry' and 'race'. Thus Florence Fenwick Muller (1902), delegate of the English United and Scottish Women's Suffrage Societies, proffered an

> English loving greeting to my Australian sister. As often happens with grown up children Australia and New Zealand have in some respects got farther on than the still hale and strong Motherland, but we rejoice in all your prosperity and progress, as we know you love and honour the home of your ancestry.

Similarly, Alice Stone Blackwell (1902), secretary of the National American Women Suffrage Association, composed some verse to farewell her 'sister in language and in blood', while the women of Colorado expressed the hope that, although 'physically antipodal', Australian and American women would 'progress spiritually side by side on the upward path of our common race'.

White Australian women saw themselves as members of the same (extended) family as white British and American women. Their sense of themselves was constituted in these early years of the nation-state within an imperialist framework in terms of the dichotomies drawn between the 'civilised' and 'primitive', the 'British race' and 'natives', 'advanced' and 'backward' peoples. Like other white Australian narratives of nation, the version of history here elaborated by 'feminist pioneers' involved a story of natural succession, in which the 'strange native inhabitants', as described by Vida Goldstein, would inevitably give way to the march of progress, as the Old World remade itself in the New.

White women's enfranchisement was explained as but one freedom enjoyed by the freedom-loving New World, a natural condition for a new and young nation. As a new nation-state in the New World, Australians were doubly rejuvenated. Thus was the youthful Goldstein greeted in the United States as the apotheosis of her nation. Alice Stone Blackwell (1902) pointed to her representative status in poetry:

> Amid this bright, progressive band
> Of women picked from every land,
> We have a youthful delegate
> To represent a youthful State.
> Australia, infant Commonwealth,
> Is full of vigor, vim and health;
> Youngest of nations gathered here,
> In some respects she has no peer.

Her delegate befits her well;
She has a stirring tale to tell,
And modestly, yet undismayed,
With facts and figures well arrayed,
She tells her tale to folks intent,
From Congressmen to President.
We view her slender girlish grace,
Her vivid, keen and sparkling face;
From her clear eyes, intelligence
Looks forth, with fun and common sense.

Ellen Wright Garrison's (1902) greeting confirmed the identification:

To Australasia all the world gives ear;
Youthful, audacious, unrestrained and free.
No immemorial bonds of time's decree
Shackle her progress nor excite her fear.
She beckons elder nations in the path
Of bold adventure and experiment.
Risking short cuts along the world's ascent
Facing unmoved the ancient order's wrath.
She gave us safer ballots, wiser laws
To lift the struggling masses, and she leads
To social heights where gain shall conquer loss.
Empanoplied to plead the woman's cause,
Armed with the record of your land's great deeds
Welcome, light-bringer from the Southern Cross!

The early narrative of national identity, the 'stirring tale' that underpinned the feminist project was racist, eugenicist and evolutionist. Yet
the new white nation-state was thought to be the very embodiment of
progress, civilisation and the advancement of women. But women's
experiment with citizenship in the new nation-state proved unsettling.
Feminist political campaigns had increasingly sought to bring together
women across the divisions of race, nation and culture, exchanging
information and ideas, achieving 'unity of action', to become 'more
valuable citizens' (Newcomb 1918). The most valuable women citizens
were deemed to be 'world citizens', respectful of racial and cultural
difference. Delegates to the third Pan-Pacific conference of women in
1932 were asked to consider for 'study' this question (*Bulletin of the
Pan-Pacific Union* 1932, 154: 11): 'Is a diversity in racial and cultural types
to be regarded as an enrichment, producing a fusion and change out of
which inventions, discoveries, improvements arise, or a contamination
of the group heritage?' By the 1930s, back in the New World civilisation of Australia, national and racial identifications had become less
certain and a feminist disenchantment with the 'group heritage' had
become noticeable. The British people, represented by the white men in

Australia, came to be depicted by some feminists as rapacious despoilers
and dispossessors.

Feminist hopes that Australia would set an example to other nations in
achieving a woman-friendly civilisation began to look foolish. Despite
numerous attempts by women, none had been elected to the national
parliament by the late 1930s. Feminist commitments and aspirations
unsettled nationalist certainties, while feminist identifications pointed to
alternative, internationalist, ways of being citizens. And in the process
new national stories of identity, more shameful than stirring, began to be
articulated.

Feminist internationalism: Beyond racialism

In order to explain their failure to achieve representation in the national
legislature, feminists revised their account of national history to emphasise the consolidation and play of masculinist politics. Formerly cast as
supporters of the women's cause, working men came to be positioned
as women's opponents.[5] Rather than achieving equal access to self-
government, women were being excluded by the institutionalisation of
men's interests in the party system. In 1903 Vida Goldstein had expressed
the hope that women would organise independently of the existing
parties which were 'controlled and directed by men'. If they joined those
parties, they would adopt 'men's methods and men's aims, and simply
help in perpetuating the old order of things' (*Woman's Sphere* 10
July 1903). Goldstein herself stood five times, unsuccessfully, as an
independent women's candidate for the Senate. Bessie Rischbieth
expressed disappointment at the triumph of men's interests and parties
in the new Commonwealth. 'A result of the early enfranchisement of
Australian women', said Bessie Rischbieth (1924), 'has been that the
woman's vote was lost almost entirely in party politics for a number of
years'. Goldstein, like Rischbieth and Mary Bennett, and Rose Scott
before them, was convinced that women's progress depended on the
work of non-party women. 'Practically every reform that has been
won for women and children', said Goldstein (*Christian Science Monitor*
4 December 1918), 'has been initiated through the political action of
non-party women'. Women's aspirations were defeated by the mobilisation and determined opposition of men, especially, in Goldstein's
view, men in the labour movement, whose New World Australia really
was. 'It seems to be a human law', said Goldstein (*Woman Voter* 8 September 1910), 'that the oppressed of one age become the oppressors of
the next'. The new order began to look, in many respects, just like the
old. Feminist visions began to seem like 'fantastic dreams' (*Woman's
Sphere* 10 July 1903). Much feminist critique began to focus more

closely on the figure of the despoiling, ravaging and discriminatory 'white man'.

Some feminists had begun to express doubts about the racial identi-fications underpinning White Australia in the discussions surrounding the introduction of the Maternity Allowance in 1912. Whereas Labor women were concerned to defend its extension to unmarried mothers, in order to defend the honour of their class, non-party feminists also protested against its racially based exclusions. The debate on this issue suggests the ways in which the identity of 'mother of the race' could be appropriated for both racist and anti-racist purposes. The 'mother of the race' was an ambiguous figure, her race sometimes taken to refer to the British race, sometimes the human race.

Feminists generally had applauded the introduction of the Maternity Allowance by the Labor Prime Minister Andrew Fisher as a recognition of the rights accruing to maternal citizenship, which they hoped to see extended. The *Woman Voter* (11 July 1912), journal of the WPA, commented:

> Five pounds is not much, but it is a beginning in the right direction. It paves the way for a wider recognition of what the State owes to the mothers and to the children. Mothers are supposed to render a supreme service to the State, and some day the State will realise that its first obligations are to motherhood and childhood.

Feminists generally were indignant at the campaigns waged by church-men and others to have the mothers of 'illegitimate' babies excluded from eligibility. Unlike women in the labour movement, the *Woman Voter* (9 October 1912) also protested against the racial exclusions, especially of Asian women:

> Women who are Asiatics or aboriginal natives are not to receive the allowance. As aboriginals are State wards, their exclusion may be justified, but we ques-tion the exclusion of Asiatic women who are residents of the Commonwealth. This exclusion is supposed to be part of the White Australia policy, but surely it is the White Australia policy gone mad. Maternity is maternity, whatever the race, and the Asiatic woman who gives birth to a child in the Commonwealth is giving birth to a British subject, and is, we think fully entitled to the allowance.

The *Woman Voter* was edited by Vida Goldstein. Her writings during these first decades of nationhood point to a troubled preoccupation with Australia's White Australia policy and racial exclusions more generally. Her concern for women, mothers and the oppressed often came into conflict with a racially based sense of national identity. Her ambivalent feelings were evident in her notes on her trip to the United States in 1902. On the one hand, she was moved to blame the influx of 'ignorant aliens' for delaying the enfranchisement of women in that country; on the other, she relished the 'cosmopolitanism' of New York and deplored the treatment of blacks in the South (Goldstein 1902b). Again, in her 'letter from Colombo' a preoccupied Goldstein (*Woman Voter* April 1911) concluded that the mixing of the races resulted in the deterioration of both: 'The coloured man takes all the vices of the white man, and the white man becomes dehumanised'.

By 1919 Goldstein's concerns about the White Australia policy led her to propose this subject for the debate regularly organised by the WPA. In her report of the convention, she was pleased to note 'that a change with us has taken place in the racial aspect of this question' and anticipated that Australia could well become more 'cosmopolitanised' (*Woman Voter* 3 July 1919). The participants were receptive to the 'growth of Internationalism'. In the edited extracts of the debate printed in the *Woman Voter* (3 July 1919), the divisions over the issue seemed to be gendered. Women generally favoured internationalism. 'No one earns [*sic*] by isolation', said Mrs Griffin. 'Australia is large enough for all.' 'Is our Internationalism only a word', asked Miss Fullerton, 'or is it a fact?' 'To shut out the Asiatic is to dethrone right for expediency', argued Mrs Paling. 'Does not Australia pride herself on being the land of experiments?', asked Miss Weekes. 'Why fear the experiment of admitting the Asiatics?' Many of the male contributors to the debate argued that coloured labour would undermine the white man's wages and conditions. 'They would use the coloured man to break down our strikes', said Mr Ross. 'Industrial control by Australian workers could alone make alien immigration safe', said Mr Cameron. Nationalist Nettie Palmer queried: 'Australians remaining undiluted and developing along their own lines may in time have a distinct contribution of their own to give to civilisation ... Should we do anything that would thwart our development?' Several of the women speakers made reference to the alleged superior morality of whites, only to cast doubt on the claim. Said Mrs Singleton: 'We hear a good deal about Japanese immorality. What about European morality in Japan?' 'Our moral superiority is a joke', confirmed Mrs Griffin. 'If we want to keep our nation on a high standard', suggested Mrs Paling, 'we should banish the undesirables of our own race'.

The national standard of morality was a key issue for feminists in these years, who were concerned especially to demand an equal moral (sexual) standard for men and women. Feminist investigations into race relations on the frontiers of settlement, in Western Australia and the Northern Territory, showed Aboriginal women to be systematically abused and degraded. Increasingly, feminists made links between masculine licentiousness and racial exploitation. Masculine desire was identified as the very source of contamination. The 'white man' – once the heroic pioneer of the New World – was transformed into an agent of destruction. The national narrative of settlement and civilisation began to be replaced by a shameful story of conquest. When reports circulated of the flogging of indigenous people in the Australian-administered territory of New Guinea, the *Woman Voter* (13 March 1919) considered this just one more 'instance of the brutality of the whites towards helpless coloured people' and asked 'whether white men [were] flogged for criminal assaults on native women and girls'. Australian claims to having a greater moral right than Germany to administer New Guinea were deemed preposterous. Goldstein (*Woman Voter* 3 July 1919) was scathing:

> The final refusal to allow Germany a mandate over her own colonies is based upon 'fear for the natives'. Fear of what? Their survival? I talked the native question over with a patriot of my acquaintance some time ago, claiming that their extermination was indefensible. She argued quite hotly that it was right and proper, and according to natural laws. The people who cannot develop a country must make way for those who can. The superior races must replace them. Well, then, we are the people. I believe we hold the world's record. Until very recent years we could not be accused of doing anything to prevent the proper substitution of the superior race. The only thing done in that direction was the work of interfering German missionaries.

Membership of British Commonwealth organisations and work with overseas women gave Australian feminists a new perspective on the exploits of the white pioneers. Commenting on an article by F. Bancroft on the position of women, white and black, in South Africa, Goldstein concurred in an analysis that focused on 'the guilty white man': 'Thus debauchery and wholesale prostitution of the black woman by the European pioneer has for many years flourished, unchecked by a single legislative act throughout the new territories under the British Crown Colony and Dutch Governments'. It was white men who had taught black men that 'no woman is safe from outrage' (*Woman Voter* 1 August 1911).

Feminists like Goldstein recognised their own complicity in the 'civilising' process. But her feminism also allowed her a critical perspective on the depredations of pioneering and colonisation that allowed her to distance herself from 'her people'. In her feminist identification with the plight of native women, the 'strange native inhabitants' became unfortunate 'sisters' and a new national history took shape, a history of brutality and extermination, in which women, white and black, were joined by the bonds of a common slavery. 'If a woman, whether white or black, has not the control of her body, she is a slave', claimed a representative of the Victorian Women Citizens Movement, Edith Jones (Conference 1929). Women in general – as wives, prostitutes, Aborigines, workers – increasingly came to be seen as 'white slaves'; that is, as sex slaves. Their bodies were not subject to their own discretion. The phenomenon of 'white slavery' made a mockery of Britain's claim to greatness. Thus 'D.A.H.' wrote in *Woman Voter* (8 April 1913): 'As Britons we are, in the mass, proud of our great and wonderful empire and of the island Motherland. We boast of our extraction and our past and present achievements'. But knowledge of the white slave traffic rendered such boasts foolish. In fact, *Woman Voter* (8 July 1913) suggested that British government officials were 'practically traffickers themselves'.

Feminists campaigning in the 1920s and 1930s elaborated on this new national story, in which Aboriginal women were positioned as paradigmatic victims, 'at the mercy of white men' (Conference 1929). The British Empire had 'seized' the whole continent as Crown lands in order to develop it as a homeland for British white people. Hunting grounds were taken up as sheep stations and the native culture was destroyed. 'The destruction of the natives', wrote Mary Bennett (1932), 'is caused by the white settlers dispossessing them of their land and by the settlers commercialising for their own advantage the native patriarchal system'. White settlement was, in fact, a process of ongoing theft and exploitation of Aboriginal land. 'We realise', said Bessie Rischbieth (1931), president of the Australian Federation of Women Voters, in a letter to Senator George Pearce demanding land rights for Aboriginal people in Arnhem Land, 'that the time is fast approaching when there will not be an acre of land in the Northern Territory or anywhere else in Australia which is not overrun by the white man'. 'Dispossession', according to this reworked narrative of nation, was crucial to settlement and the exploitation of the economic resources of the country. 'It pays the white man to dispossess the natives of their land wholesale', wrote Mary Bennett (1932) in a letter to the *Australian Board of Missions Review*, 'because the Government permits them to impress the natives as labour without paying them. The compulsion is dispossession and starvation, reinforced by violence' (see also *West Australian* 9 May 1932).

Women's rights as human rights

The destruction of Aboriginal society and the 'white slave trade in black women' – such were the achievements of the pioneers, of the average white man. 'The native women are the chief sufferers', wrote Bennett (1932).

> The worst thing I have seen is the attitude of the average white man to native women – the attitude not of the mean whites but of the overwhelming majority of white men. In the north west it is so much the accepted thing for white men to abuse native women that it is the custom of the country.

In the later narratives of national history, women, and especially black women, became the victims of men and history, rather than the figures of destiny hailed in 1902. And 'the customs of the country' were declared by feminists to be abhorrent.

Women's criticisms of these customs in overseas forums led them to be labelled as troublemakers and national traitors (see Paisley 1993). But in such forums women found their voice and a new sense of power. Denied an effective voice in the deliberations of their own parliaments, Australian feminists increasingly found excitement, stimulation and reward in international alliances. As their disappointments with the Land of Promise deepened, so their feminism and internationalism proved mutually reinforcing and women's rights came to be reconceptualised as transnational 'human rights'. Acting Prime Minister W.M. Hughes had attracted their criticism when he refused to admit the question of womanhood suffrage on to the agenda of the Imperial Conference in London in 1910, stating that it was a matter of national, domestic concern. Goldstein (*Woman Voter* December 1910) disagreed, saying that he was 'mistaken in thinking that woman suffrage is simply a question of domestic politics: it is a question affecting human rights and liberties, which we maintain enfranchised women have an absolute right to bring before the Imperial Conference'.

Between the wars Australian feminists became regular participants in international meetings. In 1919 they attended the International Women's Peace Congress held in conjunction with the Versailles conference. From 1922 they attended the League of Nations as 'substitute' or 'alternate' delegates. Stella Allen (1924), an alternate delegate in 1924, reported that she had come back with 'an almost overwhelming sense of the importance of the League of Nations. In no other place in which she had been were women and men on such equal terms as in Geneva. The mental attitude was one of absolute equality'. They sent delegates to meetings of the International Women's Suffrage Alliance and the British Dominions Women Citizens' Union, later the British Commonwealth League. They were leading contributors to the Pan-Pacific Women's Conferences held in Honolulu from 1928 on.

As a result of their dealings with Asian and Pacific women in the Pan-Pacific Conferences, some Australian feminists became more outspoken in their criticism of their country's racially exclusive immigration policy – the White Australia policy. Thus Eleanor Hinder (1930), program secretary to the first Pan-Pacific Women's Conference in 1928, wrote in excitement at the prospect of Australian women working with Chinese and Japanese women: 'I knew it to be a wholesome educative process, and for this reason among others, I was ready to put a good deal of time into planning for Australia's participation in succeeding conferences'.

She was critical of Australia defining its national identity in European terms. 'We are, as you know', Hinder wrote in a circular letter to her feminist colleagues,

> very isolated, with a population 98% British in origin: we have a national religion – the 'White Australia' policy: every organisation looks in affiliation to international groupings which centre in Europe. For the majority of the women of Australia, the women of Oriental countries simply do not exist.

Conclusion

Australian 'isolation', itself an imperialist conceit, once seen as propitious by feminists interested in distinctive national experiments, came to be redefined as a barrier to women's progress. Similarly, an over-identification with the 'familiar' stock of the British race was seen by many as impeding more fruitful affiliations with women of other cultures and races. Nationalist commitments could become a barrier to women's world citizenship. Thus the emerging critique of the depredations of the white man as exploitative 'white slaver', together with disillusionment with women's political fortunes in Australia, meshed with the growing internationalist orientation of women citizens between the wars. Concern about the conditions of indigenous people, and the advocacy of women's rights across all nations and cultures, led feminists to emphasise women's rights as a matter of human rights. Feminist political advocacy could therefore be seen as an important factor in paving the way towards the United Nations Declaration of Human Rights in 1948.

But although many Australian feminists forsook the enthusiastic nationalist and racial identifications evident in the first years of nationhood, their feminist politics remained crucially dependent on their imperial and racial status as the 'civilisers'. In their alliances with Aboriginal and Pacific and Asian women, their assumed authority allowed them to speak to and on behalf of their 'less favoured sisters' (Anon. 1933; see also Ramusack 1992). White Australian women considered they were 'favoured' with civilisation and had a responsibility to share their 'light' with 'primitive' and 'backward', or more euphemistically, 'less forward', and intrinsically 'pure', women. Feminists derived the sense of authority necessary to their reforming project precisely from their imperial sense of themselves as the most civilised representatives of the civilised races. Let down by white men who had succumbed to their perversely primitive lusts, who everywhere threatened to reduce women, black and white, to 'slavery', white feminists assumed the responsibility to maintain the white standard in the outposts of Empire. Though 'a wise Aboriginal policy is needed for the survival of the Aboriginal race', wrote Mary Bennett (1933b), 'it is equally urgent for our own survival in the

Pacific. Australia shall understand this'. Feminists had, perforce, to become the protectors of the Pacific and the saviours of their nation.

Notes

1. Sofja Livorna Friedland was a Russian delegate to the International Women's Suffrage Conference, Washington, 1902.
2. On the gendered dynamic of nationalism see, for example, Enloe (1989: 1 and ch. 3), Lake (1986a), subsequent discussions in Magarey et al. (1993) and Hall et al. (1993).
3. For a discussion of the 'hybridity of imagined communities', see Bhabha (1994).
4. Most of the periodicals and newspapers referred to in the text may be found collected in the Rischbieth Papers in the National Library of Australia (NLA) or in the Goldstein Papers at the Fawcett Library.
5. Goldstein (1902a) vacillated in her accounts of working men's relationship to the women's movement, initially stressing their support as democrats, increasingly their hostility as men. Caine (1993) attributes this shift to the influence of English feminist analysis on Goldstein, but this was but one aspect of a complex interaction.

CHAPTER 6

The Making of an Australian Civic Identity: The Bodies of Men and the Memory of War

Helen Pringle[1]

The use of and traffic in women subtend and uphold the reign of masculine hom(m)o-sexuality, even while they maintain that hom(m)o-sexuality in speculations, mirror games, identifications, and more or less rivalrous appropriations, which defer its real practice. Reigning everywhere, although prohibited in practice, hom(m)o-sexuality is played out through the bodies of women, matter, or sign, and heterosexuality has been up to now just an alibi for the smooth workings of man's relations with himself, of relations among men.

(Irigaray 1985: 172)

If only there were a way to start a city or an army made up of lovers and the boys they love! Theirs would be the best possible system of society, for they would hold back from all that is shameful, and seek honor in each other's eyes. Even a few of them, in battle side by side, would conquer all the world, I'd say. For a man in love would never allow his loved one, of all people, to see him leaving ranks or dropping weapons. He'd rather die a thousand deaths! And as for leaving the boy behind, or not coming to his aid in danger – why, no one is so base that true Love could not inspire him with courage, and make him as brave as if he'd been born a hero.

(Phaedrus, in Plato 1989: 178e–179b)

My aim here is to suggest connections between war and masculinity in the elaboration of Australian civic identity. The linkage between the violence of war and masculinity is almost too obvious to belabour. Men fight (or have fought) wars. Or so it appears. From here, it seems a short step to conjecturing a love of violence in men, a lust for destruction that finds one of its most important expressions in armed combat. In this chapter, however, I want to challenge this notion that a male love of violence and destruction lies at the basis of war. I argue that war is indeed a romance, but a civic romance conducted among men, one which constitutes women as audience or chorus to its drama. I shall argue this in relation to the formation of Australian civic identity.

While much recent feminist work on war and masculinity has seen war as an outpouring of male violence, I suggest that we look rather at the structures of communal solidarity – *between* men – by which this violence takes place. In other words, I try to see war itself as a form of communal life and love, through which masculine identity is constituted. In doing this, I am not concerned as much with the actual conduct of war, as with its commemoration: how it is remembered, represented and recreated. The memory of war relies on the invocation of communal bonds of friendship with mystical and erotic overtones. Further, I shall argue that the key role of the memory of war in the making of Australian civic identity involves a celebration of male bodies and of virile death, in a way that quite explicitly harks back to certain classical understandings of public virtue, male friendship and sacrificial death. War, then, is not a repression of love or sexuality in favour of death, but rather an arena in which both love and sexuality find place.

My argument may at times seem little more than a slightly bent reformulation of the Australian myth of mateship, centred as it is on the Anzac celebration of bonds of solidarity forged under fire. It has been noted often enough, usually half-seriously, how in war as in some sports the love of men for each other is permitted more open expression.[2] I want to take this flippancy seriously, in taking up Irigaray's point about the homosexuality of the social order, in order to argue that the homoerotic overtones of this mateship are particularly evident in war, even if such overtones must be hushed. They remain, that is, an open secret of civic identity.

Civic identity in the public life of liberalism

At the outset, however, I face a crucial problem in trying to link manhood and war to Australian civic identity. That is, public life in liberal societies like ours is not explicitly correlated with masculine virtues. The public/private division of liberal democracy is not coincident with gender distinctions. Public and private matters are rather distinguished by reference to the principle of harm. And liberalism places greatest emphasis on individual freedom rather than on public service; whereas public service may be lauded, its default is in no important sense a dereliction of obligation. To say, with the ancient Greeks, that a man who minds his own business has no business in the polis[3] does not declare the public charter of liberal democracies. In general, public rhetoric about the foundations of contemporary Australian society does not make much appeal to the values of fraternity or community between people, but rather appeals to the freedom to choose our own ways of life. Unchosen obligations, of family, kin or patria, are invisible to the universal constitutive principles characteristic of liberalism.

It is precisely on this basis that civic identity in liberal democracies has been criticised as 'thin', as providing no room for genuine moral consensus. The sharing of values by individuals is in this view a matter of convergence or compromise between individual interests and tastes, not a deeprooted conviction about the common ends of society or a lasting and durable social sympathy. The existence of fair procedures is what justifies liberal society – at the cost of substantive co-operative values.[4]

This moral portrait of liberal society has two important implications in relation to military life and the conduct of war. First, the element of necessity evident both in conscription and in discipline within the army seems not to be congruent with the liberal emphasis on voluntary and self-imposed obligations. Secondly, there is a lack of genuinely *public* values by which to justify the conduct of war by the liberal state. Nevertheless, the very *need* for substantive moral values would be diminished in a liberal society given the replacement of military life by commerce as the main occupation.[5] That is, the 'thin' public procedures and rituals of liberal democracy orient themselves around the notion of the rule of law: liberal democracy replaces the rule of force with the rule of right, of equal laws and free institutions such as the market.

While liberalism appeals to universal principles of justice, its historical development has occurred within the boundaries of particular nation-states. And in wars *between* those nation-states, individual citizens find themselves called upon to act not merely as bearers of individual interests, but as heroes prepared to kill and die for some substantive value that transcends those individual interests. Max Weber, for example, understood this as a problem peculiar to modern liberal societies, societies in which belief in gods and in values more generally becomes something private to the individual. When values are no longer public and shared, but a matter of individual choice, what is left of 'higher' moral considerations by which the state could justify its use of violence? Weber (1970: 335) argued:

> As the consummated threat of violence among modern polities, war creates a pathos and a sentiment of community. War thereby makes for an unconditionally devoted and sacrificial community among the combatants and releases an active mass compassion and love for those who are in need ...
>
> Moreover, war does something to the warrior which, in its concrete meaning, is unique: it makes him experience a consecrated meaning of death

which is characteristic only of death in war. The community of the army standing in the field today feels itself – as in the times of the war lords 'following' – to be a community unto death, and the greatest of its kind. Death on the field of battle differs from death that is only man's common lot ... Death on the field of battle differs from this merely unavoidable dying in that in war, and in this massiveness *only* in war, the individual can *believe* that he knows he is dying 'for' something. The why and the wherefore of his facing death can, as a rule, be so indubitable to him that the problem of the 'meaning' of death does not even occur to him ...

This location of death within a series of meaningful and consecrated events ultimately lies at the base of all endeavours to support the autonomous dignity of the polity resting on force.

Weber here suggests that warfare is the one area in which modern death becomes meaningful; that is, that the sacrificial community of warriors provides the only access to a 'thick' civic personality. Modern warfare does not reflect, but *creates* the thickness of civic identity.

I would argue further, along these lines, that the modern loss of a substantive moral basis for 'the autonomous dignity of the polity' goes hand in hand with a re-eroticisation of the bonds of combat. While evoking the language of classical heroes, this eroticisation is a distinctively modern development, which only appears anachronistic to the language of liberalism. To the contrary, this eroticisation of combat is in fact wholly congruent with liberalism in the sense of providing it with the thickness of a civic identity whose very disappearance it had created, but which it continually laments.

The sex of combat

Modern conceptions of the relationship between war, masculinity and citizenship have deep historical roots which are drawn upon in the Australian civic imagination. These conceptions draw upon the mythic power of Greek and Roman epic and history, in which civic personality, military capacity and masculinity are intertwined. Classical manhood was associated with military courage and domination over others, with being a warrior. The warrior's life as one of true manliness is praised in the *Iliad*, for example in the character of Achilles, who is the very prototype of hero (Weil 1977). In such classical understandings, the most beautiful friendships are formed not between men and women, but between men in battle,[6] such as the friendship of Achilles and Patroclus. The 'fine death' of warriors in battle was, in Pericles' words for example, 'the climax of their lives': 'the consummation which has overtaken these men shows us the meaning of manliness in its first revelation and in its final proof' (Thucydides 1972: 148). To die in battle was to gain a civic immortality, a glory that remained forever to inspire others. The consummation of life was 'a fine death', and for a man the place for this was in battle. In contrast, the best thing for a woman was not to leave the interior of her house (Loraux 1987: 1–30).

The conduct of war in classical times (as now) was not a stripping away of the civilised veneer of society in an outpouring of primal aggression, but was a highly stylised exercise in masculinity, with its own decorum. This decorum also bounded the ears and eyes of its spectators. In its memory, war is not presented as such violent outpouring, but as tales of heroism and self-sacrifice to a co-operative venture. As remembered, war is fought not only against an enemy but *with* comrades, and it is in this sense that its memory serves to constitute a form of communal life and of civic identity.

In this context, as a general rule, women have not been officially permitted to engage in public combat. Even today, there remains one explicit exemption to the rule of public equality, the exclusion of women from combat on the same terms as men.[7] Historically, the soldier has been constituted as a gendered *role*, involving something more than the performance of a series of tasks. Fighting is non-productive: the soldier does not produce commodities of direct value to the economy. And the labour of fighting is not done under the direct compulsion of economic necessity, but is done in reference to social relationships and loyalties.[8] Military life has a primacy to men over other jobs they may do: it involves the privileges and obligations of being a citizen.[9]

Since World War II, however, the mechanisation of warfare has meant that a lot of it is done by remote control, not by hand-to-hand fighting. The role of physical strength in warfare is now often far from decisive. This mechanisation of killing undercuts much of the rationale for the exclusion of women from combat in terms of differing strength. And the whole character of the theatre of war, with a frontline and a home front, is being redefined in an era of Star Wars. Nevertheless, our image of the warrior remains the footsoldier. It is he who forms the most poignant symbol of warfare, in the Unknown Soldier interred in the Australian War Memorial, for example. It is the infantry that in general bears the weight of civic memory as to war. Parallel to modern developments in military strategy and technology runs the extension of liberal principles such as equality of opportunity to all areas of public life, even into the military itself. That is, rationales for the exclusion of women from combat appear increasingly to be both technologically and ideologically anachronistic. Yet a deep masculinist conception of civic identity remains intractable to such changes given its continued moorings to the memory of war.

The beauty of Australian warriors

Liberal democracy is based on the idea of a public equality, from which standpoint the masculinity of war appears as an albeit tenacious holdover from the past. For example, Australia remains a society in which Anzac Day and its rituals play a significant role in national and civic identity.[10] Gallipoli is central to such rituals. In order to elucidate the peculiar quality of our civic memory, I now want to adduce some anecdotal evidence in which Gallipoli is tied back to the warrior ideal of ancient Greece and its heroes.

First, the novelist Compton MacKenzie (1929: 80–1) wrote of the Australian troops in Gallipoli:

> Much has been written about the splendid appearance of those Australian troops; but a splendid appearance seems to introduce somehow an atmosphere of the parade-ground. Such litheness and powerful grace did not want the parade-ground; that was to take it from the jungle to the circus. Their beauty, for it really was heroic, should have been celebrated in hexameters not headlines. As a child I used to pore for hours over those illustrations of Flaxman for Homer and Virgil which simulated the effect of ancient pottery. There was not one of those glorious young men I saw that day who might not himself have been Ajax or Diomed, Hector or Achilles. Their almost complete nudity, their tallness, and majestic simplicity of line, their rose-brown flesh burnt by the sun and purged of all grossness by the ordeal through which they were passing, all these united to create something as near to absolute beauty as I shall hope ever to see in this world. The dark glossy green of the arbutus leaves made an incomparable background for these shapes of heroes, and the very soil here had taken on the same tawny rose as that living flesh; one might have fancied that the dead had stained it to this rich warmth of apricot.

Noting how little the Australian soldiers were given to saluting, MacKenzie (1929: 82) went on to remark: 'They really were rather difficult; and so, no doubt, was Achilles.'

Secondly, Sir Ian Hamilton (quoted in Moorehead 1978: 192–3) wrote of the theatre of war at Gallipoli:

> you can see Turkish hand-grenades bursting along the crest, just where an occasional bayonet flashes and figures hardly distinguishable from Mother Earth crouch in an irregular line. Or else they rise to fire and are silhouetted against the sky and then you recognise the naked athletes from the Antipodes and your heart goes into your mouth as a whole bunch of them dart forward suddenly, and as suddenly disappear ... There are poets and writers who see naught in war but carrion, filth, savagery and horror. The heroism of the rank and file makes no appeal. They refuse war the credit of being the only exercise in devotion on the large scale existing in this world. The superb moral victory over death leaves them cold. Each one to his taste. To me this is no valley of death – it is a valley brim full of life at its highest power. Men live through

more in five minutes on that crest than they do in five years of Bendigo or
Ballarat. Ask the brothers of these very fighters – Calgoorlie [*sic*] or
Coolgardie miners – to do one quarter of the work and to run one hundredth
the risk on a wages basis – instanter there would be a riot. But here – not a
murmur, not a question; only a radiant force of camaraderie in action.

Hamilton again (quoted in Moorehead 1978: 356), in a preface
dedicated to the soldiers of Gallipoli, wrote:

You will hardly fade away until the sun fades out of the sky and the earth sinks
into the universal blackness. For already you form part of that great tradition
of the Dardanelles which began with Hector and Achilles. In another few
thousand years the two stories will have blended into one, and whether when
'the iron roaring went up to the vault of heaven through the unharvested sky',
as Homer tells us, it was the spear of Achilles or whether it was a 100-lb shell
from Asiatic Annie won't make much odds to the Almighty.[11]

Finally, read John Masefield (1978: 19) as he declares that the Anzacs
were:

the finest body of young men brought together in modern times. For physical
beauty and nobility of bearing they surpassed any men I have ever seen; they
walked and talked like kings in old poems and reminded me of a line of
Shakespeare:
            'Baited like eagles having lately bathed.'
... there was no thought of surrender in these marvellous young men; they
were the flower of the world's manhood, and died as they had lived, owning
no master on earth.

Throughout such passages,[12] the Australian army is presented not as a
well-disciplined fighting machine, but as robust men of strong passions.
Rather than parade-ground soldiers, they are warriors, 'naked athletes',
the sight of whom produces acute aesthetic pleasure in the spectator.
The beauty of the Australians is of the flesh, a virile flesh which assumes
an almost sublime moral quality, a 'radiant force'. This force asserts
claims on its spectator, which can only be acquitted justly in classical
allusion.

    To draw attention to the homoerotic overtones of these passages is of
course to confront the paradox of the exclusion of homosexuals and
homosexuality from the armed forces. The usual rationalisation of
taboos on homosexuality in the army, involving its alleged compromise
of operational effectiveness (morale, discipline and cohesion) and
creation of security risks,[13] seems lacking in explanatory power. It may
be that military discipline relies on creating a certain sexual tension
in soldiers through the cultivation of homoerotic attachments, while

denying its release: in Irigaray's terms, 'reigning everywhere, although prohibited in practice'.[14]

Klaus Theweleit (1987: 52–63, 1989: 306–45), in his study of fascism, has dismissed the idea that a latent homosexuality lies at the base of (fascist) armed bonding. Theweleit argues that the apparent homosexuality of the fascist warrior is 'strictly encoded; and for this very reason, it never becomes sexual':

> Like the opposite from which it flees, it is rigidly codified – as escape, transgression, boyish mischief, perverse game, or indeed ultimately as act of terror. In all these forms, it is far more likely to be definable in the terms of the fascist system than in terms of such things as love relationships between men. (Theweleit 1989: 323, 325)

In terms of its wider implications, Theweleit's point rests on a distinction between real homosexuality, marked by 'the potential for actual *homosexual* pleasure', and fake homosexuality, based for example on the attraction of transgression. This seems to me to maintain a spurious distinction between the codified camaraderie of soldiers and real homosexuality – which is, however, no more natural and uncodified than any other form of sexuality.[15]

A soldier's love is certainly not a simple psychological disposition. It is a carefully cultivated spiritual and corporeal discipline, a highly ritualised form of male solidarity whose expression as beauty takes form around such virtues as chivalry, sacrifice and fidelity. The language in which such camaraderie is praised, the classical allusions of MacKenzie, Hamilton and Masefield for example, betray a vision of erotic relations between fighters, a vision whose 'pleasure' is consummated through being reserved as narrative to its spectators, an audience in which women loom large.

Narratives of war and bodies[16]

It may seem paradoxical to implicate women in an activity from which they have been so effectively quarantined. Many feminist writers on war, for example, have argued that the state is not a 'gender-neutral' space but a masculine 'barracks community' needing to be transformed before real sexual equality can be attained (Hartsock 1982: 283–6). Feminists have accepted that national military service is tied to the privilege of a citizenship predicated on the willingness to assume the rights and burdens of the defence and protection of the community in war. Citizen privileges were and are justified by the military burdens borne by men and not by women. Here I shall not go into any detail on the proposals of Sara Ruddick and similar writers for the creation of what Ruddick calls a 'peaceful army' (Ruddick 1983: 471–89). For writers like Ruddick, however, the basis of this redefinition of war and military life is that women are more peaceful than men, perhaps not as a matter of biology but as a style of thought and feeling learned in a 'private' world of gentleness and of the heart well removed from that of men.

Feminist explorations of war such as that of Ruddick have counter-posed the notion of 'maternal thinking' to the violence-ridden mascu-linity of war and army. I think that this sets up a false dichotomy, which misunderstands the interplay between love and violence in *both* the combatants and the spectators of war. I would argue that the main symbolic 'benefit' of the spectacle of male solidarity in war is related to the response it calls forth in its spectators. Nancy Huston (1982: 273–4) has noted that, even more than making war, men love to talk about it (which today means making films about it). Huston argues that the tears and lamentations of women are not just the unintended consequence of war, but its very goal. Women are called into play in the theatre of war pre-eminently as chorus or commentary on the main action in which civic identity is performed.

In this context, Ross Poole (1985: 78) has noted that the com-memoration of war celebrates

> mutual caring, comradeship and readiness for selfless sacrifice amongst those who fought ... War is not so much the construction of a new and virulent form of masculinity, as the recovery for masculine identity of that relational form of identity constructed within the family. It is, in this sense, the return of the feminine.

While I agree with the somewhat Weberian terms of the first part of this passage, I take issue with its conclusion. The 'return of the feminine', I would argue, comes in the constructing of women as spectators: neither females nor femininity find their place in the theatre of war in its actual conduct. The memory of war, I would add, constructs both a male sacrificial body and a feminine body. By no means passive, this feminine body is constituted through a community of spectators, called upon to lament or to cheer.

Vera Brittain (quoted in Segal 1987: 172) reluctantly recognised this exhilaration of the spectator as the appeal of war, in writing:

> It is, I think, this glamour, this magic, this incomparable keying up of the spirit in a time of mortal conflict, which constitute the pacifist's real problem – a problem still incompletely imagined, and still quite unresolved ... while it lasts no emotion known to man seems as yet to have quite the compelling power of this enlarged vitality.

While Brittain is seemingly talking here about the experience of actual combat, it is only as spectator that she had access to it. This 'enlarged vitality' is the pleasure of the spectator, a pleasure in a masculine drama.

Poetry and the media in Australia, as Carmel Shute has noted, presented the defeat at Gallipoli not only as a milestone of battle, but as the victory of masculinity. Shute cites news clippings in which the Anzacs are said to have displayed a masculinity which had 'never been surpassed in the history of democracies'. Again, the *Lone Hand* of 1 March 1919 noted (quoted in Shute 1975: 19):

> The Australian comes out of the great war looking the most virile thing on earth. The tasks other men could not do, he went into with a laugh, and though the laughter died in the bitter strain of the front trenches in the rush across 'no man's land', his achievements remain ... Australian manhood is our chief asset.

C.E.W. Bean (quoted in Shute 1975: 20) set the seal on this type of remembrance:

> To be the sort of man who would give way when his mates were trusting to his firmness ... to have the rest of his life haunted by the knowledge that he was set his soldier's task and had lacked the grit to carry it through – that was the prospect that those men could not face. Life was very dear, but life was not worth living unless they could be true to the idea of Australian manhood.

In this context, one theme of feminist writings that I wish to challenge is that male violence and, in particular, war rest on contempt for and abstraction from the body.[17] This theme draws on a line of feminist thought which argues that woman has historically been defined as body, and (masculine) civic identity defined as triumph over the body. It is certainly true that one of the most common *philosophical* images used to picture manhood is the idea of the whole body, impermeable to outside influences and unaffected by the fortune of the world.[18] In the narratives of Gallipoli, however, the bodies of men are glorified in thoroughly mystical ways such that war is not the triumph over the body by the soul, but the triumph *of* the male body. Male identity may be defined *philosophically* as domination over the body, but in civic terms this identity is as much a flight *into* physicality as away from it.

Again, this is consistent with the language of the classical Greeks, in which the practice of citizenship and war is centred around the celebration of the male body, the gloriously wounded body, punctured, bleeding, and vulnerable to wounds which let blood. A glorious civic blood, that is, not the blood of women's time. Two Australian poems

from World War I cited by Carmel Shute illustrate this theme. The first is
'The Test' (Shute 1975: 10), addressed to the 'Shirker', which seems to
refer as much to the reluctant mother as to the reluctant soldier-son:

> Is it that you are fearful of the bayonet's stabbing bite?
> Is it that you are shrinking from shells that shriek in the night?
> Shells that shriek their triumph through bodies bloody and torn
> Does the shriek of shrapnel scare you?
> Better you were never born.
> Those who are God's true mothers, those who are worth wives,
> Think you they value their honour, or only sloth-stained lives?

The second is a poem praising the Anzacs (Shute 1975: 19):

> Bravest where a world of men
>   Are brave beyond all earth's rewards
> So stout none shall charge again
>   Till the last breaking of the swords.
> Wounded or holed, home from war
>   Or yonder by the Lone Pine laid,
> Give him his due forever more –
>   'The bravest thing God ever made'.

The moral or spiritual qualities of honour and bravery are here *seen*
through the marks they leave on the bodies of soldiers. Indeed, the body
is perfected by the marks upon it: male sexuality, warlike prowess and
public honour are alike vindicated in the ceremonial wounding of war.
In this sense, the love of men for each other is made as spectacle for
women to feast their eyes upon.[19]

In this way we can perhaps better understand the curiously ambivalent
stance of armies towards homosexuality, a stance which at once celebrates male friendship and deplores its explicitly sexual consummation.
Virile wounding and death are visible to the community through
narratives that create a civic imaginary about the bodies of men. The
death of warriors becomes public in its narrative repetition, through
which the beauty of sacrificial death satisfies the 'lust of the eye'.[20] The
sacrifice of men in war is food for thought, for tales and tears and
imagination, in which men acquire a virile civic body and women's
bodies become the site of spectatorial pleasure. Archbishop Duhig in a
service commemorating Anzac Day in Brisbane in 1916 made the remark
that Australia had had 'her birth and her baptism in the blood of her
sons' (quoted in Shute 1975: 20).[21] The civic birth of Australian
manhood through the blood of war replaces the merely mundane birth
of men through mothers. And the maternal body itself is now witness to
this second birth.

Conclusion

The larger point of this paper is to suggest that war does *not* rest on the suppression of eros or love or passionate attachments, but plays out male desire in the ethical and political ordering of virility as civic identity. The memory of war as constructed in such narratives does not present war as an outpouring of violence, but as tableaux of heroism and self-sacrifice by male bodies – tableaux meant to be repeated and responded to. If we see war simply as violence, we risk nailing what Phaedrus would identify for us as the real culprit – love and its sight. A love, that is, among men. Such themes are evident in the historical and literary narratives of the Anzacs at Gallipoli. These texts demonstrate the role of images derived from World War I in the making of an Australian version of civic identity.

Notes

1. This is a revised version of a paper presented to the Australian Civilisation and Mythologies of Australian Cultures Conference, organised by the Sir Robert Menzies Centre for Australian Studies, at Eötvös Loránd University, Budapest, 15–16 May 1992. I wish to thank the conference participants and Grant Hilliard for their helpful comments on my work, and I am indebted to Hugh Smith for giving me useful material on homosexuality in the armed forces.
2. A simple example: the statuette of the Winfield Cup, depicting Arthur Summons and Norm Provan entangled, wounded and covered in mud, bears a striking resemblance to one of Damien Parer's more famous war photographs.
3. See for example Pericles' Funeral Oration in Thucydides (1972: 143–51).
4. The works of Sandel (1982) and Unger (1976) are characteristic examples of such critiques of liberalism.
5. For example, see the remarks of John Stuart Mill, quoted in Howard (1978: 37).
6. Note here the remarks of Michel Foucault (in Barbedette 1982: 41): 'The Greeks never admitted love between two *adult men*. We can certainly find allusions to the idea of love between young men, when they were soldiers, but not for any others.'
7. In Australia, women are now permitted in combat-related duties (since 1990) and in many combat duties (since December 1993) although, significantly, not in the infantry. The *Defence Legislation Amendment Act*, making selective conscientious objection possible, also makes women (and Aborigines) subject to compulsory military service: see Australia (1992: 1453–4).
8. Note for example the exchange in the film *Casablanca*, in which Rick claims that he ran arms to the Republicans in the civil war because he was paid well: the Major replies that the other side would have paid him a lot more. Or recall Rousseau's dictum that no man ever walked up to the breach out of self-interest.
9. For historical background, see Kantorowicz (1957: 232–72).

10. Sara Dowse and Pat Giles (1984: 63–8) characterise Australia as a 'warrior society', and argue that the celebration of 'mateship' and male bonding linked to the birth of a nation on Anzac Day is founded on the exclusion of half the population from national identity.

11. I am indebted to Taussig (1987: 123, 125–6) for the references to Hamilton and MacKenzie.

12. I should note that such classical allusions were not only made by British men. For example, in 1917 the Women's Compulsory Service League initiated a petition in favour of conscription in Australia which read: 'Sparta stands not alone in the heroism of its women. The spirit which said "Return with or on your shield" is burning brightly in the land' (quoted in Shute 1975: 10).

13. See Bérubé (1989: 383). Under pressure from the Human Rights Commission, the Australian Defence Forces reviewed their policy on homosexuality, and after some prevarication the ban was lifted by the Australian government in November 1992 (Diaz 1992). The situation in other countries varies (Whelan 1992).

14. See also the work of Eve Kosofsky Sedgwick (1985: 1–5), which posits a continuum between the homosocial and the homosexual in order to stress the erotic implications of the former.

15. Theweleit's analysis echoes the usual response of the armed forces to any characterisation of 'mischief' in the ranks as latent homosexuality. For example, allegations of bastardisation at the Australian Defence Force Academy in May 1992 involved accusations against cadets of bullying and sexual intimidation, including being forced to simulate sex in a position known as 'reverse Vienna oyster' and to lick cream from the underpants of other cadets. Brigadier Adrian D'Hage noted, 'There were sexual undertones', but he described the events as 'misguided revelry' (Wright 1992).

16. Note that I am using 'narrative' in a very inclusive sense, although my examples are primarily literary. For architectural examples, see Astbury (1992) and Edwards (1991).

17. See for example Hartsock (1984: 125) and Ruddick (1983: 484).

18. Plato is probably the originator of this notion. The central image of the wounded Christ introduces into philosophy itself a novel view of the value of the wounded body. St Augustine for example notes that at the resurrection we 'reach the perfection of manhood, the stature of the perfect maturity of Christ'. St Augustine writes that the body will be resurrected in the perfection of manhood, although the martyrs for example will still manifest the scars of the wounds they suffered in Christ's name: 'For in those wounds there will be no deformity, but only dignity, and the beauty of their valour will shine out, a beauty *in* the body and yet not *of* the body.' That is, the resurrected bodies will certainly not lack defects, but 'proofs of valour' are not to be accounted as defects. See Augustine (1972: 1061–2), and more generally, Steinberg (1983).

19. Where women refuse to serve as enthusiastic spectators, these homoerotic overtones of war emerge very explicitly and even bitterly. For example, Sandra Gilbert (1983: 424) has examined the ambivalence of men to women behind the lines in World War I, documenting homoeroticism in writings on the experience of war.

20. Cf. Gray (1970: 28–9).

21. Some writers have argued that conceptions of male virility appropriate the pains of childbirth to a new civic birth: see for example Loraux (1981) and Huston (1986: 127).

CHAPTER 7

(Homo)sexual Identities, Queer Theory and Politics

Dennis Altman

It is tempting to wish that identity politics would go away. Faced with the human misery which results from the violent assertion of racial, ethnic and religious differences in Bosnia, South Africa and India, the liberal Enlightenment appeal to a transcultural humanness, whereby we are all seen as individuals equal before the law, can only be an improvement. Yet the post-Cold War world has reminded us of the stubborn persistence of national and ethnic identities as a basic fact of political life and source of political conflict. Such identities are of course social constructions: one is not born Azerbaijani or Afrikaaner, these are identities which are historically determined, socially reproduced and changeable through political action. Nonetheless, such identities remain central to most of political life, and we know very little about the conditions under which people would willingly surrender a strong sense of identity based on race or belief. Indeed, some ethnic ties appear so persistent that an argument for an instinctual human need for communal (tribal) identity becomes seductive.

Two points should be made in relation to current postmodern critiques of 'identity politics'. First, it is perfectly reasonable to recognise that identities are socially constructed while also acknowledging their apparent resilience as political forms. Postmodernists tend to assume that 'identity politics' are a form of essentialism (see e.g. Fuss 1989). But this sort of essentialism has been out of fashion in the social sciences for far longer than the new literary imperialists, who believe they invented both cultural studies and social theory, recognise. Second, politics based upon the assertion and protection of identity assume the importance of human agency. Such politics are often linked to the formation of social movements, based on particular concepts of identity, which are effective precisely because they assert the primacy of certain identities over others (cf. Winant 1993: 170). The tensions for those – black lesbians are the commonly cited example – who feel pulled between the assertion of several identities simultaneously are obvious.[1] Cindy Patton (1993: 175) argues that identity politics assume that 'a preconsciousness of an intrinsic condition existed prior to the group', but like Douglas Crimp (1993: 314) I doubt that this need be the case.

Human agency may apply both to those asserting an identity and to their enemies; the history of the invention of 'the homosexual' is one of complicity between those defined as such and those (doctors, psychologists, lawmakers) with an interest in defining certain behaviours as identities – all the better, as Foucault might argue, to control them. (In the same way, those most attracted to an essentialist view of homosexuality are likely to include both homosexuals and homophobes, even if the latter often simultaneously cling to a view that homosexual seduction is an ever present threat.) Nonetheless, without the invention of certain forms of identity and community, the creation of alternative sites of power and expertise, of dissident voices to those of the recognised orthodoxies, would be impossible.[2] The assertion of identity by marginalised and stigmatised groups strengthens the definitions which can be used to control them, but at the same time creates the possibilities to address those factors which maintain their stigmatisation.

It is easy for university-based critics to underestimate the hunger for 'identity' that is experienced by those who feel dispossessed, ignored or stigmatised. All social and political discourses of identity combine elements of the 'real' and the imagined, the mythological culture of one's forebears and the over-rehearsed claims of present grievances. Think of the way these come together in the tragic expressions of nationalist identities in the former Yugoslavia – and their somewhat pathetic, if troubling, echoes in ethnic communities in Australia. (Similar mechanisms may be at work in the construction of individual identity, but the vast psychological literature on identity is beyond the scope of this chapter.)

Over the past twenty years 'identity politics' have come, as L.A. Kauffman (1990: 6–7) has argued, to imply

> not only organising around shared identity, as for example classic nationalist movements have done. Identity politics also expresses the belief that identity itself – its elaboration, expression or affirmation – is and should be a fundamental focus of political work. In this way, the politics of identity have led to an unprecedented politicisation of previously nonpolitical terrains: sexuality, interpersonal relations, lifestyle and culture.

Most significant of these expanded formulations are those of the lesbian and gay movement. Indeed, one is hard pressed to think of other 'lifestyles' or 'interpersonal relations' which have become players in the political realm.

There is a sense in which the idea of a discrete 'lesbian or gay' identity runs counter to what is likely to be true about human sexuality. If one accepts that there is some validity to the Freudian view of sexuality, which sees homo-sexual as much as hetero-sexual desire as part of the human potential, then Gore Vidal was right when he insisted that 'homosexual' should only be used as an adjective but never as a noun (see Altman 1983: 295). Many societies, of course, accept this view. The construction of a cohesive set of identities and communities, summed up in the term 'the modern homosexual',[3] is largely an invention of modern western societies. The idea that people are either 'straight' or 'gay' is a convenient fiction, which ignores the far more fluid nature of sexual desire and fantasy.

Among the self-identifications of homosexuals an essentialist view of homosexuality – 'I was born this way' or 'I've always known I was gay' – has co-existed through much of this century with a constructionist view, as expressed in more radical gay liberationist arguments and, particularly, in radical lesbian positions (see Altman 1993; Hocquenghem 1993; Mieli 1980; Rich 1980; Wittig 1992). If the dominant discourse of gay and lesbian scholars has been constructionist, that of the wider community has often been essentialist, a position which, at least in the United States, was attractive as a defence against psychiatric attempts to change sexual orientation (see Epstein 1994; Vance 1984). This explains the seeming attraction of genetic explanations for homosexuality among at least some American homosexuals. Both positions came together in supporting the creation of 'gay' or 'lesbian and gay' identities as political, social and cultural constructs, so that the idea of homosexuality as the basis for a whole set of socio-cultural relations, behaviours and styles has become common to most western countries. In the global marketplace the 'gay lifestyle', 'the lipstick lesbian' has become a recognised and exploitable consumer group.

These shifts in (self) definition seem the result not only of action by those involved in the burgeoning lesbian/gay movements of the past few decades, but also of larger socio-economic changes which have increased the cultural and political space available for a broader range of social and sexual arrangements than was true in previous periods of history. Social constructionism recognises the interaction of human agency and social (and indeed biological) forces. As Claudia Card (1992: 46) puts it: 'Institutions partially "construct" the lives of those they govern, and they are in turn "constructed" by human behavior.'

Consider the rapid transition from the definition of 'the homosexual' in the early 1960s as an individual 'deviant', 'criminal' or 'sinner' to the current status of the 'gay' or 'lesbian' as a member of a community perceived by many politicians and the media to be a significant and legitimate player in at least some aspects of social life. Of course, the transition is neither complete nor even in its impact. Politicians may well court the gay vote in the electorates of Bligh and Melbourne Ports, but they are more likely to attack homosexuality in Gunnedah or Toowoomba, as the furore over the ABC telecast of the 1994 Gay and Lesbian Mardi Gras revealed. Nonetheless, the changes are significant, and have forced some change in the broader Australian self-image that ours is a particularly homophobic and intolerant society. I have argued elsewhere (Altman 1994) that the changes have been eased in Australia by the fact that they have coincided with the development of multi-culturalism as an official national definition (and one that is used some-what differently from the way that term is used in the United States, with its echoes of 'political correctness'). In some ways 'gay' has become another part of the multicultural mosaic, and events such as the Gay and Lesbian Mardi Gras can be easily encompassed as another ethnic festival.

Without some concept of a shared identity, the creation of the sense of community that makes the Mardi Gras possible could not have occurred. Of course, this sense of identity and community are not merely the result of lesbian/gay agency. Increasing affluence, changes in the social expectations of gender, the commodification of much of what was previously regarded as private, and overseas influences, have all played their part in opening up space for new sexual identities (see Altman 1987). But in the end, the most single important factor was the creation of a sense of shared identity and commitment based on homosexuality and the common experience of social stigma. The small and seemingly marginal sexual radical movements of the late 1960s and early 1970s were an essential catalyst for the vastly larger gay/lesbian worlds now apparent in most large cities. (So too, it is important to note, was the sort of hostility towards gay self-assertion symbolised in recent years by the Reverend Fred Nile. It has often been claimed that lesbian/gay movements emerge where there are clear-cut symbols of oppression, and most particularly in English-speaking societies where legal restrictions were the major focus of the gay movement before the onset of the HIV/AIDS illness, and remain so in Tasmania.) Without obvious enemies, whose major role for homosexuals and the media alike is to personalise 'homophobia', it would be far harder to develop homosexuality as a basis for political mobilisation.

The size of the contemporary gay/lesbian population is of the order of larger ethnic groups within Australia. In his autobiography Robert Dessaix (1994: 164) writes of discovering the 'Annandale to Bondi belt':

A stroll up Oxford Street in those days revealed a flourishing subculture, not just homosexuals on the prowl. To the out-of-towner it was comfortingly clear that in these seedy, down-at-heel streets and lanes and in the nearby suburbs people were experimenting with a new set of rituals and rites, new value-systems, new readings of history and new political agendas, and they were talking to each other about them in their own newspapers and books and in their own cafes and pubs.

Nor are such phenomena restricted to Sydney, although that city is the undoubted gay capital of the south Pacific. In the 1990s smaller cities, such as Hobart, Townsville or Darwin, also have their own pubs and cafes, lesbian and gay radio programs and information lines.

In some ways the creation of lesbian/gay identities and communities has analogies in the creation of a sense of nation. Indeed, the concept of 'nation' is echoed in the rhetoric of the movement from Jill Johnston's *Lesbian Nation* (1973) through to 'Queer Nation' in the 1990s. Some gay men have also used the term 'tribe' to describe themselves, a term which I think was first used by Christopher Isherwood. There is the same emphasis on shared values, history, 'sensibility'; the same claims that homosexuality – like nationality – is a 'master identity' which transcends differences of class, race or age. This moves easily into a romantic ahistorical essentialism, summed up in a very revealing passage from Patricia Nell Warren's (1979: 86) novel *The Beauty Queen*:

> America had acknowledged all the immigrants who had come pouring up that channel, past the Statue of Liberty, through the now-decaying buildings at Ellis Island – all the immigrants but one. America had never honored the homosexual. The gay sailors who haunted the first waterfront bars, the lesbian governesses who taught the first children of the rich straights. The gays too had come over on the Mayflower, had first glimpsed New York Harbor from the decks of the Half Moon.

Recently the emergence of 'queer theory' has been presented as a challenge to the existing concepts of 'lesbian' and 'gay' identity, and the term has unleashed considerable passion, above all in the politically charged confines of inner Sydney. 'Queer' is a term which was asserted as a political label by younger lesbian/gay activists in the United States, who had been radicalised by AIDS and official responses to it, and also by a feeling that the existing lesbian/gay institutions were incapable of adequately responding to current crises. In an odd transmogrification, a term originally used to assert gay identity became used to deconstruct that very identity, and 'queer' came to mean any form of sexuality which was outside the conventional heterosexual norm.[4]

As an aesthetic term 'queer' is very useful; one might characterise films such as *Orlando* or *The Crying Game* as 'queer'. As a political term, however, it is less so. The idea that there are large numbers of people outside the heterosexual mainstream who can come together under the queer umbrella seems unlikely. Most homosexuals do not feel any particular community with sex-workers, trans-sexuals or straight fetishists. It is perhaps not surprising, therefore, that a number of those who have been involved in the creation of lesbian/gay politics scorn 'queer' inclusiveness as a return to the sort of coded coyness of the closet where specific homosexual political demands could be camouflaged in vague references to 'sexual liberation'. Theoretically, 'queer' is closely linked to postmodernism, and sometimes seems to owe more to current academic fashion than to any form of political activism. As Lisa Duggan (1992: 26), who on the whole is sympathetic to the queer project, noted: 'There is a tendency among some queer theorists to engage in academic debates at a high level of intellectual sophistication, while erasing the political and activist roots of their theoretical insights and concern'.[5]

Without some sort of assertion of shared identity, the huge changes in the status of homosexuals over the past several decades could not have occurred. Identity politics created a lesbian/gay movement and at the same time gave the larger society a means to incorporate homosexuals into respectability. Once homosexuality could be defined in social rather than individual terms, it became possible to conceive of homosexuals as another part of the multicultural fabric, with the same rights to protection from discrimination and access to government services as other minorities. The idea of a distinctive gay identity may well be a myth, but like other myths of identity it has been an important component of individual self-esteem and assertion. As long as considerable homophobia exists, as long as people fear rejection, persecution, even violence from others because of their sexuality, there is a need for a political concept of lesbian/gay identity which cannot be easily assimilated under 'queerness'.

Postmodern critics of identity politics, however, would claim that identities are too fluid and provisional to form the basis of a politics. These claims seem part of a larger scepticism about the possibilities for political action. As David Harvey (1990a: 53–4) put it:

> Modernism was very much about the pursuit of better futures, even if perpetual frustration of that aim was conducive to paranoia. But postmodernism typically strips away that possibility by concentrating upon the schizophrenic circumstances induced by fragmentation and all those instabilities (including those of language) that prevent us even picturing coherently, let alone devising strategies to produce, some radically different future.

The deconstruction of identity thus tends to go hand in hand with a certain disdain for political organising. Chris Atmore (1993: 13) has noted that 'post-structuralist critiques of identity politics have substituted the lone rebel motif for the embarrassing "movement",' thereby revealing a general lack of interest in conventional political activity. 'Queer theory' seems to discuss politics very much in terms of cultural rather than institutional representation, to show little interest in the electoral or interest-group type of activities which have been the mainstay of gay/lesbian political activity since 1980.[6] In Australia there has been remarkably little written by political scientists which reflects the political debates around the decriminalisation of homosexuality (and how the different itineraries of such debates in, say, South Australia, Tasmania and Queensland might throw light on state political cultures) or which analyses the impact of 'the gay lobby' in, for example, the career of New South Wales Independent MLA Clover Moore.[7]

Ironically, the universalist liberal concept of politics, which sees it as an arena in which individuals come together unmediated by group loyalties, is also criticised by postmodernism, which (rightly) points to the extent to which all universals are the product of particular interests and ideologies. Yet, for all their limits, *both* of these concepts seem to me worth defending, both on moral and on pragmatic grounds. In the end, engagement in identity politics is justified where it contributes to greater individual freedom and self-esteem. Indeed, I would argue, it ceases to be legitimate where it subordinates the interests of the individual to some vague notion of community good. Judith Butler's (1993: 18) comment is pertinent: 'The critique of the queer subject is crucial to the continuing *democratisation* of queer politics.'

Identity politics needs to recognise that the liberation of any particular group is related to the liberation of the larger society, that an identity politics which does not simultaneously encompass some vision of a general interest is a threat to a genuinely democratic society. Martha Nussbaum (1994) has called for a greater cosmopolitanism in American education, in part in response to the fragmentation of academic discourses into identity-based studies ('women's', 'Afro-American', 'Hispanic', etc). Such cosmopolitanism needs to extend to a recognition that a democratic society necessitates an acceptance – not merely the toleration – of different values and lifestyles. Where identities are asserted to rectify historical wrongs and structural oppression – perhaps most clearly in Australia in the case of Aboriginal claims for self-determination – they can contribute to a broadening of the base for a genuinely participatory civil society. Where, however, identity discourse becomes a rationale for oppressing others – as is clearly the case in the resurgence of tribal loyalties in the former Yugoslavia and Soviet Union

– it poses a threat to the democratic order. There are less striking examples of identity as oppressive from the gay movement, which has tended to be supportive of the claims of other groups. One case would be Richard Mohr's (1988) specious argument that gay men with AIDS should be treated better than others. But it is certainly true that like all 'communities', the lesbian/gay worlds impose their own pressures for conformity, as exemplifed in all those jokes about lesbian humourlessness or gay men who hate Judy Garland.

'Identity politics', wrote Barbara Epstein (1992: 154), 'forces people's experiences into categories that are too narrow and also makes it difficult for us to speak to one another across the boundaries of these identities – let alone create the coalitions needed to build a movement for progressive change'. For these reasons, the contemporary emphasis on identity-based politics threatens to obliterate any concept of a shared public space, of the ideal of a common citizenship which is increasingly portrayed as no more than the ideological invention of dominant middle-class white men. Nevertheless, to recognise that the discourse of citizenship has historically been dominated by certain interests does not mean it is irrelevant to other groups, nor that we should not seek to expand its meaning. The trend in the United States towards seeking political balance through a politically correct mix of gender, race and ethnicity means ultimately a denial of the political: our views are assumed to arise necessarily from our identities, which is to take esssentialism to its logical conclusion. There are some interesting examples in the development of women's, black and gay studies, where the identity of those involved is taken to be more significant than their understanding of ideologies of gender, race or sexuality. To assume, for example, that only women should teach courses related to gender is to deny the ability to transcend one's immediate experience, which is to deny the possibility of imagination, empathy and scholarship.

In the name of empowering previously suppressed groups, identity politics threatens to silence others. Nothing is more destructive than the game of comparative oppression, whereby one group tries to claim a greater degree of suffering than another, a claim which in recent years has been turned against the gay movement. Thus in some of the political rhetoric around AIDS, one detects a nasty tone in the frequent references to 'middle-class white gay men' which ignores the point that they are the people (at least in this and similar countries) who are most affected by the epidemic (see King 1993; Watney 1989).

Postmodern views of the contingency and fragility of identity are important concepts, but they must be measured against the strength with which many people assert their communal identities as a central part of their being. Of course, some of those who advocate postmodernism recognise this, as in the comment by Steven Seidman (1993: 142) that: 'The kind of postmodern approach I am recommending favors pragmatic, justificatory strategies that underscore the practical and rhetorical character of social discourse.' In the age of AIDS, gay identity has become more, not less, important for large numbers of people. It is also becoming a more important mark of self-definition for people outside the rich western world, with the development of a recognisable gay culture in most of those countries of Eastern Europe, South America and South and East Asia where the conditions allow for its emergence. The rhetorical flourishes of queer deconstruction have little meaning for groups in Bombay, Buenos Aires or Budapest who have seized on the idea of lesbian/gay identities as a way of carving out certain social and political space in rapidly changing societies.

'It seems', as Jane Gallop (cited in Weeks 1991: 69) has put it, that 'identity must be continually assumed and immediately called into question, or alternatively, constantly questioned yet all the time assumed.' The real problem is how to ensure that identity politics contributes to a larger social good, rather than simply protecting the interests of entrenched minorities, which is arguably the dominant form of multicultural politics in Australia today. Here the history of lesbian/gay politics becomes of far wider relevance than to its immediate constituency. Just as Freud, Havelock Ellis and Foucault all found in homosexuality a crucial metaphor for a larger discussion of sexuality, so the social and political movements based upon homosexuality help elucidate some of the central problems of political action in the contemporary world. The self-reflexivity which is a mark of lesbian/gay life, the very recentness of the creation of lesbian/gay communities, indeed of the word 'gay' itself, all make apparent the sorts of issues raised by politics based upon particular identities. As fashionable postmodern interpretations make such identity politics seem narrow, limited and, above all, old-fashioned, it becomes necessary to reassert the point that identity politics has the potential to be both liberatory and repressive. In both cases, however, identity politics is about organisation, movements and interaction with the state, and hence deserves greater consideration than has usually been accorded it by mainstream political science.

Notes

1. See the writings of hooks (1990) and Moraga and Anzaldua (1984).
2. This is discussed with relation to psychology in Sampson (1993).
3. The phrase is Ken Plummer's (1981).
4. On 'queer', see Duggan (1992) and de Lauretis (1991).

5. Compare the criticisms by Morton (1993).
6. For an example of how 'queer' theorists conceptualise the political, see the articles under the rubric 'Politics and Representation' in Abelove, Barale and Halperin (1993). None of them deal with what are conventionally viewed as political institutions or processes.
7. AIDS policy making is something of an exception. See Altman (1992) and Ballard (1989).

Race, Place and Citzenship

CHAPTER 8

Racialism and Democracy: The Legacy of White Australia

John Kane

Assertions of national identity aim to anchor cultures or nations in time, orienting them towards a future and linking them to a real or imagined past.[1] Cobbled together from a variety of textual and symbolical materials as national identities usually are, they are frequently riddled with paradox and contradiction. This does not, of course, necessarily diminish their utility; coherence and truth are less essential here than practicality. But even identity claims which have long proved their usefulness can become impractical if societal values change or novel challenges arise. In these circumstances, dominant conceptions of national unity may seem to demand revision or renewal. Readings of history may become controversial as people plunder the past for values, characteristics or qualities that might be conscripted into present service.[2] A nation's past may constitute a 'repository of treasures'[3] to be drawn upon as circumstances require, but the value of any particular treasure is always contestable and frequently contested. The difficulty for those seeking to redefine a national identity lies not merely in choosing what aspects of the national heritage to retain and what to discard, but also in determining what elements contemporary society can be persuaded to embrace and what it wishes to repudiate. This chapter examines these issues of recovery and repudiation, with reference to arguments about White Australia.

The rhetoric of repudiation

Australian governments have been committed for some years to the repudiation of the institutional racialism which characterised the nation's past, most notoriously in the immigration laws known as the

117

'White Australia' policy. Measures such as the ending of racial discrimination in immigration in the early 1970s, the passage of the *Racial
Discrimination Act* in 1975 and various Aboriginal land rights acts, and
the legislation with respect to native title and social justice for
Aborigines that arose out of the High Court's *Mabo* case, attest to the
strength of this commitment. This process has been partly driven, no
doubt, by a perceived need to brush up the national image for the
benefit of potential trading partners.[4] But also at stake is the country's
moral perception of itself, and of its standing in the international
community.[5]

In repudiating the doctrine of 'White Australia', Australians have
done much more than just change an attitude: they have relinquished a
national political identity which served for more than half a century. It
was an identity that had grown obsolete in an increasingly heterogeneous society and a world of altered values. The present policy of
'multiculturalism' reflects these changes, and seeks to assure all Australia's ethnic groups of their rightful place in the national fold. The
rhetoric of Australian egalitarianism extends now to citizens of all
backgrounds. In multiculturalism, the official break with a racialist past
appears complete.

Yet such a break presents problems for Australians as they consider
the attitudes they should adopt to their national history. It is natural,
perhaps, looking across the break, to feel a sense of unease or guilt
about the past (or, the other side of the coin, a defensive impulse to
deny guilt).[6] Australians are no longer sure what to claim and what to
disclaim in their inheritance. The radical rupture also has consequences
when we consider the historical and rational foundations of multiculturalism. Its 'negative' foundation is the repudiation of racialism, but
what are its positive bases? Not knowing these, how is it possible to
translate multiculturalism into social and political practice? How, in
particular, are we to reconcile diversity with the need for social
and political unity, and to understand what it means now to be an
'Australian'?

It will be the contention of this chapter that some perspective may be
gained on such questions by an understanding of the positive elements
that informed the doctrine of White Australia. Humphrey McQueen
(1986: 268) observed that a full understanding of the power of racism
in Australia will require recognition that White Australia 'expressed a
code of civic morality ... (It) was a doctrine full of affirmative values,
offering much more than a negative rejection of other peoples.' Elaine
Thompson (1994: 46) has recently endorsed this claim in her book
on Australian egalitarianism, where she writes: 'More than a single
policy [White Australia] was the ideological foundation of Australian

democracy. Notions of equality, representation, rights and justice were all laid on it.'

Thompson shows clearly that the political ideals of Australians at Federation were inseparably linked to deep racialist beliefs, and that both found expression in the policy of White Australia. This chapter, in laying out the logic of linkage, will echo and extend Thompson's analysis, but will try to avoid the tendency evident in that work (and much more marked in McQueen's) toward historical judgementalism. I will argue that it was a *virtue* of White Australia to recognise that a democratic polity can only be founded on a conviction of the essential *equality* of its citizens. The problem for colonial Australians was how to reconcile this conviction with their profound, if erroneous, belief in human inequality. The particular solution they arrived at was to argue that the preservation of democratic values required the strict maintenance of a racial homogeneity, in which whiteness was the governing principle. Thompson (1994: 40), however, calls this a 'perverse egalitarian logic', and argues that it was 'deeply flawed' in two respects: 'first, the belief that a society based on exclusion could be democratic, and that there could be a democracy founded on the denial of equality and justice; second, the absolute belief that a multiracial society could not be democratic' (1994: 46).

The first of these 'flaws' involves, I think, a misjudgement. To accept Thompson's point would be to deny that white Australia was a democratic nation, which is plainly absurd. It would also mean, of course, denying the title 'democracy' to ancient Athens, originator of the concept, because it failed to grant that women, tradesmen and slaves were equal to the men of property who formed its citizenry. Certainly democracy requires equality of the citizens who comprise the *demos*, but who is to be included in the category of citizen is a different and prior question. Ancient Athens, and white Australia at Federation, gave different answers to this question than most of us would give today, but they thought their answers were founded on sufficient reason and therefore quite just. It might seem, in retrospect, 'perverse' to found a defence of equality on exclusion of those regarded as inherently unequal. Nonetheless, as Thompson's own work shows, the racialist beliefs of white Australians were widely and deeply held, and were, moreover, held by most people not merely as moral opinion but as proven 'scientific' fact. These beliefs must indeed be judged, from our historically advantaged position as deeply flawed, indeed as profoundly wrong, but the *logic* was not flawed if the premises be accepted.

The second 'flaw' identified is a belief that also follows logically from white Australia's racialist premises, as Thompson's own following passage demonstrates. She concludes that 'Australia's democrats could not conceive of a society in which different races, especially if they differed in colour, could live together under conditions of equality' (1994: 46). Thompson, however, goes on to argue that Alfred Deakin was wrong when he declared unity of race was an 'absolute essential' to the unity of Australia. In terms of abstract argument, Deakin may well be judged wrong, but in terms of his historical situation – a situation which included precisely the deep racialism of the time – he may well have been right. Thompson (1994: 97) claims that 'racial heterogeneity would not automatically have meant conflict', but her own account of the devastation wrought on indigenous peoples and on Chinese immigrants by racially motivated whites should give some cause for doubt. White Australians also had very clearly in their minds, as the records show, the terrible examples of the American Civil War and strife-torn South Africa to bolster their fears. Indeed, a glance at the inter-group conflicts of the late twentieth-century world should demonstrate that commitment to a peaceful, democratic and heterogeneous community remains, to some extent, an act of moral and political faith.

We are right to find certain aspects of our past abhorrent, and to face them squarely, but a certain sensitivity is required when attempting to *judge* the past from the privileged perspective of the present. The racialism of white Australia (shared by almost all whites everywhere at the time) could only be effaced by the passage of time and historical experience (it still awaits erasure in the minds of many today). We fail to learn from the past when we are concerned only to condemn what could not, feasibly, have been otherwise. It is this difficulty of historical judgement that makes the political acts of repudiation and retrieval problematic but nevertheless worthwhile. We cannot evade our past, but we need not be prisoners to it. If it is to be of any positive use to us, we must accept it with all its crimes and achievements, determined to outgrow the evils and to build upon the goods. I will argue, at any rate, that some of the values embedded in the doctrine of White Australia are recoverable from the grip of racism and remain relevant to a modern multicultural society, and to modern notions of national identity.

Certainly, the changes to Australian society in the past half-century have ensured that the White Australian conception of a unified national identity based on racial homogeneity is no longer possible, even if it were still thought desirable. This chapter therefore takes a cue from Donald Horne (1994b), who argues what is now required is an Australian 'civic identity'. Certain elements of this civic identity already exist, I will argue, in the doctrine of White Australia. Their recovery demands that we move from a 'thick', descriptive conception of identity, based on allegedly common national and racial characteristics, to a 'thin' one, based on a firm commitment to a democratic polity. It is the argument of this paper that, in rejecting this principle, the new policy of multiculturalism takes up a particular challenge. This is to demonstrate the possibility of a liberal-democratic civic identity which can reconcile two beliefs in apparent tension, namely, the need to respect cultural diversity on the one hand, and the need to preserve political unity on the other.

The following analysis begins by considering the British-Australian origins of the concept of a White Australian national identity, and shows why Australians thought the policy based on it provided an answer to many fundamental questions posed by the founding of a new nation. I then proceed to outline the economic, moral and political arguments that underpinned the defence of White Australia. I contend that our political forebears were right in their belief that a successful democracy required social cleavages to be contained within a unifying civic sphere, and further, that conflicts which could not be accommodated within that sphere threatened the destruction of democracy. Given that the radical solution of racial simplification adopted by White Australians is no longer morally defensible or feasible in practice, I outline the path from 'thick' racial identity to 'thin' civic identity. The latter, I argue, is implicit in the multiculturalist policy that has displaced that of White Australia.

British-Australian identity and nationhood

The doctrine of White Australia asserted the existence of a positive Australian identity that needed to be rigorously protected if certain worthy political and social goals and values were to be achieved – or, in more glorious flights of fancy, if 'higher', white or British, civilisation itself was to survive on the face of the earth (see Pearson in Crowley 1980: 69–70). This identity, as explicitly conceived at the time of Federation, comprised three parts – 'whiteness', 'Britishness' and 'Australianness' – and functioned at each level to guard security and assert dominion (Cole 1971). The whiteness of Australians, 'not only white, but whiter than white: the best people in the world at being white', according to Horne (1994a), was asserted against all the coloured races of the world who might by sheer force of numbers usurp them in their settled land. The Britishness reinforced the superiority claim of whiteness, and called forth Imperial protection from both Asian hordes and other European powers. Australianness indicated that the British character had been modified by colonial levelling and toughening (whether towards improvement or degeneration was sometimes a matter of debate; see Cole 1971: 518–22) and could be asserted against the whole world, including, if necessary, Britain itself.[7]

The vigour with which this tripartite identity was asserted and legis-latively defended in 1901 was a measure of its importance and of the depth of fear which underlay it. The relevant pieces of legislation (see Palfreeman 1971) enacted by the new Commonwealth parliament to safeguard it were known under the collective title of 'White Australia Policy'. Writing in 1924, Sir Frederick Eggleston (Yarwood 1968: 121) called this policy 'the formula which the Australian people have framed as the only solution of a number of very complex problems which affect their security and welfare'. The speed with which the policy was put in place upon Federation demonstrated that the matter had already been politically determined. The federal legislation on immigration was a preventative measure among whose principal targets was the newly industrialised and increasingly powerful nation of Japan (see Yarwood 1962: 258). (Chinese immigration had already been effectively excluded during the 1880s by co-ordinated colonial legislation.) Despite problems with the Colonial Office in Whitehall and objections from the Japanese government, the measures that would largely govern the composition of the nation for the next two-thirds of a century were in place very shortly after Federation.

'White Australia' provided an answer to certain fundamental ques-tions about the sort of polity and society that the new nation would become. Australia, it asserted, would be a unified British society; it would be democratic and egalitarian; it would be a predominantly Christian society but with a secularist polity; it would be capitalist, with the conflict between capital and labour safely regulated; and it would be a society which aimed at providing and securing a high and growing standard of living for *all* its members. In the eyes of the founders of the Commonwealth, each one of these aims and ideals would be threatened by a policy of unrestricted immigration. It followed to their minds that Australian society must be, first and foremost, a *white* society.

The case for White Australia

The descriptive characteristics that defined the national identity de-fended by the White Australia policy included both racial and cultural elements. These characteristics were partly inherited – from 'good British stock' – and partly acquired – as that stock adapted itself to the new social and geographic environment. Conceiving of themselves as members of a superior British 'race', white Australians held themselves naturally endowed with virtuous qualities – physical, mental and moral – absent from or less developed in other races. As inheritors of British political traditions and values, they felt themselves possessed of certain ingrained capacities for living under a liberal democratic constitution.

The racial and cultural strands were, to their minds, inextricably linked. It was precisely the possession of unique racial characteristics that had enabled the British constitutional achievement, and that also ensured that white Australians were morally and psychologically fit to appropriate that achievement and to develop it further in distinctive and progressive ways (Huttenback 1976: 15).

It should be remembered that the racialist outlook of Australians in the late nineteenth century was far from unique. It was, in fact, a ubiquitous feature of white colonial nations, for this was the heyday of 'scientific' racialism and social Darwinism (see Goodwin 1964; Huttenback 1976). The doctrine of the 'equality of man', when measured against the alleged 'facts' of racial difference, was held to be invalid except insofar as it might apply *within* races, but really only within those races thought to be sufficiently advanced to warrant and demand equality.[8] In fact, the realisation of egalitarian ideals depended, it was argued, precisely on the preservation of racial and cultural homogeneity. Early Australians maintained that a society of mixed race would benefit neither dominant nor inferior groups, and would have profoundly adverse effects on the economic order, on the moral-social order, and on the political order.

The economic order

The likely economic consequences of unrestricted immigration were a contentious issue. Ever since the practice of assigning convicts to landowners had come to an end in the 1840s, there had been those who saw the importation of cheap 'coolie' labour – Indian, Chinese or Islander – as the antidote to scarce, expensive (and uncontrollable) European labour. With regard to the inhospitable tropical north, this strategy was often depicted as the *only* solution to the problem of development. Such a policy would also, according to Governor Bowen of Queensland (Yarwood 1968: 42), positively advance the prospects of European immigrants.[9] But only the big landowners of the coastal strip, who would be the obvious beneficiaries, accepted this. Members of the labour movement argued that, on the contrary, the 'coolie option' was a plot by employers and some liberals to destroy the unions and lower workers' standards of living. Trade unionists saw a threat not only to wages, but also to the entire social contract between labour, capital and government which was developing in the colonies.[10]

In one of those paradoxical contortions that are common in attempts to delineate 'thick' conceptions of identity, the racial inferiority argument was in the economic sphere turned on its head. Here it was the *superiority*, in some respects, of the Chinese (and later the Japanese) that was perceived to be the problem. 'Asiatics' appeared to live on next to nothing and would work not only for less money, but longer and harder than a European (see Gibb 1973: 63–4). In the first Commonwealth parliament, Senator Staniford-Smith (cited in Gibb 1973: 117) argued that the admitted virtues of thrift and industry of Asians, transplanted into Australia, became economic vices which 'would cause an enormous amount of wretchedness and misery amongst our labouring classes ... For these and many other reasons the people are determined that Australia shall be kept for the white race'. These sentiments also required that local Australian industry be 'protected' from Asian industriousness exercised *outside* the country. 'White Australia', therefore, went hand in hand with a policy of thoroughgoing protectionism.

The moral-social order

The moral and social costs included not only the inevitable degradation of the inferior group, but also the corrupting effects of inequality on the dominant race. Part of the case was made by Eggleston, who argued that the homogeneity required for stability and order was difficult enough to achieve even among the Caucasian races of Europe. He considered it impossible among mixed races where differences of colour indelibly discriminated the alien. In such societies, 'the coloured races become pawns, depressing the standard of life and removing the white race from a healthy contact with manual labour ...' (cited in Yarwood 1968: 121). To mix the races was, in effect, to become a society divided into virtual slaves and slave-owners, with all the moral ill-effects that implied. According to Australia's first prime minister, Edmund Barton (cited in Huttenback 1976: 287), this was unavoidable because: 'The savage employed by the white man is, in our judgement, more or less a slave, even under an agreement, because of the intellectual inequality between them'.

The political order

The ideal of democratic citizenship implied the maintenance of the political equality and liberty of the citizenry. This could only be achieved in a unified society. For Alfred Deakin (cited in Gibb 1973: 103–4), this meant one of united race, whose members could intermix and intermarry without 'degradation', and who were qualified to live under the Australian Constitution ('the broadest and most liberal the world has perhaps yet seen') without abusing it. The implication here was that the 'inferior' races were not competent to fulfil the political duties that a democracy expects.[11] This argument had already been forcibly put in 1888 by Sir Henry Parkes, who made it clear that the alleged inferiority justified withholding political rights from other races (cited in Yarwood 1968: 94).

The most extreme political and social consequences of mixing the races could be seen, it was held, in the great negative examples of the United States of America and the colonies of Southern Africa. The necessity of maintaining a vast and permanent under-class, which, according to racialist theory, could not without loss of purity and power be assimilated, produced a potential for devastating conflict. The advocates of White Australia sought to avoid the racial problems which they perceived as having plunged the United States into the violence of civil war (see Crowley 1980: 488).

Civic identity and democratic politics

The fears of Australia's founders concerning the formation of irreconcilable social divisions should not be too lightly dismissed. The greatest problem for democratic government, after all, and its greatest achievement when it works, is the accommodation of social cleavages within a structure of cultural values that are shared by the principal antagonists (Touraine 1991: 265). Liberal democracy accepts the existence of such cleavages and also the legitimacy of the conflicts they give rise to, but endeavours to contain conflict within a political sphere of mutual respect and tolerance. We should not need the recent horrors of Bosnia or Rwanda to remind us that in the absence of strongly shared common values conflicts may degenerate into civil war. We have the history of the twentieth century, on the other hand, to teach us that the result of *suppressing* social conflict may be totalitarianism and the loss of the power to oppose. Liberal democracy attempts to avoid the evils of both excessive unity and excessive conflict by providing a civil arena in which the inevitable conflicts of social division can safely be played out (Touraine 1991: 265–6).

A fundamental condition for the success of this strategy is the establishment of a responsible citizenry. Democracy resides on an ethical view of people as self-reliant and autonomous individuals capable of making decisions (including social and political decisions) for themselves, as opposed to having them made for them by 'expert' others. It assumes that all citizens have the right to participate in the political process. By virtue of its acceptance of social conflict, it also grants to its citizens the right of opposition, in respect to other social groups or to political decisions (see Shapiro 1994: 5). It is obvious, then, that the participants in a democracy must be granted rights of political *liberty* and *equality*.

Alain Touraine (1991: 265) claims that democracy's attempt to combine particular interests and the general interest 'is impossible if the conviction does not exist that all human beings are *equal*'. I argued above, however, that it would be more accurate to say that *those who are granted the rights of citizenship* must be admitted as equal. This issue was a real and grave one for colonial Australians. They desired the maintenance and strengthening of their newly won democratic rights, and they recognised unreservedly that this required a free and equal citizenry. But the democratic ideal had to be accommodated to racialist beliefs and fears which portrayed humanity in terms precisely of radical *in*equality. The choices appeared stark. They were:

- admit a significant population of coloured peoples but deny them citizenship (as is still widely practised in Europe and elsewhere);
- admit these people and grant them citizenship (perhaps after providing them with the educational and cultural resources necessary for the acquisition of citizenship capacities); or
- avoid the whole problem by refusing to admit them in the first place (and by encouraging the departure of those already here).[12]

The first choice was unacceptable because it would produce a rigidly stratified society of 'slaves and slave-owners', with moral ill-effects on the white caste and an inherent potential for violent conflict. White Australians were sufficiently committed to a self-reliant egalitarian society to be willing to forego any improvements to economic development and social status that an inegalitarian one might afford. While most of them might profess pride in their British political heritage, very few wished to see reproduced in Australia the kind of stratification that existed in British class society.

The second choice, of granting citizenship to 'inferior' races, was equally unthinkable. Here all the fears – social, spiritual and sexual – associated with racialism came fully into play. Equality of citizenship introduced the prospect of social intercourse with the despised races and, worse, of intermarriage; the result could only be the degradation of the sturdy white stock. When pure and impure were mixed, the pure was inevitably sullied without noticeable improvement to the impure. And, besides, what could be gained from giving rights to people believed constitutionally incapable of using them properly? The mutual tolerance that democratic government required would not exist in such circumstances. Myra Willard (1923: 196) put the matter clearly more than seventy years ago:

> For the maintenance of their free social and political institutions – the concrete expression of a democracy – Australians felt that all resident peoples must be treated alike. But to grant equality of social and political status to

resident Asiatics, allowed to enter freely, would destroy the very conception that made such a society possible.

For most white Australian writers and politicians, it seemed plain that the only possible option was the third – the creation and preservation of a homogeneous white society.[13] It was a matter of avoiding potential problems by simplifying the situation. It must also be noted that significant commentators at the time regarded the establishment of 'radical' democracy itself as a threat to the social order (see Melleuish 1994). To complicate the Australian political experiment further by adding the potential for racial disharmony must have appeared unacceptably risky. Given the prevailing climate of racialist opinion, the possibility of the formation of a permanent under-class defined by colour was undoubtedly real. So was the danger, in hard and competitive times, of racial victimisation, rioting and physical violence such as had occurred on the goldfields a half-century before. The policy of enforced homogeneity appeared to many federating Australians as the one which would most certainly avoid these dangers. It was the only one, they believed, which could prevent the formation of social cleavages that might prove fatal to the democratic social order they wished to maintain.

From racial identity to civic identity

If there were inevitable economic costs associated with this choice – for instance in the retardation of development of the tropical north – then white Australia was ready and willing to bear them. A higher principle was at stake (see Deakin in Gibb 1973: 103–4). The white-British-Australian identity was to be preserved within a homogeneous society for the sake of maintaining progressive, liberal democratic institutions that could be bequeathed to future generations (Cole 1971: 512–13).

But such a 'thick' conception of national identity, based on alleged racial characteristics, was clearly vulnerable to the changes in beliefs and attitudes that occurred during the course of the twentieth century. The discrediting of 'scientific' racialist theory, the terrible lesson of Nazi Germany and an increasingly liberal and more widely accessible education system in western countries (including Australia) after World War II led ultimately to a vigorous reassertion of belief in the fundamental moral equality of all humankind. Further, it became apparent that the simplifying strategy of homogeneity could not, given demographic and geographic realities, be maintained forever. The changes in the ethnic composition of Australian society after the war (and the granting of citizenship rights to indigenous peoples) provided an additional challenge to the 'thick' conception, one that could not be wholly met by policies of 'assimilation'. Governments aimed to present naturalised groups as bona fide Australians, yet the diverse traditions and characters of these groups were not those of Anglo-Celtic Australia, nor would they ever wholly be. In these circumstances, a national identity based on the alleged possession of distinctive racial characteristics ceased to be a viable political option.

There remained, however, the democratic political ideal that the now obsolete identity was supposed to have guaranteed. It was an ideal which could, as it turned out, be logically dissociated from the racialist premises of White Australia and shine all the brighter for that. The repudiation of racialism implied that no person should, on the grounds of colour or ethnicity, be excluded from participative citizenship in the liberal democratic polity. Yet, in this first stage of the repudiation of White Australia, the cultural policy was essentially assimilationist. It was based upon a view of citizens as free and equal persons capable of making their own political choices; that is, as individuals who were strictly indistinguishable in political terms but who would eventually merge socially and culturally into Anglo-Celtic Australia.

The policy of multiculturalism, however, seeks to go beyond assimilation. Like its predecessor, the White Australia policy, it insists on the salience of cultural difference, though unlike its predecessor it does not portray such difference in terms of moral superiority and inferiority. Rather, it tends by implication to assert that a comparison of cultures in such terms is invidious and lacking in rational foundation. But there is a potential dilemma here that proponents of multiculturalism are bound to address. The fact is that the question of the moral equality of human beings is logically distinct from the question of the moral equality of human cultures. Traditions and values may be not only diverse across cultures, but also radically contradictory or antagonistic. Ideally, multiculturalism presumes that respect for individuals must be extended to the cultures and traditions they are formed by and inhabit. It tries to embody such respect in an extended principle of tolerance. Yet there must be inevitable limits to this tolerance. Whatever philosophical and moral problems may be encountered in any attempt to compare cultures in terms of value-ranking, a polity has no choice but to set and enforce its own value boundaries. For instance, it must assert its right to forbid a cultural practice that it considers morally abhorrent – the infibulation by Sudanese Australians of their daughters, for example – however deeply and historically entrenched in a culture such a practice may be.

For individuals, there will always be the possibility of tension between the demands of their cultural group or community (which may be more or less closed and defensive) and the demands of the democratic collective (Touraine 1991: 266). The modernising state, democratic or otherwise, tends to dissolve and reshape the ties that bind 'traditional' groups together, often with very painful consequences for those involved. Cultural groups may resist this dissolution as best they can, but there are necessary limits to the measures they may take in such resistance (Arneson and Shapiro 1996). Thus, if it is true that a democratic state needs to recognise that a principle of individual equality must include respect for the cultures from which different individuals spring, it is equally true that cultural groups, for their part, must recognise that their sovereignty over their members is limited by the legitimate demands and legal requirements of the liberal democratic polity. In particular, it is limited by that polity's necessary insistence on the right of individuals freely to choose their own destinies, and to stand in opposition not only to the state itself, but also to their own communities. Touraine argues that giving a minority group a choice only between assimilation or marginalisation is an attack on its human rights. On the other hand, if each group defines itself solely on the basis of its difference from others, then estrangement will occur, and civil war or racist violence may follow (Touraine 1991: 266).

The only means of ensuring unity in diversity in such circumstances is to demand the commitment of all groups to the very polity which affords them such liberty and respect. There is a necessary mutuality in this. All groups need to be united in their adherence to the overarching framework of a democratic constitution which, while it grants them rights and liberties, also imposes a duty of tolerance and adherence to its own fundamental values and goals. Multiculturalism must, in other words, make clear the obligations it imposes on groups as well as the rights it grants them. This is essential if multiculturalism is to succeed in uniting the various cultural identities which people may choose to maintain within a common civic identity.

Conclusion

The policy questions surrounding identity in a multi-ethnic society are complex ones. The luxury of simplification through enforced homogeneity, even should we desire it, is no longer available. The expectation of multiculturalism is that diverse groups with their particular 'thick' identities may be bound together within a 'thin' civic identity shared by all. This thin civic identity has been a public feature of Australian nationalism from the beginning, a central rationale for the maintenance of the thick, racial identity which sometimes obscured it. It remains now as the principal hope for achieving unity across diversity.

Although slight in content it cannot therefore be regarded as negligible. The deeper and more numerous the divisions and cleavages within a democratic society, the more profound its need to inculcate in its citizens an awareness of a civic identity which embodies both the citizen's rights and the citizen's responsibilities. The political challenge is to deliver on the promise of multiculturalism and confirm the strength of an Australian democracy which is no longer based on the social conformity of White Australia or cultural assimilation. By finding ways to promote both civic unity *and* cultural diversity among citizens, Australia may yet consolidate the next 'experimental' stage in its democratic evolution. By repudiating the original racialist foundations of its polity, Australia will have both recovered and renovated its democratic heritage.

Notes

1. I am speaking here of 'positive' identities that a culture may create for itself, rather than 'negative' ones that may be imposed on it by more powerful groups, and which may be partly embraced, partly resisted.
2. Witness the indignation aroused in Queensland in 1994 over the description in school educational material of Australian colonisers as 'invaders' rather than 'settlers'.
3. I am indebted to Geoff Stokes for contributing to this line of thought.
4. This is undoubtedly a real need for a nation with an explicitly racialist past which is trying to woo Asia. See Suryakusuma (1994) and McKenzie (1994).
5. Justice Brennan, in his judgment in the Mabo case, expressed the principle clearly on the law's behalf when he declared that 'it is imperative in today's world that the [Australian] common law should neither be nor be seen to be frozen in an age of racial discrimination' (*Mabo v Queensland* (1992) 107 ALR 1 at 28).
6. Opponents of multiculturalism, like Geoffrey Blainey (1985/86: 16), argue that 'too many supporters of the multicultural industry dismiss Australian history ... as hardly worth celebrating ... They have a deep sense of grievance about ... the past treatment of the Chinese, of Aborigines, of women (etc.) ...'
7. It was an irony of the situation that, for the sake of the British 'race', Australia should find itself defying British authorities anxious to avoid the insult implied by discriminatory immigration policies to coloured citizens of the Empire. See Yarwood (1962: 263–4).
8. Free trader Bruce Smith was a rare voice raised in the parliamentary debates of 1901 in opposition to this narrow reading of the principle. He criticised his colleagues' liberal use of the phrase 'equality of man' because when he asked, 'What man?', the reply was 'Australians', not human beings in general (Yarwood 1968: 99–100).
9. 'The introduction of Asiatic labour', Bowen (in Yarwood 1968: 42) argued, 'would be to Queensland what machinery has been to England, elevating the European labourer to the rank of a mechanic, and the mechanic to

that of an employer, and contributing in a marvellous degree to the well-being of every class of society'.

10. Such fears were, of course, bolstered by, and imbued with, the deep racialist sentiments characteristic of the age, sentiments which cut across classes and infected even the most radical of labour leaders (see Mansfield 1954; Markus 1973).

11. Nevertheless, there is evidence to indicate that some Chinese immigrants were aware of the requirements for democratic citizenship (Meng, L.K. et al. in Crowley 1980: 98–9), and the need to join trades unions (McQueen 1978: 34).

12. Such issues remain with us today. See Davidson (1993, 1994).

13. One might feel tempted to add another option, namely a change of Australian attitudes to admit the essential moral equality of all humankind, but this, of course, was precisely what prevailing opinion held to be untrue. Admittedly, liberals in the British Colonial Office and Joseph Chamberlain, Secretary of State for the Colonies, for example, may have held different views, but these were firmly rejected.

CHAPTER 9

Immigration and National Identity: Multiculturalism

James Jupp

National governments have usually had first claim on the right to form national identities. In seeking votes or public support for their policies, political leaders have commonly made reference to national identity, as it was thought to be or as it could become. For example, in April 1993, newly elected Labor Prime Minister Paul Keating (1993e) argued that 'Australia will be taken more seriously as a player in regional affairs if we are clear about our identity and demonstrate that we really mean to stand on our own feet practically and psychologically'. The first Australian prime minister to advocate a republic, he related his position to those demographic changes producing an Australia 'where a growing proportion of the population has few if any ties with the United Kingdom; where our future increasingly lies within our own region; and where our identity as a nation is no longer derivative but our own' (Keating 1993e). This eminently rational approach does, however, beg the question of whether governments *can* develop a clear and coherent identity in a society with many origins, and whether indeed they *ought* to do so.

Australian governments have typically sought to shape and reshape national identity by two means. First, they have set restrictions and conditions upon foreign immigration into the country. Second, they have set criteria for granting citizenship and have framed domestic policies around such principles as integration or assimilation by which it was hoped to achieve social harmony, or even social justice. Identity politics, that is, conflict and contest over the preferred types of national character and citizenry and how best to promote them, has been at the core of Australian politics, whatever their form, since 1788. Debates over the official policy of multiculturalism are simply the latest manifestations of this type of identity politics. Somewhat like other forms of national political ideology, multiculturalism offers a rudimentary social and political vision of an ideal Australian society, as well as a range of policies for its attainment. For these reasons, multiculturalism has attracted criticism from a number of quarters. This chapter outlines the evolution of the ideology of multiculturalism, examines a range of claims about it, and offers a number of responses based upon the available empirical evidence.

Historical background

On one reading of history, Australia has been searching for its national identity since the 1820s. The most intense period of this quest was probably between the 1880s and the 1940s, which largely coincided with the implementation of the White Australia Policy and the establishment of the Australian Labor Party (Alomes 1988). It was also the period during which Australians fought in two British wars, creating the national myth of the Anzacs at Gallipoli. Although World War II was of much greater direct interest to Australia than the Boer War or World War I, it was still governed by Prime Minister Menzies' famous fiat that British entry into war automatically meant Australian entry.

Over this period Australia became increasingly, but never entirely, monocultural. The overriding assumption was that the best society was one in which citizens were as much like each other as possible. Despite the continuing religious dualism between Protestantism and Catholicism, white Australians of British and Irish origins became completely dominant. Other ethnic minorities, most notably the Aborigines, Chinese and Germans, steadily declined in numbers. The old Australia also embraced Irish Catholics who could be Australian nationalists without being British imperialists. Plans for postwar reconstruction after 1945 assumed that British immigration would be officially favoured, as it had been during the great migration waves of the 1880s, the 1910s and the 1920s. It was thought that monoculturalism would be further strengthened, especially as Catholic Ireland was no longer a significant reservoir of potential immigrants. Yet Australia always exhibited certain dualisms – Protestant and Catholic, settlers and Aborigines, and British and Australian.

The early dream of a monocultural White Australia was not realised. And it was Arthur Calwell, one of its strongest political advocates, who instigated further moves away from it by recruiting displaced persons from eastern Europe in 1947. In terms of accommodating a plurality of ethnic cultures, Australia became increasingly 'multicultural' through immigration from that date, whatever the official rhetoric of assimilation. Any sense of a uniform 'national identity' created by the two previous generations inevitably eroded. Since 1947 much of the debate on

Australian national identity has centred on two contradictory objectives: preservation of the apparently uniform identity already established; and its replacement by a new multicultural identity not requiring homogeneity but adherence to values, institutions and forms of behaviour (see Foster and Stockley 1988; Gardiner-Garden 1993; Goodman et al. 1991; Sawer 1990; Zubrzycki 1991). This second objective is much closer to that sought by other immigrant societies, most notably the United States and Canada.

Official definitions of multiculturalism

Contest over definitions is central to identity politics, and the official policies of multiculturalism have set many of the parameters for debate over the evolution of Australian national identity. Yet conservative critics of multiculturalism such as Geoffrey Blainey (1984), Lauchlan Chipman (1980) and Leonie Kramer have frequently asserted that it is undefined or that such definitions as exist are meaningless. Recourse is often made to the normative definition given by the *Macquarie Dictionary* that it is 'the theory that it is beneficial to a society to maintain more than one culture within its structure'. This may be the view of many supporters of a multicultural society (defined by *Macquarie* as a 'society which embraces a number of minority cultures'). But it is not the universally agreed formulation of governments since the term first came to Australia from Canada in the early 1970s. Zubrzycki (1968: 6), as early as 1968, used the term 'cultural pluralism' to mean 'the retention of ethnic identity and continued participation of individual settlers in minority group activities'. Al Grassby (1973: 5), as Minister for Immigration, first defined multiculturalism officially in 1973 as enshrining the 'family of the nation'. He advocated the idea of 'permanent ethnic pluralism', by which he meant that 'each ethnic group desiring it, is permitted to create its own communal life and preserve its own cultural heritage indefinitely, while taking part in the general life of the nation' (Grassby 1973: 5).

In its early stages the official definition of multiculturalism was counterposed to the previously dominant assimilationist ideology (Australian Ethnic Affairs Council (AEAC) 1977; Ethnic Affairs Commission (EAC) of NSW 1978; Zubrzycki 1982). As that older ideology began to recede, in public rhetoric if not among the public, it became necessary to redefine multiculturalism in order to sustain more concrete references to certain programs and policies. This became the task of committees and official inquiries. Individual scholars such as Zubrzycki (1982) and Smolicz (1991) were influential, and a redefinition by Stephen Castles and his colleagues at the University of Wollongong was also significant (Castles et al. 1988; see also Jakubowicz 1984). But essentially government has dictated the terms of reference since 1980. The most important of such official definitions was outlined by the Galbally review of migrant programs and services in 1978. This urged four guiding principles of which the following two were of general application:

> all members of our society must have equal opportunity to realise their full potential and must have equal access to programs and services; every person should be able to maintain his or her culture without prejudice or disadvantage and should be encouraged to understand and embrace other cultures. (Galbally 1978: 4)

These principles were broadly echoed in the Jupp report on programs and services (Jupp 1986).

A major shift in definition, however, took place in 1988 in reaction to the criticism of the concept by John Howard when he was parliamentary leader of the Liberal Party of Australia, and by Stephen FitzGerald, chairman of a major inquiry into immigration. Both were concerned essentially with dual loyalties and with the persistence of activities and beliefs deemed incompatible with Australian values. Howard, addressing the Western Australia Liberal Convention at Esperance on 30 July 1988, developed the theme of 'One Australia' and the risk to 'national unity' of Labor's Aboriginal, multicultural and trade union policies. He shared the view of many conservative critics of the Bicentennial celebrations that Australians were apologetic about their national identity. Howard favoured:

> an Australian society that respects our cultural diversity and acknowledges that we are drawn from many parts of the world, but requires of all of us a loyalty to Australia at all times and to her institutions and her values and her traditions which transcends loyalty to any other set of values anywhere in the world. (quoted in Jupp 1991: 146)

The idea of an overriding commitment to Australia was reiterated in the FitzGerald report on immigration policy later in the same year (FitzGerald 1988).

Soon after these debates, the *National Agenda for a Multicultural Australia*, launched by Labor Prime Minister Bob Hawke in July 1989, introduced several caveats into its otherwise strong endorsement of multiculturalism. Its three dimensions of multiculturalism went beyond the Galbally definition, especially in stressing social justice and economic efficiency. But its endorsement of cultural identity added the words 'within carefully defined limits' to the standard approval of cultural, religious and linguistic diversity (Office of Multicultural Affairs (OMA) 1989a). The agenda went on to set some limits on multiculturalism.

These included the 'premise that all Australians should have an over-riding and unifying commitment to Australia, its interests and future first and foremost'; a requirement that all Australians should 'accept the basic structures and principles of Australian society – the Constitution and rule of law, tolerance and equality, parliamentary democracy, freedom of speech and religion, English as the national language and equality of the sexes'; and the point that multiculturalism imposed 'obligations as well as conferring rights; the right to express one's own culture and beliefs involves a reciprocal responsibility to accept the right of others to express their views and values' (Jupp 1991: 151). These modifications also extended the social liberal conception of the state by recognising that effective participation and citizenship might require the accommodation of diversity rather than homogeneity.

These changes represent a concession to FitzGerald and an attempt to pre-empt conservative criticism that Australia risked becoming a 'nation of warring tribes'. The notion that citizens had a duty to Australian values, rather than to the monarchy or the country, was embodied in the new pledge of commitment for naturalised citizens which became effective from January 1994 (*Australian Citizen Amendment Act 1993*): 'From this time forward (under God) I pledge my loyalty to Australia and its people, whose democratic rights I share, whose rights and liberties I respect, and whose laws I will uphold and obey.' It was now accepted formally that a commitment to certain institutions and values rather than ethnic inheritance ought to be at the core of national identity.

The critics

Since its inception in 1974, multiculturalism has attracted criticism from diverse political and intellectual perspectives which have queried its rationale, political character and social consequences. The most controversial views have emanated from conservatives like Professor Geoffrey Blainey who claimed that Australia's immigration policies were threatening the social homogeneity he considered vital for maintaining a stable social and political order. He writes:

> People need to feel they belong to their country. ... the people who are hardest hit by a depression, who feel that their children will suffer, look for loyalty from the rest of the community and the government. The present immigration programme, in its indifference to the feelings of the old Australians, erodes those loyalties. The multicultural policy, and its emphasis on what is different and on the rights of the new minority rather than the old majority, gnaws at that sense of solidarity that many people crave for. (Blainey 1984: 153)

Multicultural policies are thought to erode that 'crimson thread of kinship' which links us to our British heritage. The historian John Hirst (1990: 9) criticises what he sees as 'separatist' multiculturalism that denies 'any superior legitimacy to the host culture' and deploys public funds so that migrants can retain their own culture. In his view, this approach risks perpetuating intolerance between ethnic communities and also promoting favouritism and inequalities. Such consequences would also be 'offensive to the liberal and egalitarian elements of our culture' (1990: 10) – Anglo-Celtic values which ought to be maintained. Governments have no place in promoting ethnic diversity, since this is seen to undermine important liberal, pluralist values and to encourage social and political conflict (see also Chipman 1980; Cooray 1986; Knopfelmacher 1982). The conservatives therefore repudiate government efforts to promote such diversity by the use of public funds for language teaching or special schools.

Although some conservatives see multiculturalism as a product of the radical left (Chipman 1978: 53), it is important to note that left academics have produced a number of the strongest critiques of the policy. In some respects, these critiques tend to confirm conservative claims about the fostering of division, but for quite different reasons. Those who derive their critical insights from political economy (e.g. Collins 1988; Jakubowicz 1984; Wong 1992) argue that multiculturalism is a state ideology whose function is to smooth the inevitable class and labour conflicts that arise from the process of capital accumulation. By its stress on social cohesion, multiculturalism mystifies and obscures the underlying structural features of social and economic inequality, and class exploitation at work. Nevertheless, instead of fostering social cohesion, multiculturalism has often produced the opposite. As Jakubowicz (1984: 28) puts it: 'Multiculturalism has become an ideology that maintains divisions within the working class, either consciously or not.' Whereas the public rhetoric of multiculturalism celebrates diversity and toleration, this only serves to disguise the fact that most migrants remain a lower paid under-class performing menial labour at lower rates of pay than the rest of Australian society. According to its later critics (Castles et al. 1988: 78), by co-opting ethnic elites multiculturalism has become 'a necessary ideology' which has 'created its own constituency and institutional basis'.

Women writers have also pointed out how a strong multiculturalism may not only keep women at the lower end of the socio-economic scale in terms of income and conditions of work (de Lepervanche 1992), but also entrench sexist social and cultural practices (Kalantzis 1990). By encouraging the retention of ethnic heritage, multiculturalism reinforces patriarchal forms of authority in the family and community, and so infringes upon those individual liberal rights that are normally taken for granted in Australia. Indeed, in terms of personal identity, it is argued that multicultural rhetoric establishes the family and 'tradition' as the primary locations for the expression of migrant women's identity (Martin 1991: 119, 122). On this account, multiculturalism situates ethnic women as 'objects of, and never actors in, democratic society' (Martin 1991: 122). State promotion of diverse ethnic and cultural identities may result in the strengthening of negative female identities and the further marginalisation of women (see also Bottomley 1991). Yet feminists remain aware of the diversity among women from non-English-speaking backgrounds, and that they 'also frequently live in a uniquely women's culture which is itself countercultural to the dominant ethos of success in late industrial society' (Kalantzis 1990: 58).

Certain liberals accept that ethnic and cultural diversity is unavoidable, but they reject calls for the promotion or retention of any strong sense of national identity since this will inevitably misrepresent the 'diversity of identities' in any society (Kukathas 1993: 157). If the preservation of cultural identities is thought important, it ought to be attempted through the private and voluntary activities of ethnic communities, not through the state. In short, the maintenance of cultural identity ought to be the province of the private, not the public, sphere of social life. The best guarantee of cultural diversity, however, is considered to lie in the maintenance of free, liberal democratic political institutions. For this reason, the only common identity worth preserving is that relatively weak political one which is based upon a 'shared or common institutional and historical inheritance'. Similar arguments have been proposed by what could be called liberal nationalists. Australians, they argue, need to develop and strengthen their 'civic identity', in which allegiance to liberal democratic values and institutions is central (e.g. Horne 1994a, 1994b).

Many of the conflicting claims, whether empirical or normative, are not easily resolved by simple appeals to evidence (see Jupp 1994). Nevertheless, a number of general demographic facts about Australia may prove instructive. They suggest that the worst fears of the conservatives may be unfounded. As for the liberals, the revised oath of citizenship has already accommodated a few of their concerns.

Australia: Multicultural demography

Since the beginning of the postwar immigration program in 1947, the population has increased 2.3 times. In 1991, 23 per cent of Australians indicated that they were born overseas, compared with only 9 per cent in 1947. Those from non-English-speaking birthplaces now account for about 14 per cent; and those of Asian and Middle Eastern birth are now 20 times as numerous as they were in 1947 (Moss 1993). Catholics now outnumber Anglicans and form the largest group of practising believers. Australia is overwhelmingly urban and metropolitan, and occupations such as miners, transport workers or small farmers are now much less numerous than teachers, office workers or public servants, as are their trade unions. The current composition of the population by birthplace, summarised from the 1991 Census, is set out in table 9.1.

Australia is no longer overwhelmingly 'British' in its geographic origins, as it was in 1947. Nonetheless, it is still predominantly 'European', and there are large immigrant populations derived from Britain, Ireland, New Zealand, the United States, Canada and South Africa which have the same origins as past generations of British Australians.

Australia is still overwhelmingly Christian in nominal adherence, though there are much larger numbers now refusing to give a religion or stating 'no religion' than in the past. There are a higher proportion of Catholics than before and a small but growing number of non-Christians. The religious composition of the population, as summarised from the 1991 Census, is presented in table 9.2.

Despite fears of Islamic fundamentalism (and exaggerated numerical claims by Muslim leaders), Australia is still a 'Christian country' in nominal terms. The number of Muslims recorded by the Census is the same as the number of Pentecostalists, who are possibly more fundamentalist than the majority of Australian Muslims. The overall impact of mass migration since 1947 has been to increase the proportions of Catholics, Orthodox, Muslims and Buddhists, but the shift has not been comparable to the rising numbers declaring themselves to have no religion. Moreover, all these increasing denominations come from a variety of source countries which often have quite differing languages

Table 9.1 Population by birthplace, 1991

Country of birth	%
Australia and New Zealand	79.0
UK and Ireland	7.0
Italy, former Yugoslavia, Greece	3.3
Germany and rest of Europe	3.5
Viet Nam and Southeast Asia	2.4
China and East Asia	1.1
Middle East and North Africa	1.1
The Americas	0.9
India and South Asia	0.6
South Africa and rest of Africa	0.6

Table 9.2   Religious composition of the population, 1991

Religion	%
Catholic	27.3
Anglican	23.9
Major Protestant	14.0
Orthodox	2.8
Other Christian	5.9
Muslims	0.9
Jews	0.4
Other non-Christians	1.3
No religion/Not stated	23.1
Total Christian	73.9
Total non-Christian	2.6

Source: Bouma 1993: Table One

and cultures, making Islam, for example, much less unified than many believe (Bouma 1994).

In summary, Australian multiculturalism is based on a very large number of quite small fragments of cultural diversity embedded in a larger Anglo-Celtic cultural environment (Martin 1981). Within those fragments there are further divisions based on ideology, generation, experience and organisational rivalries. Even when second and earlier generations are added to the total, giving a proportion of about one-quarter of the population who are not of Anglo-Celtic descent, the collective cohesion of those from non-English-speaking backgrounds is not particularly great. Moreover, as an immigrant group operates within an English-language, nominally Christian and British/Irish-derived culture, it is always subject to assimilation and erosion. It must fight constantly for legitimacy and acceptance. These are many of the general consequences of official multiculturalism, despite the exaggerated and alarmist attacks of people such as Geoffrey Blainey or John Howard. Multiculturalism is a liberal policy aimed at the integration of immigrant minorities *and* their equitable treatment. Conservative critiques drawn from the United States experience are therefore quite inappropriate to Australia. In part this is because the American terminology refers primarily to affirmative action employment programs directed towards long-resident black and Hispanic populations.

The political significance of Australia's changed 'ethnic' population is that many popular assumptions central to the notion of national identity can no longer be sustained. Politicians in metropolitan elec-torates know that half or more of their potential voters do not derive from the British Isles and have no necessary loyalty to either British or historic Australian symbols and beliefs. As I have argued elsewhere, the measurable power of the 'ethnic lobby' depends to some degree on the myth of the 'ethnic vote' and has been most influential on the ALP (Jupp 1993). Equally, conservative fears about 'warring tribes' or 'loss of identity' are reactions to changes in the ethnic composition of the population and the adoption of official multiculturalism since 1973. What such conservative accounts fail to explain is how there could be such effective solidarity among a wide range of ethnicities as to challenge the mainstream majority practices, beliefs and institutions of Australia.

The remarkable feature of mass immigration is that its impact on political institutions and practices has been so slight. During the 1980s, it probably contributed to Labor's long run of electoral successes not only in national politics, but also in New South Wales, Victoria and South Australia, states which have received the most immigrants. Since immigrant membership of unions numbers about one-quarter of all unionists, and up to 80 per cent for some unions in manufacturing, multiculturalism may also have sustained manual-worker trade unions. Mass immigration has furthered the shift of political influence away from the rural sector and thus from the National Party, as few immigrants have gone to rural Australia in recent years. It has limited the (already declining) influence of organisations like the Returned Services League (RSL) and now makes it impossible for any influential people or organisations to effect a return to White Australia, a policy which all parties officially endorsed prior to 1965. But the 'ethnic' composition of elected parliaments has changed only slightly. The total from all non-English-speaking birthplaces in the Australian national parliament is only 3.1 per cent, and it is little higher in the legislatures of Victoria, New South Wales or South Australia. Not until the appointment of Con Sciacca in March 1994 did a postwar non-British migrant enter the Commonwealth ministry. By comparison, in the US House of Representatives there are 39 blacks, 19 Hispanics and 7 Asians and Pacific Islanders, comprising almost 15 per cent of the total. This is quite apart from the large number of those of Continental European descent.

There is little question that the agenda in Australian public debate is still controlled by the native-born and British-derived majority. Multicultural, immigration and Aboriginal policy are almost the only areas in which this is not the case. Native-born Australians, for example, have very little interest in, knowledge of or commitment to multiculturalism. Outside the areas of multiculturalism, immigration, Aboriginal affairs and the access and equity aspects of social justice, it would be hard to think of a policy area in which Australia's ethnic or indigenous minorities have any significant impact other than simply as citizens. Their presence may, however, change the more popular notions of 'national identity' in ways that are hard to measure by the usual social scientific methods (see Price 1991).

Multiculturalism and national identity – An assessment

At the official and political level it is generally agreed that Australia is significantly 'multicultural' in the simple descriptive sense of including in its society a wide variety of language, religious and birthplace groups, largely resulting from immigration after 1947. Assimilation, in the sense of complete adoption of 'Australian' characteristics, is acknowledged as unlikely in the first generation of adult migrants. Australian society, it is widely accepted, has become much more complex and varied over the past fifty years. Despite all these changes, few would disagree that Australia has been remarkably peaceful and harmonious. There is some disagreement on whether this fortunate condition is the result of multiculturalism or has come about in spite of it.

Governments and policy-makers also generally accept that the imposition of cultural uniformity is undesirable and probably impossible. Racial prejudice and discrimination are not tolerated in the public arena, the mass media or the education system and are, in general, illegal or liable to compulsory arbitration. It is also widely accepted that all Australians should have equitable chances of social improvement, and this particularly involves mastery of the English language through public institutions. Recognising gross inequality, insecurity, shortage of resources and the alienation of minorities as the major causes of disharmony in other societies, those who stress social justice try to ensure that these conditions are avoided for ethnic minorities here.

The overall benefits are generally held to outweigh the costs of having to teach English to migrants, to interpret and translate, to modify programs and practices for those who cannot effectively conduct business in English, to consult with the multicultural constituencies and to create monitoring and advisory agencies to supervise these processes (Jupp 1989; OMA 1992). Most other alleged costs of multiculturalism cannot be effectively distinguished from costs relating to the population as a whole (Sestito 1982; Rimmer 1988). The most expensive of all multicultural provisions are those which support religious schools, hospitals and charities, and whose clients are drawn mainly from the native-born population.

There is now a solid body of informed opinion in Australia which accepts multiculturalism as inevitable and desirable, although this view is not universally shared with the wider public (McAllister and Moore 1989; Bell 1992). All nine Australian governments hold to this opinion, as do the four major national parties and most of the mainstream media. Mass public opinion has moved more slowly. Both the FitzGerald inquiry and the later Liberal Party survey *Towards 2000* reported considerable disquiet about multiculturalism and immigration. Nevertheless, the only large-scale, professional survey on issues relevant to multiculturalism (conducted in 1988 by the Office of Multicultural Affairs) provided results which were fairly reassuring about tolerance for variety. Where 'special privileges' were suspected, which included, uncharitably, special nursing homes for elderly immigrants who do not speak English, the results were less encouraging (OMA 1989b).

Despite the abandoning of White Australia, the racism and violence which characterise many other developed societies undergoing ethnic transformation have not occurred. In that sense multiculturalism has worked, and those who say it 'does not work anywhere' are simply wrong. The odd outbreaks of graffiti, firebombs or soccer brawls are disturbing, but hardly a sign of serious social dislocation. Although ethnic violence is quite rare, it always attracts media attention. While such events are undesirable and damaging to multicultural and immigration policy, they do not signify the end of the world (Milburn 1994). Finally, in terms of political and cultural identity, it is arguable that multiculturalism has played an important role in developing a distinctive 'Australian' outlook freed from its British origins and its backward-looking nationalism.

Conclusion

Given these relatively positive outcomes, we may question whether Australians need a strong sense of national identity. Might not Australia now be in a postmodern phase where national loyalties are redundant (e.g. Castles et al. 1988; Docker 1994)? Answers to such questions are not as simple as much of the public debate on multiculturalism and national identity might suggest. In an important sense, multiculturalism and a uniform conception of national identity are incompatible. Yet governments which inherit delimited territories cannot accept this. In the United States, Canada, India, Malaysia, Singapore, Switzerland, New Zealand and the United Kingdom, states have successfully developed collective loyalty from their multicultural populations. In the Soviet Union, Yugoslavia, Sri Lanka, Ethiopia and Lebanon, they have failed to do so. Over most of Latin America for the past 150 years and most of Africa for the past forty, the record has been less than inspiring, despite a strong emphasis on national symbols and leaders. Australia, as a rich, peaceful and rather remote society does not face most of the serious dilemmas confronting other states. Multiculturalism has worked very well because its only serious challenges came from conservatives who were looking back to a monocultural and conventional society which had ceased to exist. It was never challenged by secessionists. Whatever may appear to be true of a radical strand of Aboriginal politics, separate development has never been sought or advocated by ethnic groups created through immigration.

The ideology and policies of multiculturalism have created a public space for cultural diversity in official conceptions of Australian identity where none had existed before. Where a more unified identity has been sought, the practical outcome has been the reaffirmation of expressly political values or civic traditions, instead of those deriving from ethnicity or 'culture'. These achievements, however, raise several problems for those who would want Australia to project a 'clear identity' into the Asia-Pacific region. Perhaps the most defensible unity is that contained in the commitment to liberal democratic values and the respect for liberty and human rights. Yet it is the articulation of these sentiments in Asia which has attracted the caution that to continue to do so would impair our trading opportunities in the region (see e.g. Nason 1994). On the other hand, to promote a clear identity in cultural terms would be to risk suppressing recognition of those ambiguities and diversities that have been among the greatest achievements of Australian multiculturalism.

CHAPTER 10

Australia and Asia: Place, Determinism and National Identities

Wayne Hudson and Geoffrey Stokes

For most of the last two hundred years, 'Asia' and 'Asianness' were feared by Australians. Previous Australian discussions of national identity employed the word 'Asia' as a dialectical contrast term, consistent with a Romantic poetics (see Hudson 1991). 'Asia' and 'Asians' were often constructed not only as 'other', but as opposite: as cruel, barbarous and treacherous, qualities that supported claims to the apparent superiority of Australian character and the values of British civilisation. Today Australian understandings are generally more refined and the images of Asia are more positive. Such shifts have been prompted as much by greater personal contact, though travel, trade and immigration, as by better academic knowledge.

Indeed, Australia's increasing trade with countries in Asia has provoked a reappraisal of our cultural, economic and political identities. It has been argued that the dependence of Australia's economic security upon trade with Asian countries is a reason for shifting our cultural orientation more towards Asia. Advocates of closer ties with Asia have called upon Australians to learn Asian languages and even to become less critical of human rights abuses among our close neighbours and 'trading partners' (see e.g. Nason 1994; Woolcott 1993; Wrigley 1994). Where the 'shift to Asia' is presented as valuable, the debate also involves historical priority disputes over who initiated the process (see e.g. Hill 1994; Murray 1993; D. Walker 1994). In the public rhetoric about Australia's relationship to Asia may be found various perceptions of Australian identity, its determinants and what it could or should become.

Such concerns are given further credibility when 'Asia' is beginning to be defined in political and trading agreements, and when Asian political leaders call for the recognition of 'Asian' values (Goh Chok

Tong 1994) and 'Asian' forms of politics (Lee Kwan Yew 1993). Influential Asian leaders and newspapers have also queried whether
Australia and Australians can really be part of Asia and have suggested
the conditions for acceptance into the region (Lee Kwan Yew 1994;
McGregor 1994). An editorial of the *Japan Times Weekly* (13–19
December 1993: 20), for example, argued that Australians would have
to master a distinct set of cultural norms and linguistic forms defining
Asian diplomatic decorum if they wanted to join the Asian club: 'But
one cannot become an Asian merely by wanting to be one ... A set of
cultural tests must be met.' Clearly, what is at issue here, however
overstated, is the question of cultural values and behaviour.

In controversies about whether Australia is, or ought to be, 'part of
Asia', the Australian participants often assume that 'Asia' is a place. In
particular, advocates of cultural engagement with Asia often rely upon at
least two conceptions of 'place', both of which bear evidence of
determinism. In the first, physical geography provides the constraints
upon what Australia and Australians can become. In the second, the
economics of a region (or perhaps its economic geography) are thought
to set limits and provide opportunities for our economic advancement.
When Leader of the Opposition, John Howard (interview in Sheridan
1995a) exemplified both appeals: 'There is no doubt that we are
incredibly fortunate that our geography has cast us next to the fastest
growing region in the world.' Australians are urged to make choices
about the future according to the perceived demands of our geographic
or economic location. That is, both types of political rhetoric resort to
'place' as a means of predetermining political agendas and influencing
key decisions about Australia's national and cultural identities. This
chapter outlines the problematic nature of these particular conceptions
of place in recent Australian discourses about identity. We argue that
such discourses often rely upon unsophisticated (or untheorised)
notions of place that cannot provide a coherent rationale for changes in
national identity.

Asia and geographic determinism

Arguments for a shift in Australian attitudes and policies towards Asia
became more frequent after 1945. A characteristic geographic determinism regarding Australia's place in the world is evident in the words
of Anglican Bishop E.H. Burgmann published in 1947 (1973: 173):

> We have to remind ourselves that geographically we are Oriental, we are not
> European. We are an island just off the south east coast of Asia, and are part
> of the Oriental world. There our fate is set. We are there geographically and
> there we will stay.

Burgmann's objective was the worthy one of reforming the White Australia Policy and the racism thought basic to Australian national identity. But the geographic determinism is clear. Some forty-five years after Burgmann, Jamie Mackie (1992: 11) makes a somewhat similar point:

> There can be little disagreement over the basic facts. Geographically Australia is located immutably just off the southeastern coast of Asia ... Our political destiny, as well as our economic prospects, have become bound up inexorably with the great developments happening in the main Asian countries since the end of the colonial era ...

Although he wants to overcome the misleading polarities generated about Australia's place in Asia, Mackie's argument also has a geographical or historical geographical determinist tone to it (see also Fitzgerald 1995). That is, it assumes there are some historical trajectories that we cannot escape, if only because of our geographical place in the world. Such arguments are common in much contemporary Australian political rhetoric and are contested by those who feel threatened by them and their consequences. The opponents often draw upon a sense of place that is related to, but not bound by, physical location, and that expresses certain philosophical and cultural values. To exemplify further this resort to place, we offer critical readings of arguments and statements by Stephen FitzGerald, John Passmore, and Alison Broinowski. In each case, however, our reading is strategic and does not pretend to do justice to the complexity of their views.

The Asianist and former diplomat Stephen FitzGerald has put forcefully the argument that Australians should regard themselves as 'part of Asia'. FitzGerald's merit is to refuse to fudge the issues and to warn Australians that deciding to stay emotionally European and strategically American may not be good enough. His insight is that we have to choose, and that joining Asia may be the best choice. FitzGerald (1993a) advocates a strong, cohesive and singular Australian identity in contrast to a multiculturalism, which is 'at best only a process'. He opts for Australian national plus Asian regional identities. On FitzGerald's (1993a) view Australians can have two identities:

> The challenge is to hold passionately to the Australian identity, because it is so singular and attractive, and at the same time to develop a regional identity as Asian. To see ourselves as citizens of a broader neighbourhood, which for all its diversity is feeling its way forward to becoming a community and find what it has in common to shape a regional identity as Asian. The challenge for us is to have two identities. Double identity. Believing both, and comfortable with both, and finding no contradiction between the two. To be one with people from around the region, who will become 'The New Asians'.

FitzGerald celebrates 'a society' which is literate, cultured and creative in the tradition of both Europe and Asia, brilliantly cosmopolitan: 'the honey-coloured society'. In effect, Australians are to be hybrid in culture, cuisine and genetics.

FitzGerald explicitly privileges geography. He believes that our geography is Asian and that we should face up to the realities of that geography. According to FitzGerald, Australia should decide once and for all to be part of Asia and modify its ethical culture accordingly. Of course, he knows many Australians are not convinced, and rightly notes that there is a residual racism operative in their views (FitzGerald 1993b: 2, 12).

FitzGerald's stance reflects the finesse of the former diplomat as well as his own expert knowledge of commercial and political perceptions in East Asia. But when he declares that after he left university he became 'Asian' (FitzGerald 1993a), one detects an Orientalist refrain (see Said 1978). At times an Old Left anti-Americanism seems allied to his preferred version of 'Australianness', witness his references to 'the quiet Australian' (FitzGerald 1994). FitzGerald is fearless in pressing for the moral values and the cultural possibilities to which his own biography alerts him, but he plays down the diversity of Asian cultures. If he were not to do so, it would become clear that our choices of some and not other Asian cultures may be strongly determined not by geographies but by political and economic interests.

Putting the case against construing Australia as 'part of Asia', the Australian historian of philosophy John Passmore argues that we should regard ourselves as a European country 'close to Asia', not as 'part of Asia' (1992: 12). According to Passmore, we should choose to regard ourselves as 'Australian Europeans'. In support of this option he appeals to the fact that our historical memories are European (1992: 15):

> What do I mean when I say that we are European? The most important events in our history, the ones which have done most to make us what we are, occurred in Europe, albeit a Europe itself profoundly influenced by Egypt and the Middle East. They occurred in Ancient Greece and Rome, both in the form of classical literature, philosophy and law and, with the conversion of gentiles, in the form of Christianity and the formation of the established Churches; they occurred in Europe generally with the Renaissance, the Reformation, the French and the Scottish Enlightenment, the birth of the concept of toleration and of representative government, the industrial and agricultural revolution, the Chartist movement, the rise of feminism, the penal reforms under the auspices of Bentham and Beccaria.

Challenged to answer 'of what is Australia a part', he replies (1992: 14–15): 'We are part of Europe'. Specifically: 'we should try to establish ourselves as a modest European country, which tries to appreciate the differences in, and between, Asian countries, so much more notable than they are between European countries'. Passmore (12–13) defends this verdict by arguing that the obvious rebuttals of his views are compatible with our putative status as a European country. Thus,

- there is nothing peculiar in a European country having special interests and problems;
- most parts of Europe are closer to large areas of Asia than we are to any part of Asia except Indonesia (here Passmore uses 'Asia' in the Eurocentric sense of 'the Orient', which would include Turkey and what is usually known as the Middle East);
- to study Asia is not to make oneself less European.

Having Asian and indigenous populations does not make us non-European either, just as being influenced by Asian food, art, music and theatre is nothing un-European.

Should these arguments not suffice, there are others based on 'Australia's distinctiveness'. Being European apparently does not prevent us from being 'distinctly Australian' (1992:14). Indeed, 'some of our differences with Asian countries are characteristically Australian' (18). For Passmore, however, *cultural* identity is what really counts. The 'breasts that gave us sustenance' were and continue to be largely European (12). And we remain universalist (that is, European) in our moral attitudes, unlike Asians (18). Australia is not part of 'Asia' because 'Asians' do not share Australian beliefs in freedom of the press, freedom of information, lack of censorship and so on (19). Passmore's arguments suggest a contrast between Europe and Asia which glosses over important variations among countries of both areas. His wider historical claims are also undermined by recent studies which show that European and Asian cultures were sometimes more interdependent and influenced by each other than the older scholarship assumed (Abu-Lughod 1989; Chaudhuri 1990).

Passmore's contribution, however, is to emphasise that physical geography is not decisive. Commenting in an earlier article on how far it makes sense to speak of Australian philosophy as opposed to philosophy in Australia (Passmore 1988: 17), he argued that it was the character of the culture, not geography or place, which was crucial, and that in the course of Australian history different 'minds' had flourished under the same skies. Nonetheless, these 'minds' are linked for Passmore with geographies: with where the cultures came from. Nonetheless, he does not theorise the relations between different types of geography (physical, cultural, social, economic) in any systematic way.

Another former diplomat, Alison Broinowski, author of a major study of Australian impressions of Asia (1992), takes a more explicitly constructivist approach. Like most Asianists, at least in private, Broinowski takes the point about 'Asia' being a mythical European construct, but then argues for a pragmatic attitude (1994a: 62):

> In the 1990s, just as Australia is renegotiating aspects of its identity, detaching itself from Europe and seeking to engage itself more with Asia, Asian countries are also defining their region and their place in it for themselves. 'Asia' will be used in the mid 1990s by Asians to mean what they choose it to mean, and to exclude whomever and whatever they choose to exclude.

Australia may not be part of 'Asia' but, according to Broinowski (1994a: 62), Australia should capitalise on its relative geographic position by becoming a powerhouse of information about Asia:

> Australia is uniquely positioned to collect the most reliable, up-to-date information on Asia across all fields, and to make it available in English. The task involves continuing research in all Asian countries, consistent Australian presence there, and well-organised activities on many fronts. The challenge and the opportunities are Australia's alone.

In more explicitly voluntarist terms, however, whether Australia can be part of Asia depends on whether Asians want us to be (1994b).

Broinowski stresses the need for making decisions and policies that are based on perceived interests. Accordingly, she argues that Australia should create its 'difference' by relating what it does to the Asia-Pacific hemisphere whenever possible. Broinowski also accepts that, to be persuasive, political and cultural rhetoric may not have to represent accurately the political and cultural circumstance. In effect, she recommends using cultures found in particular geographies to create identities that are 'different', even if this involves some departure from strict matters of fact. Such identities can then be traded and exchanged as commodities. In simple terms, if difference sells, Australian identities could be constructed in ways which are more productive.

Once it is conceded that 'Asia' is a term with multiple and conflicting meanings, the subject of multiple and often misleading rhetorics, not a belatedly discovered geographic area, better promotional strategies can be formulated. Rethinking the resort to place is not merely a matter of academic niceties: it is also a matter of thinking about economic and other opportunities in ways which increase the chances of practical success. One such rethinking may be seen in the economists' references to the 'Asia-Pacific'.

The 'Asia-Pacific region' and economic determinism

Recently a more powerful notion has attracted public attention, namely that of an 'Asia-Pacific region', to which Australia 'belongs' and, more importantly, which exhibits its own historical or economic logic. For Ross Garnaut (1992: 359) this region offers an economic destiny and 'journey' for Australia:

> Australia has in recent years resumed an Asia-Pacific journey, to reconcile powerful economic and geo-strategic interests with its European history, traditions and culture. Australians have spent much of the twentieth century seeking alternatives to, and for a while derailing, the Asia-Pacific journey. But in the last one-third of the twentieth century, and particularly in the last one-sixth, necessity has been more clearly understood.

Garnaut's earlier influential assessment (1989: 2) of Australia's place in that part of the region deemed 'Northeast Asia' had an almost millennial tone about it: 'The Northeast Asian economies are more closely complementary to Australia in their resource endowments and in their commodity composition *than any other economies on earth*' (emphasis added).

Garnaut (1992: 359) is adamant that Australia's journey is not an 'Asian' one, for 'there is no such thing as "Asia"'. For both Garnaut and his co-editor Drysdale (1994: 2) there is, however, an Asia-Pacific region which is a trade region with a geographic name: 'The "region" of Asia Pacific trade expansion has defined itself as the set of East Asian and Pacific countries joined by intense trade and investment ties.' It is argued that the Asia-Pacific is a region in a technical sense of a collection of countries characterised by their economic integration with one another. This is a very specific claim about actual patterns of trade and economic organisation and should not be confused with notions of a geographic region. Significantly, the Asia-Pacific Economic Co-operation (APEC) process is conceived as an institutional forum for strengthening and developing such ties (Garnaut 1992: 374). Within the economists' rhetoric there is a quasi-realist conception of the Asia-Pacific which 'defines itself' in terms of a) trade and investment links and b) institutional links based upon APEC. The institutional links map almost automatically upon, and are designed to encourage further, the economic ones. By its participation in such institutions, Australia is presented as able to adapt to economic 'necessity' in the region.

In response to such claims we must ask where, or perhaps what, is the Asia-Pacific, and whether it is an economic region. The answer to the first question is that the Asia-Pacific is not geographically determinate, despite attempts to promote beliefs to the contrary by distributing maps.

Much of Asia does not appear on such maps (see e.g. Australia, Asia & APEC 1994: 4–5): most obviously India, Pakistan, Bangladesh and Sri Lanka. Micronesia and Polynesia are played down to insignificance, and Antarctica is also excluded. Canada, which has rather little Pacific coastline, is allegedly part of the Asia-Pacific, as is the huge United States; whereas according to some maps Russian Asia does not belong, even though it is a vast part of Asia, and a major military Pacific power. Vietnam, Burma, Cambodia and Laos are also missing. Obviously, it is difficult to be precise about the location of an area which includes extensive areas of empty ocean and countries whose land masses extend far from their coastlines. It is especially not easy to show where the Asia-Pacific ends.

Nor is it clear that the Asia-Pacific is an economic region. Even those who argue that it is frequently change their terminology at crucial points, referring, for example, to 'the Pacific rim' (e.g. Trood 1993: 15). But the Pacific rim also turns out to be problematic even when maps are supplied (Dangler 1993), especially since the bits on the rim are not the only bits that matter for China, Japan and the United States (see also White 1992b). In essence, the 'region' is an abstraction based on trade and investment aggregates, allied to a specific reading of the direction of the world economy, according to which regionalism (that is, regional economic integration) rather than globalism is the dominant emerging pattern. Such economic regionalisation defines itself, and is allegedly occurring as a result of market processes. Regional economic integration has the theoretical status of a utopian possibility which the free market is bringing about. The evidence for this is complex, and not always grounded in specific industries, let alone factories.[1]

Assuming the optimistic scenarios for Australian trade advanced by the economic regionalists to be true, and they are not without critics (e.g. Gastin 1994), the issue then becomes whether Australia should continue to concentrate on being part of such an economic region. Here the experts argue the merits of regionalism versus multilateralism (e.g. Kruger in Garnaut and Drysdale 1994). The Garnaut/Drysdale position, however, offers a third path: the path of 'open regionalism' whereby a loose institutional organisation is set up, the members of which move towards free trade but without discriminating against non-members (Garnaut and Drysdale 1994: 2). The Bogor declaration (1994) of the APEC meeting in Indonesia represents a prima facie triumph for this option, although there are divisions between those countries who favour open regionalism and those who hope for discriminatory regionalism in due course.

As yet, there is no agreement about who the members of the economic region should ultimately be. In practice, of course, the members of the economic 'region' may be the countries who join APEC. Garnaut and Drysdale (1994: 3) themselves do not take it as obvious that Latin American countries should belong to 'the region', and note that the spread of internationally oriented policies in the East Asian style has raised new and difficult questions about the natural boundaries of the economic region. Related slippage is visible when Garnaut and Drysdale (1994: 1) declare that the Asia-Pacific is the world's most dynamic centre of growth in trade and economic output, without explaining how the area they construct from their figures can be a centre of anything. It is also important to note that Canada, the United States, Mexico and Chile do not appear in the 1994 *Asia-Pacific Profiles,* and that Thailand and Malaysia have already signalled major reservations about complying with any free trade goal to be reached by 2020.

The uncertainties surrounding any attempt to link the Asia-Pacific to the fortunes of APEC show that attempts to tie economics to geography may prove tenuous. The precise role of APEC is unclear in the longer term. It is hard to predict exact political and economic alliances over the next half-century. No one knows what the role of the United States will be, especially if the boom in the US southeast continues. Nor is it certain that regionalism in the sense of regional economic integration will be the long-term organisational pattern. Even if prospects for a new global political order are grim (Sato and Taylor 1993), economic global-ising processes may well eventually transform current regional eco-nomic integrations. Clearly there were tensions between former Prime Minister Keating's conviction that decisive leadership could push Aus-tralia into greatness and the pessimism of observers who argued that Australians were failing to crack Asian markets, that percentage trade with Asia was falling, and that Australian manufacturing would be destroyed by free trade with Asian competitors. The economist Helen Hughes (1994) may have been too pessimistic in arguing that APEC could at best be a 'talking shop' and at worst a regional bloc which discriminated against others (see also Sheridan 1994a, 1994b). But Australia, at any rate, will have to pursue both bilateral and multilateral global strategies rather than concentrate on a single 'region' (Stokes 1994b).

Finally, it is important to note that economic regionalism does not necessarily underpin attempts to renegotiate Australian identities in terms of the completion of an alleged single Australian nation. On the contrary, in an essay distinguishing the various different notions of regionalism which are currently often confused, Heinz Arndt (in Garnaut and Drysdale 1994) argues that all of them imply the rejection of the national economy as the sole module of the world economic system. That is, in economic terms the entities that integrate may not be nations. Moreover, some of the economic activity that evidences integration may belong to the 'sub-regional level'; that is, integration within triangles or proximate areas such as Singapore, Johor and Riau. Hence economic integration could flourish in ways which do not help a nation-state to consolidate a separate identity.

This problematic possibility is not one usually considered by Australian political leaders. Former Prime Minister Keating (1994c) argued that, although Australia was not an 'Asian' country it ought to be integrated into the 'region around us'. On the other hand, Keating argued that Australia must operate as a united nation with a single identity. Just what that identity would eventually be remains opaque. Nevertheless, some consequences of such an international economic strategy are clear for Australian economic identities. To be a successful part of the region, Australians must cast off their old economically inadequate (lazy and inefficient) identities requiring 'protection', and develop new ones, those which would enable greater competitiveness, economic efficiency, flexibility, individual initiative, and productive output. The 'others' in such narratives of identity are our former selves, and Anderson and Garnaut (1987) have provided the requisite history of our misguided ways.[2] The new identity and economic strategy also require greater familiarity with economic opportunities in the Asia-Pacific region and 'Asian' ways of doing business, as well as educational programs and industrial relations policies designed to further those goals.

Australia may succeed in enunciating other types of cultural identity through its involvement with countries to the north of it and its involvement in a large trading group. But we must not confuse the former with the latter, or confuse a major trade grouping with a place. Belonging to a trade group called a region may be advantageous in a range of diplomatic and economic contexts. But we should not allow ourselves to believe that 'the region' is there in any simple untheorised sense or that it requires us to act in one way more than another, let alone that it has uniform cultural features which we must attempt to emulate.

If we concede that Australians may need to transform their identities and cultures to maximise their advantage as an international trading country, our argument is that attempting to organise the relevant decisions around notions of 'a region', let alone 'the region', whatever it is called, may not be sensible. 'Regionality' is a matter of context, and the contexts are multiple. Thinking of Australian identities as involving membership of a single 'region' may not help us to get our relations with proximate countries right, especially since three of the countries that Australian political leaders get most excited about – China, Japan and Korea – are not proximate. Hence the notion that we should integrate our defence strategies 'with the region' also only makes sense if 'the region' is defined relative to security contexts, not in terms of an economic 'region' or a trading group which includes Mexico and Chile. Insofar as globalisation turns out to involve real organisational changes in the world economy, it may be a mistake to gear Australian policy exclusively towards the inculcation of a 'regional' identity.

The official search for Australia's place in the world reached another stage when the former Minister for Foreign Affairs argued that Australians should see themselves as part of East Asia (Sheridan 1995b; Whiteman 1995). Gareth Evans' innovation was to recognise that Australians could usefully regard themselves as part of a number of different 'places', namely the Asia-Pacific, South Pacific and Indian Ocean, all within the East Asian hemisphere. Such recognition offered the advantage of encouraging Australians to identify with whatever place (read 'region') that may be needed for diplomatic, economic or security reasons. Such pragmatism, however, required more careful attention to be given to its consequences for national identity *within* Australia. Projecting multiple identities may be productive for external affairs, but it may also be internally destabilising and confusing. In the wake of the economic dislocation brought on by Labor government programs to 'rationalise' the Australian economy and integrate it further with the relevant Asian economies, the official calls to diversify Australian identities may not have offered much comfort to those who had to bear the personal and social costs of such 'reforms'.

Australian identity and place

On the analysis above, Australian discourses about 'Asia' need to change. The terms in which policy options are constructed need to be sharper, and not muddled by resort to vocabularies with determinist assumptions. Depending on their interests, Australians may now have to construct and negotiate multiple identities, new and old, and to learn to deploy them in different contexts. This means moving beyond notions of a single identity tied to a nation-state. There is a growing view that the survival of 'nations' in the ethnic sense will weaken the long-term viability of the nation-state as a vehicle for their management (Boutros-Ghali 1994: 7). It may be ventured further that in the contemporary world our rhetorics of place and identity fall behind the new spatio-temporal possibilities unleashed by electronic media and advanced technologies. The point here is that 'place' needs to be understood today in terms of a virtual topography of space and time, and not in terms of proximity on maps, especially when maps are interpreted uncritically – that is, without taking account of the politics and projections they assume (see e.g. Wood 1992). It may be argued, however, that it is natural to assume that culture will be determined by place and that populations should take their cultures from where they are or from those nearby (see Keith and Pile 1993). But this is not self-evident, as any study of Jewish, Chinese or black diasporas confirms. Nor does it work for the Islamic world at many levels of description. If we are right, then Australians will increasingly live in a world where such 'exceptions' become much more common.

For these reasons, Australians may need to represent themselves in a number of different ways. Essentialist accounts of 'Australia', 'Europe' and 'Asia' also need to be replaced by dynamic interpretations sensitive to changing political and economic contexts. There is a new inclusionist use of the term 'Asia' in Japanese and Indonesian discourses, even though many Japanese did not think of themselves as 'Asians' well into the 1980s (see Tamamotu 1994; Funabashi 1994). If today a sense of 'Asia' is spreading, it is the result of the impact of globalisation on the economies and media of various countries and of the relative declining importance of relationships with former colonial powers (see e.g. McGrew and Lewis 1992). Neighbouring countries are looking to neighbours as possible trading partners, but only where and when economic advantage follows.

Conclusion

This chapter criticises the geographic and economic determinism that conditions the terms in which contemporary debates over Australia and its place in Asia are conducted. Those who use the rhetorics of 'place' invoke an external authority that will deliver a more secure and certain basis for identity and public policy. We argue that 'place' is not such an authority and cannot deliver the certainties it seems to promise. On the contrary, 'place' itself has become a complex theoretical matter (see Cochrane 1987; Entrikin 1991; Keith and Pile 1993; Spain 1992), and cannot be reduced either to physical geography or to economic region. Although it is widely assumed that identities and locations are closely linked, this too may not always be the case (Bhabha 1994). Like so many other foundations of identity, such as 'history' or 'heritage', the content and meaning of 'place' are subject to dispute, especially among those who hold or contest political power.[3]

Our somewhat naive and undertheorised conceptions of place need to be replaced by politically explicit accounts which explain clearly how place, space and conflicting geographies (physical, political, economic, social and cultural) are related to one another.[4] Nothing in our argument denies that place is important or that geography or economics may be significant for the construction of identities. We simply advocate a more theoretically complex understanding of place, and question the current resort to place as a form of closure that limits discussion of other political, economic and cultural possibilities.

Notes

1. For the detail on trade relations, see Garnaut and Drysdale (1994). For country profiles and comment on individual Australian States, see *Asian Business Review* December/January (1995: 128–71).
2. For an alternative interpretation of Australian economic history, see White (1992a).
3. It is also arguable that particular conceptions of place are formed at intersections between physical geography and multinational capitalism (Harvey 1990b), even if attempts to show how various spatialisations are connected may be optimistic (contra Soja 1989).
4. For the history of different approaches to geography, including geographic Romanticism, see Bird (1993) and Bowen (1981).

CHAPTER 11

Citizenship and Aboriginality:
Two Conceptions of Identity
in Aboriginal Political Thought

Geoffrey Stokes[1]

Until recently, indigenous people in Australia were not considered to have had the ideological power to challenge the prerogatives of the Australian state (see Howard 1982: 1). This chapter aims to revise this interpretation and demonstrate how Aboriginal people have deployed a number of distinctive political ideas and arguments. In their attempts to influence the policies of the Australian state, Aboriginal activists have engaged in a struggle over ideas in which notions of Aboriginal identity have played a key role. The question of who is a 'real' Aborigine or Torres Strait Islander is central to conflicts over access to political and economic resources. For this reason, the practical problem becomes one of how indigenous people present themselves to Australian governments, as well as to each other.

From the beginning of white invasion, the very category 'Aborigine' assisted in the process of colonisation. By categorising Aboriginal people as a 'primordial or primitive other', whites also asserted the superiority of their own collective European identity (Attwood 1992: iii). Such conceptions provided part of the rationale for the dispossession and removal of Aboriginal people from their lands, their violent elimination, and the denial of their political rights. Early European conceptions of an inferior Aboriginal (human) nature, character or identity were later reinforced by scientific theories of nineteenth-century biology and anthropology (see Attwood and Arnold 1992). Such ideas served as the ideological cornerstones for the colonial repression of Aborigines. By representing the indigenous peoples as a homogeneous group, the term 'Aborigine' also suggested a uniformity of culture and identity that was largely unknown to the original inhabitants.[2] The indigenous peoples were not without self-conscious group identities, but these were associated more with culture, genealogical ties, and place (Tonkinson 1990: 191-2).[3]

These conceptions of an inferior Aboriginal character and identity retained their force long after the termination of formal colonial status. Aboriginal people are well aware of the functions these ideas perform, as the following statement makes clear:

> Every time we're put down as savage or primitive or hopeless, white people are reassured that they are civilised, modern and successful. Aboriginal people are tired of being used as a sounding board for white society to bounce off ideas about its own identity. (West 1994: 14–15)

To the extent that European ideologies of Aboriginal identity become myths, believed by both whites and Aborigines, and become institutionalised in laws, programs of protection, segregation and education, they continue to be powerful instruments of domination.

A continuing political task for Aboriginal politics has been to criticise and attempt to overthrow the received European conceptions of Aboriginal identity, and then to replace them with more appropriate ones. At different stages, the critique has required Aboriginal people to engage with, adapt and use European political ideas like those of citizenship, justice or self-determination, while at the same time drawing upon indigenous Aboriginal traditions. This project required Aboriginal people to create ideologies employing notions of change, time and progress that were largely alien to earlier forms of Aboriginal politics and culture (see Kolig 1973/74, 1982, 1989). In so doing, Aboriginal people have developed a distinctive tradition of Australian political thought.

This chapter discusses two historically and conceptually divergent conceptions of identity in Aboriginal political thought, and demonstrates their significance for Aboriginal politics and the relations of Aborigines with different levels of the Australian state. Arguments for full citizenship rights in the 1930s and 1940s relied upon a conception of identity that suppressed notions of Aboriginal difference from Europeans. After 1967, however, Aborigines increasingly made political claims on the dual basis of equal citizenship rights *and* cultural differences.[4]

The quest for citizenship

Until the 1960s few Aboriginal political activists wrote or published systematic treatises or texts in support of their views. The sources for Aboriginal political thought may be found instead in the claims and arguments made in petitions, letters and reports of speeches, and in articles in the few Aboriginal periodicals such as *Australian Abo Call, Smoke Signals,* or *Identity.*[5] Heather Goodall (1994: 14–15) shows that in the 1920s Aboriginal activists in New South Wales justified demands for land rights by referring to the values of their culture and the differences between Aborigines and Europeans. One such activist in Victoria, William Cooper, worked assiduously for the creation of a special Aboriginal seat in the Commonwealth parliament (Markus 1983). In taking this approach, he followed the lead of New Zealand that had created parliamentary seats for Maoris in 1867.

By the 1930s, however, Aboriginal calls for the recognition of their traditional culture and their prior rights to land became more muted. The later arguments stressed the essential similarities between Aborigines and Europeans.[6] One of the most sustained and eloquently written examples may be found in the pamphlet *Aborigines Claim Citizen's Rights!* published in P.R. Stephensen's monthly magazine *The Publicist*.[7] Written in 1938 by Jack Patten (1904–57) and William Ferguson (1882–1950), this brief political tract attempted to counter the colonialist stereotypes of Aborigines, and argued for granting them full citizenship rights.[8] The pamphlet was part of a broader response to the crisis over land and resources in which Aborigines found themselves in New South Wales in the 1920s and 1930s (see Goodall 1988; Markus 1983). The tract made a vigorous protest against the extensive loss of economic and civil rights suffered by Aborigines in New South Wales during the 1930s depression (Goodall 1995: 10–12). The political objective was to publicise the social, political and legal conditions under which Aborigines lived, and to persuade those in power to reform the legislation that governed them. The coming 150th anniversary of the landing of Governor Phillip provided the opportunity for publicising their case.

The primary issues for these writers were the widespread denial of justice and equality, and the limited conceptions of Aboriginal identity upon which state governments based their policies. Patten and Ferguson's tract contained numerous arguments that confronted the conventional opinions and argued for new government policies. They contended that Aborigines were much the same as whites, except that they were treated more poorly. These Aboriginal activists argued for their equal capacities for citizenship with the white. An essential task was to explain historically how Aborigines came to exhibit some of the negative characteristics observed by whites, and why they often lived in such dreadful conditions.

Part of the significance of Patten and Ferguson's argument lies in their use of European liberal democratic discourse and their abandonment of claims for special treatment founded upon 'Aboriginal' needs. They also stressed the need for whites to listen to Aborigines directly, rather than to any religious or scientific intermediaries. That is, they made a distinct claim for the authority of Aboriginal voices to interpret Aboriginal problems (1938: 3, 10). By these means, Patten and Ferguson hoped to shift the white perception of the problem.

Patten and Ferguson particularly criticised the principles underlying the policy of 'protection', and pointed out its devastating impact upon Aboriginal people. With Swiftian irony, these writers observed that the policy had been so successful that the numbers of full-blood Aborigines had declined to the point where there were fewer of them needing 'protection'. Furthermore, they claimed that the protection legislation itself had kept Aborigines 'backward' (1938: 6). Thus these writers provided a revised account of the 'facts' of the case about 'protection' and demonstrated the arbitrariness of government policy. Patten and Ferguson pointed out the contradiction that, whereas Aborigines were treated either as a criminal menace to the community or as incapable of looking after themselves, they were still given a vote and allowed to serve in the armed forces (1938: 8). The authors also pointed to the economic exploitation of Aboriginal domestic and rural labour.

Patten and Ferguson supplied an alternative account of the history of Australia and the place of the Aborigines in it. Their opening words are striking:

> You are the New Australians, but we are the Old Australians. We have in our arteries the blood of the Original Australians, who have lived in this land for many thousands of years. You came here only recently, and you took our land away from us by force. You have almost exterminated our people, but there are enough of us remaining to expose the humbug of your claim, as white Australians, to be a civilised, progressive, kindly and humane nation. By your cruelty and callousness towards the Aborigines you stand condemned in the eyes of the civilised world (1938: 3).

Accordingly, 26 January was not a day of celebration for Aborigines, but one of mourning. Australia Day 1938 represented '150 years of misery and degradation imposed upon the original inhabitants by the white invaders of this country' (1938: 3). Patten and Ferguson rejected both the content and the consequences of official, scientific and popular definitions of Aboriginality, as well as the arbitrary administrative procedures for defining it. They offered a critical account of how governments and social scientists had represented and defined Aborigines. For example, the New South Wales *Aborigines Protection Act* (1909–1936) defined an Aborigine as 'any full blooded or half-caste Aboriginal who is native of Australia, and who is temporarily or permanently resident in New South Wales' (1938: 6). The Aborigines Protection Board had power to control those who were designated Aborigines, that is 'any person *apparently* having an admixture of Aboriginal blood' (my emphasis), and to require them to live on an Aboriginal Reserve (1938: 7).

Patten and Ferguson repudiated the way their status has been reduced to that of 'scientific or anthropological curiosities', objects which are 'to be "preserved", like the koala bears, as exhibits' (1938: 9). Both religion and science were held responsible for their condition. Accordingly, Patten and Ferguson (10), urged the 'New Australians' to avoid guidance from 'religious and scientific persons, no matter how well meaning or philanthropic they may seem.' They (6) rejected the official definitions of Aboriginal people as 'outcasts', 'backward' and 'inferior', as beings who need constant supervision by government officials. They pointed out how cartoons, popular jokes and ridicule reinforced the official stereotypes (10). These writers were well aware of the political implications of the official ideology of Aboriginality (11): 'You, who originally conquered us by guns against our spears, now rely on superiority of numbers to support your false claims of moral and intellectual superiority.'

Central to the Aboriginal case was the claim to an equal humanity with whites. By contrast to the official and popular definitions, they presented Aborigines as human, as educable, and as potentially good citizens. Patten and Ferguson (1938: 4) acknowledged, however, a diversity among Aboriginal people, referring to those blacks who were 'nomadic, or still uncivilised or only partly civilised'. Yet they (10–11) pressed the New Australians to 'realise that the typical Aboriginal or half-caste, born and bred in the bush, is just as good a citizen, and just as good an Australian as anybody else'. The claim to a common humanity allowed a moral appeal to the white Christian 'conscience', and to the principles of democracy, citizens' rights, equality and justice (3–4, 9): 'We ask for equal education, equal opportunity, equal wages, equal rights to possess property, or to be our own masters – in two words: *equal citizenship!*' (9).

Such arguments supported a political program that required abolition of the Aborigines Protection Board and the holding of a royal commission into the conditions of Aborigines. Nonetheless, their politics were assimilationist (9): 'We have no desire to go back to primitive conditions of the Stone Age. We ask you to teach our people to live in the Modern Age, as modern citizens.' Reflecting the scientific prejudices of the time, they argued that a 'mixture of Aboriginal and white races was practicable', and further, that the black race could be absorbed into the white race within three generations, 'without any fear of a "throw-back"' (11).

Patten and Ferguson initially opposed any 'special rights' for Aborigines. At the Sydney meeting on 26 January 1938, however, Ferguson (cited in Horner and Langton 1987: 31) took a different stance on the question of land:

We ask for the right to own land that our fathers and mothers owned from time immemorial. I think that the government could at least make land grants to Aborigines. Why give preference to immigrants when our people have no land, and no right to own land?

At other forums the pair disagreed further over political strategy. Patten for example, saw the need for a 'stepping stone' to modern civilisation and argued that Aborigines should not simply be thrown out of the reserves (Horner and Langton 1987: 31–2).

Patten and Ferguson criticised and rejected the specific Australian ideological version of white superiority, which justified domination of blacks by whites. If there was any general Aboriginal identity, it was located within a shared history of oppression. Any notion of essential difference from whites was absent. Patten and Ferguson recognised both the historical causes of their *apparent* difference and certain distinctions between uncivilised tribal blacks and civilised ones. There appeared to be little of value that could be recovered from the past or from traditional indigenous cultures. As McGregor (1993: 568) notes, the Aboriginal political activists of the time 'based their demands for human rights not on any concept of Aboriginality, but on an ideal of civilisation'.

Patten and Ferguson constructed a relatively uniform conception of Aboriginal identity, one that would support their political claims for full citizenship rights. Given the political circumstances, there would have been little else that they could do. Pointing out the complexity and diversity of Aboriginal society and culture would probably have been counter-productive to the political task they set themselves. Patten and Ferguson saw the future for Aborigines primarily as one in which they would exercise equal citizenship rights in a homogeneous and 'civilised' society. The assimilationist social vision reflected the liberal democratic and universalist assumptions of their white supporters from Christian groups and left-wing organisations. Although the influence of the dominant racist ideology is discernible in their work, it does not go unchallenged. Patten and Ferguson rejected or shifted the meaning of certain ideas, and accepted the plausibility of others.

The political values that Patten and Ferguson adopted were virtually synonymous with those of liberal and social democracy, in particular citizens' rights and equal opportunity. The pair presented Aborigines as members of a common human race – in terms that whites could readily recognise – so that they could be treated according to principles also recognised by whites. Patten and Ferguson's stress on rights constitutes a significant departure from the rhetoric of utilitarianism commonly observed as characteristic of Australian political culture (e.g. Hancock 1961 and Collins 1985). Indeed, any appeal to the greatest good for the greatest number carries the risk that the majority can legitimately override minority interests. Since white Australians clearly constituted the greatest number, recognising Aboriginal rights in any form would probably have been to the economic detriment of the majority. These conceptions of citizenship rights were therefore unavoidably universalist, appealing to values that transcended the dominant conceptions of a British (or possibly Australian) justice. In this respect, Patten and Ferguson have arguably made a distinctive contribution to Australian political debate.

In the short term, however, their political and ideological program had minimal success. Although Ferguson was elected to the Aborigines Protection Board in 1943, he died in 1949 with few of the reforms he had advocated having been attained. Furthermore, the pair's efforts could not bring unity to the diversity of opinion even among the small elite of Aboriginal activists in New South Wales and Victoria. Patten and Ferguson's achievement, however, was to begin the business of articulating a number of basic truths about white 'humbug', truths that Australian governments eventually acknowledged and acted upon. They demonstrated clearly, for example, the different degrees of citizenship that existed, and the arbitrariness of state power. By helping to promote a 'Day of Mourning' they contributed a dramatic symbolic reminder of the status of Aboriginal people.

The quest for Aboriginality

Passage of the federal constitutional referendum in 1967 gave the Commonwealth government primary responsibility for Aboriginal affairs and required the inclusion of Aboriginal people in the national census. These changes allowed the Commonwealth to enact uniform electoral laws, and are widely thought to have brought full citizenship rights to Aborigines. Nevertheless, new problems have confronted Aboriginal people, and old problems have reappeared in bolder relief. After 1967 the problem of identity becomes more prominent in Aboriginal political writing, but the stress shifts to Aboriginal uniqueness and difference from whites.[9] The term 'identity' itself, in association with the term 'heritage', has been evident in Aboriginal political writings, since 1966 at least (see Kabarli 1966: 21). The following analysis is based upon a broad survey of Aboriginal writings on identity taken from the late 1960s to the 1990s. Although detailed analysis of the various forms of Aboriginal political argument, especially after the Mabo judgment in 1992 (e.g. Rowse 1994; Blaskett and Smith 1994), is needed, it is beyond the scope of this chapter. My aim here is simply to demonstrate the centrality, character and significance of the quest for identity in Aboriginal political thinking.

Aboriginal political commentary after 1967 indicates that Aborigines remained deeply conscious both of how whites saw them and of the effects this had on their lives. In the pages of the magazine *Identity* (1971–82), there are numerous references to problems of personal and political identity. In a letter to a regular 'Forum', Stan Jenkins (1972: 11) wrote: 'Some of the popular prejudices held about us are that we are stupid, lazy, irresponsible, not to be trusted or relied upon, primitive, of low mentality and even degenerate.' Once internalised these conceptions often became a source of shame to Aborigines, which in turn operated as a form of discipline and self-regulation. This is not to deny that in some Aboriginal communities derogatory labels have been 'inverted and transformed', and thereafter taken up as means of expressing group and individual identity (Carter 1988: 65). Nevertheless, such strategies do not overcome all the problems associated with the outside imposition of negative colonialist stereotypes. A continual difficulty was that of dealing with whites in daily life. In the words of Jack Davis (1974: 10):

> For the average Aboriginal today whether he be tribalised or not, life is one continuous struggle. Although he pays his taxes, if he is a town or city dweller the electric light and rental bills, he is at a distinct disadvantage because of his inheritance of his Aboriginality from the WHITE MAN'S PAST.

Because of the psychological, even pathological, consequences of their identities, many Aboriginal people were unable to take full advantage of their formal citizenship rights. Kevin Gilbert (1971: 23) explains:

> The principal social-recognition trauma is caused by shame – the inferiorised racial-cultural image with which Aboriginal People have been forcibly indoctrinated. The main problem is one involving loss of a valued identity. Such identity can only be re-established by according dignity and justice to the Aboriginal, by recognising his national, self-viable status by according him land rights and right of participation. Without this the 'Citizens' Right' is still, in the Aborigines' eyes, a Bill of no value, without substance or honour.

Aboriginal people of virtually all political persuasions have written of their sense of inappropriate or lost identities and the need to recover or reconstruct them. Paul Coe (in Tatz 1975: 105), an early advocate of 'Black Power', has written: 'The whole policy of Black Power in Australia is a policy of self-assertion, of self-identity.' And again (Coe in Tatz 1975: 107): 'If you can give these people a past you will give them a future. This is the whole point of cultural identity.'

More recently, Natasha McNamara (1990: 98) has argued: 'Aboriginal [people] and Torres Strait Islanders need an identity which allows them to move forward without forgetting the past and its lessons.' For Noel Pearson (1994c), former director of the Cape York Land Council, racialist assumptions of Aboriginal inferiority are central to white beliefs about Aboriginal people: 'Who can say that notions of racial inferiority rooted in a violent past do not still infect our national psyche?' The political objective remains one of rejecting white stereotypes and recovering, reaffirming and re-creating Aboriginal conceptions of character and identity (see also Bourke 1994).

The process of constructing Aboriginality has often occurred almost spontaneously in response to particularly significant political events. Important among these events were the establishment of the Aboriginal Tent Embassy on the lawns of Parliament House in 1971 and the design of the Aboriginal flag. The Tent Embassy provided a powerful symbol of pan-Aboriginality that drew Aborigines together from all over Australia, and enabled a common set of claims to be made upon the Commonwealth government (see Newfong 1972). The Aboriginal flag also provided a new cultural artefact that symbolised unity against white society, Aboriginal sovereignty, and marked 'things and events as Aboriginal' (Tonkinson 1990: 197).

The struggle to redefine Aboriginal identity required the recovery of philosophies and ideologies from the past. Kevin Gilbert (1981), for example, draws upon his conception of the 'dreaming' to explore the 'Aboriginal Question'. In Gilbert's writing, the idea of justice is broader than that of fairness or proceduralism. Justice acquires a cosmological dimension that implies the possibility of restoring order, balance and harmony to the whole Aboriginal universe. The theme of an enduring Aboriginal identity given meaning by a larger cosmological order is also evident in the National Aboriginal Conference's (1989) account, 'Aboriginal Ideology and Philosophy of the Land'. This tract explains the significance of the Dreaming and that of religion and land to Aboriginal social relations. Like other nationalist narratives of identity, these Aboriginal writings refer to an idealised past, one that existed in Australia before invasion (see e.g. Foley 1988; Larbalestier 1991).

Like their Aboriginal predecessors, the later writers on identity also draw upon a shared history of suffering and oppression since invasion, one that creates unity of experience and common bonds. But they depart from the earlier writers in several ways. Greater recognition is given to the old Aboriginal philosophies, as well as to the diversity of Aboriginal experiences and of their identities. The later writers acknowledge that Aboriginal identities are maintained on at least two levels, that of a pan-Aboriginality and that of local and regional identities associated with place. Having access to multiple identities allows for greater political flexibility.

Since the 1960s Aboriginal activists have reclaimed authority to speak about Aboriginal matters and to define the category of Aborigine and Aboriginality (see Dodson 1994). In addition, they have sought control over various symbols and artefacts of Aboriginal culture. An early (and eventually successful) claim was that anyone was an Aborigine who claimed to be one and who was accepted by others as an Aborigine (see e.g. Perkins 1968: 34; Bonner cited in Burger 1979: 89). Such strategies helped overcome the divisions among Aborigines engendered by colonialist references to proportions of 'blood'. Struggles to recover authority over such matters from state bureaucracies and from social scientists are political ones in which Aboriginality is constantly developed and reinterpreted. One important consequence of this is that Aboriginal people have succeeded in reforming the terms and procedures through which the state deals with them.

Aboriginality and the state

With these new cultural resources different arguments and political objectives became possible. Along with the usual rights due to them as Australian citizens, Aborigines and Torres Strait Islanders could claim further rights because of their different or special needs. The 'sameness' of contemporary Aborigines to the original inhabitants underscores their 'difference' from whites, which in turn can be used to demand special *political* recognition.[10] Aboriginal activists have expanded their claim to equal justice beyond that of equal welfare entitlements so that it now embraces various notions of self-government, self-determination, and even national or sub-national sovereignty.

The central role played by assumptions about Aboriginality is evident in the report by Michael Dodson (1993: 9), the commissioner for Aboriginal Social Justice, who invokes identity as the main justification for special citizenship rights:

> The historical origins and the present existence of disadvantage motivate for [*sic*] special measures to redress past injustices. But the fundamental rationale for current policies of social justice should not rest on the past absence of rights or on plain citizenship entitlements. It should rest on the special identity and entitlements of indigenous Australians by virtue of our status as indigenous peoples.

Expanding notions of citizenship, alongside the success of claims to differential treatment, have created problems for the state in dealing with Aboriginal groups. Given its rationalising tendencies, the Australian state has preferred to deal with unitary constituencies, and has established various institutions to encourage unity and uniformity of Aboriginal representation. These institutions have created their own problems – both for the state and for Aborigines (see Rowse 1991).

On certain issues, like land rights, the state accords special entitlements if it is convinced of the cultural authenticity of the claimants. Those who have been able to unite and present themselves in terms that the state recognised have been more likely to win certain concessions. In this regard the High Court of Australia's judgment in Mabo represents perhaps one the greatest achievements of the politics of identity. The unity and identity claimed by the Murray Islanders of the Torres Strait helped persuade the High Court to recognise that Aboriginal rights to land had survived the imposition of British sovereignty. The state, however, must also deal with the political divisions that its decisions and policies have engendered among Aboriginal people. These include serious differences of opinion within key organisations like the Aboriginal and Torres Strait Islander Commission (ATSIC), and between it and other Aboriginal critics like Michael Mansell (1990, 1993) and the Aboriginal Provisional Government. Further ideological conflict has occurred between Aboriginal women over the best political strategies for dealing with rape and women's issues in Aboriginal communities.[11]

Partly because of the success of cultural heritage arguments, select groups of Aborigines and Torres Straits Islanders have gained greater entitlements to, and control over, certain economic resources. Depending on the state or territory concerned, the variety of these resources has expanded or contracted over time. Among these resources are access to land and land rights, shares in certain kinds of welfare programs, and even forms of self-government. Those Aborigines in urban areas who could not or would not make such cultural claims can be neglected, or their political demands overridden. The Commonwealth Bill (1994) for an Aboriginal Land Fund was designed to compensate those Aboriginal people who could not claim land under the *Native Title Act 1993*. The original intention was to make land available to Aboriginal communities and not individuals. When certain Aboriginal groups lobbied for amendments to allow for individual claims, such proposals attracted criticism because of their impact upon Aboriginal identity. Michael Dodson (quoted in J. Walker 1994) was adamant: 'By amending the bill to allow individuals to purchase land ... the essence of Aboriginality is shattered.' As this example shows, the present discourse around identity has practical significance both for unity of purpose among Aboriginal political activists and for their relations with the state.

Addressing the problem of political differences among Aborigines, Noel Pearson (1994a, 1994b) has argued for the forging of a new Aboriginal political ideology. He points out that Aboriginal activists themselves are generally described in terms (e.g. Uncle Tom or Malcom X) taken from the United States. For Pearson (1994b: 99) the political identities of Aboriginal activists are 'largely white constructs':

> The colonists have defined the way in which our struggle is to be understood – they, the media, the wider colonial society, define our struggles as moderate or radical, conservative or activist, to suit themselves, and we have internalised these characterisations and made them our own.

Accordingly, Pearson (1994b: 100) calls for Aboriginal people to change the language in which they speak about themselves and their problems, and to move beyond the 'politics of victims'.

Conclusion

Conceptions of Aboriginal identity are crucial to an understanding of Aboriginal political thought and practice. Arguments for citizenship rights in the 1930s and 1940s combined analysis of the social conditions of Aborigines with a universalist liberal discourse about justice. They rejected notions of any essential Aboriginal difference from Europeans. After 1967, in the growing climate of racial tolerance and recognition of cultural diversity, Aboriginal writers relied on accounts of Aboriginality that emphasised key differences between European and Aboriginal cultures. Such conceptions have been instrumental in allowing Aboriginal people to extend their citizenship claims in Australian democracy. Although founded on cultural difference, the later strategy has extended the boundaries of the cultural domain, enabling Aborigines to promote economic and political interests. In contemporary Australia, as elsewhere in the world, the processes of cultural renewal and political self-determination occur together (Archer 1991).

Although the conceptions of Aboriginality are diverse, evolving and contested, they have been catalysts both for indigenous political ideas and institutions and for creating new forms of political solidarity. Yet Aboriginality is also a source of political struggle both within Aboriginal communities and between them and the Australian state. On balance, however, this chapter confirms an earlier claim by Rowse (1985: 46) that 'The doctrine of "Aboriginality" has a rationale in a particular practice of political mobilization in the two decades since the referendum of 1967'. Such practices are examples of 'ethnogenesis', a political process involving the construction of a common culture out of cultural diversity (Jones and Hill-Burnett 1982; see also Morris 1988a; 1989).

It is important to register that the 'construction and use of an ideology of Aboriginality is a specific attempt by Aborigines to regain and retain control over both things and ideas' (Keefe 1988: 67). Such an ideological project offers opportunities for overcoming a variety of forms of discrimination, and for regaining control over land, cultural artefacts and skeletal remains. Nevertheless, given their previous disparate Aboriginal identities and the uneven spread of colonial forms of domination throughout the country, these strategies have often brought conflicts of interest among Aboriginal people. The problem remains one of continually reconstructing a previously absent general identity, while devising strategies that accommodate the diverse Aboriginal identities associated with place or region. There is, too, a risk that appeals to Aboriginality may confine political struggles to those issues deemed narrowly 'cultural', and thereby exclude economic ones.

The larger political problem of whether such strategies constitute either resistance to, or incorporation into, the values and practices of the white society has received much attention in recent anthropological literature (see Cowlinshaw 1993; Hollinsworth 1992; Keefe 1988; Lattas 1993; Morris 1988b; Rowse 1993; Thiele 1984). Although Aboriginal political ideas draw upon previously alien cultural categories, it is arguable that Aboriginal people have creatively adapted white political discourse to their own ends, albeit unevenly and with mixed political success. This is not just a matter of random individual resistance, nor uncritical consent to European ideas, but represents intelligent appraisal of viable strategies within different political contexts. Ultimately, whether these strategies have benefited Aborigines will depend upon practical outcomes and, in part, upon how Aboriginal people themselves assess the outcomes.[12]

Notes

1. Research for this paper was aided by an Australian Research Council grant. I would also like to acknowledge the research assistance of Kevin Blackburn and Jeremy Chenoweth, discussions with Karen Gillen, John Kane and Tom Wilson, as well as the comments offered by members of the Australian Political Thought Research Group to which an early version of this chapter was presented in 1992.
2. See Fesl (1990: 35), Mansell (1989: 11) and McNamara (1990: 96). My use of the term is based upon the fact that many, if not a majority, of the indigenous people in Australia who are not Torres Strait Islanders find it convenient to continue to refer to themselves as 'Aborigines', 'Aboriginal people' and even 'Aboriginals', and that there is no generally accepted replacement.

3. It is doubtful that colonialist policies would have entirely eroded more narrow self-definitions of Aboriginality in terms of place and clan (Attwood 1989).

4. These conceptions of identity do not exhaust the range of political ideas deployed by indigenous people, but they illustrate certain patterns of public intellectual response to colonial and postcolonial forms of domination. For an account of the early evolution of the citizenship status of Aborigines, see Stretton and Finnimore (1993).

5. One valuable selection of letters and articles may be found in Markus (1988). Oral histories (e.g. Rintoul 1993) and Aboriginal literature (poems, plays, novels and autobiography) would also provide relevant sources (see e.g. Ariss 1988), but I am here primarily concerned with relatively formal kinds of political statement set out in written form.

6. Similar themes are treated by McGregor (1993).

7. Stephensen was an Australian nationalist, anti-Semite, and white supremacist who, on the basis of a diffusionist anthropological theory, believed that Australia and its Aboriginal people were the original home of the Aryan race (Munroe 1992: 123–4). Although Munroe (1992: 183) claims that the pamphlet bears the 'unmistakable marks of Stephensen's aggressive style', there is little evidence that it was not primarily the work of the two authors referred to, or that it was unrepresentative of Aboriginal political ideas of the time.

8. William Ferguson was an ex-shearer and organiser in the Australian Workers Union and long-time member of the Australian Labor Party. In 1937 he organised the foundation meeting of the Aborigines' Progressive Association in Dubbo, NSW (*ADB* 1891–1939: 487–8). John Patten worked as a labourer and a boxer, and served as a soldier in World War II where he was injured in battles in the Middle East. A powerful orator, he was an activist for Aboriginal causes in NSW and Victoria (*ADB* 1891–1939: 162–3).

9. Goodall (1994) locates a rejection of equality and a shift towards reasserting cultural differences in some areas in NSW from 1957.

10. For an earlier anthropological discussion, see Jones and Hill-Burnett (1982: 233).

11. See Bell and Nelson (1989), Letters to the Editor (1991) and Pettman (1992).

12. On the problem of who ought to speak about Aboriginal issues, see Rowse (1994/95).

Culture: Literature and Film

Political Identity in Contemporary Australian Literature: David Malouf and Peter Carey

M.D. Fletcher

Much has been written about Australian national character and national identity. Images of the latter have often been based upon responses to the Australian landscape, generally perceived as hostile, as a place of exile as well as emancipation. Bush heroes have commonly been depicted as men who survived the hardships and hostility of the Australian outback through courage, stamina, independence and rejection of authority, but especially mateship. As national icons the bushman and later the 'digger' (a term for active and returned soldiers) have been Anglo and male, and as such have contributed to a narrow masculinist conception of Australian national identity (Turner 1986 and, especially, Shaffer 1988). Two major Australian authors, David Malouf and Peter Carey, each challenge these characterisations – in different ways – in recent novels. Those challenges are the focus of this essay.

While questions of national character and identity have political implications, political identity itself, as opposed to individual identity or social or cultural identity, has received little attention in Australia, especially before the recent public debate on republicanism and the so-called 'millennium fever' over possible changes to the Constitution.[1] In an attempt to make clear and concrete the political (and not just the cultural) nature of the identity discussed in this chapter, two classical political science texts are invoked to ground but hopefully not to constrain this discussion: W.J.M. Mackenzie's *Political Identity* (1978) and Almond and Verba's *The Civic Culture* (1963). Mackenzie focuses on the concepts of shared physical space; shared race, class and religion; and shared 'language in an extended sense' – including myth, symbols, ritual and ideology – and the way these concepts contribute to shared political interests. Almond and Verba, however, articulate a distinction between participant and subject political culture which is germane to

Carey's *The Tax Inspector*. A participant political culture is one in which citizens participate actively in the responsibilities of government and governing. A subject political culture is one in which individuals and groups avoid direct participation, and whose political activity is limited to adapting to the demands that governments make upon them.

Mackenzie has provided a starting point for discussing the novels, especially if we revise his approach in light of contemporary theorising. In analyses of postcolonial literature there is a particular emphasis on identification via exclusion; that is, on the obverse of Mackenzie's focus on shared characteristics. Identity is defined as much against 'the other' – that is, in terms of what we are not, as by positively shared characteristics. Exclusion on the basis of race, for example, is central to Malouf's *Remembering Babylon*.

As a second caveat, the question of language is perhaps more complex than Mackenzie's discussion would imply. On the one hand, language per se is perceived as more problematic in these 'poststructuralist' days than Mackenzie suggests. That is, language can no longer be seen simply as a transparent instrument of communication, but is itself assumed to be an active producer of meaning. On the other hand, postcolonial Australia has faced in at least two directions in the development of political identity. Early writers extolled the virtues of imperial Great Britain and the civilising effects of the English language, while the displaced and dispossessed indigenous people symbolised what was to be avoided or overcome in progress towards higher civilisation and establishing a liberal democratic polity. In postcolonial analyses, both the colonising effects of English and settler destruction of indigenous culture have been at issue. These points also have relevance to the analyses below. Finally, the obvious should be stated: these are 'readings' of *Remembering Babylon* and *The Tax Inspector*, focusing on political identity, and quite different emphases are possible.

Remembering Babylon

Malouf's *Remembering Babylon*, like much Australian 'political' literature, is a story of origins, set in the nineteenth century. The novel is instructive, however, for its portrayal of the complex origins of political identity in the emotional fears of communities. When Gemmy, a white who has lived among Aborigines for years from the age of 13, bounds out of woods he is 'captured' by the McIvor children – Janet and Meg and especially their cousin Lachlan – and Jock and Ellen McIvor take him in. His presence in the community is unsettling, kindling fears of the blacks with whom he might be in contact. When he is visited by two

Aborigines to invite him back to the tribe, fear turns the community against the McIvors as well as against Gemmy. The points for focus are Malouf's attention to 'place and race' (Gunew 1990), to language, and to sites of collective decision-making linked to the notion of formal political institutions.

Landscape has loomed large in Australian literary culture, primarily as hostile and usually including Aborigines as part of the hostile environment, a landscape that is alive and confronting in contrast to the peace and serenity of the English garden. In *Remembering Babylon*, Malouf uses that trope to a different conclusion. He does not simply depict a hostility of place including Aborigines, nor does he simply depict the perception of the landscape (including Aborigines) as hostile and then challenge that perception. He does both of these; but he also includes a recognition that whites experienced real fears, as well as real hardships, and were not motivated simply by brutality or negativity (Truax 1993). Still, in querying that perception, he provides alternative views of both the landscape and the Aborigines.

The characters do see the land as alien, and the attempt to make it more like 'home' (England = Babylon) means long hours of extremely difficult work that might not be necessary if they were prepared to adjust. The fact that blacks prefer grubs to potatoes and mutton marks their alienness and links to the hint that they are or recently were cannibals (Malouf 1993: 77).[2] The entire notion of *terra nullius* rests on European assumptions about the nature of property as involving the exploitation of resources rather than simply living with the land. At the same time, the life *is* hard and, even for Ellen, 'open' country can mean empty country – an absence of things, of history and of previous lives or ghosts (110). In addition, the unknown beyond the clearing can swallow you up. Contrary to myths of exploration that permeate Australian history, the settlers stay in the clearing, afraid of the bush.[3] It is left to the minister, Frazer, on the basis of his 'botanising' with Gemmy, and to Gemmy's own experiences of living with the Aborigines, to provide the alternative case for the beauty and hospitality of the land.

In terms of the broader politics of spatial practices (Shapiro 1992), locations are given meaning, which in turn conditions one's perception of appropriate responses. As depicted in *Babylon*, the settlers' perception of the landscape as hostile results in a constant emphasis on survival and an intensity that leaves no space for play or distance for reflection. Ellen's efforts to remind Jock of his younger days only highlight the intensity and hardships of their life. These difficulties contrast with the laughter they later find by reliving Ellen's memory of a humorous tightrope episode after a split with their neighbours over Gemmy has pushed them closer together again.

Aborigines are seen as part of the hostile landscape and thus as less than human. In fact, only two Aborigines are sighted by the community, and then only by the unreliable Andy, and their appearance is very dignified. All knowledge of the Aborigines is 'pre-knowledge' or 'prejudice', assumed before the fact, and no Aborigines speak to or interact with the white community.[4] At the same time, Gemmy himself acts as a surrogate black. He is a 'black white': despite his blond hair he does not look like a white (40) and 'smells like a myall' (a disparaging term for Aborigine) (41). He is even called a 'nigger' (15) and a 'bloody coon' (98) in anger. Gemmy is not threatening to the community, as the unseen blacks are perceived to be, but neither does he act 'properly'. Socialised to survive in marginal situations, he is not assertive, becoming characterised as skittish and unmanly. Even Ellen originally refers to him as if he were a pet: ' "He'll be nae trouble – Lachlan'll see t' him" ' (70). Failing to fulfil the community criteria for white male behaviour, he is easily seen as black, and the reader shares this perception. It is worth noting that identity is being derived from perceptions of what 'we' are not, but without clear knowledge of the other, just as in Malouf's *The Great World* (1990), identity by inversion occurs without an explicit exploration of the nature of the Japanese who guard, brutalise and kill Australian prisoners of war. Further, in the latter novel Malouf attacked the idea that Australian character may be set, as opposed to still developing.

The unknowable induces fear, and that applies both to the bush and scrub beyond the clearing and to Aborigines. For Malouf, the unknowable is symbolised by an unknown language.[5] In his first encounter with Gemmy, Lachlan is frightened only by the unknown language in which Gemmy speaks (4), and the entire community is frightened by the idea of an unknown language (65). By way of contrast, Gemmy had been able, easily, to learn the language of 'his' tribe and to fit into the black community (26). Essentially, the experience was little different from those of his earlier lives in which he had to adapt to alien and difficult conditions in London, and later at sea.

To pursue further the manner in which these considerations relate to political identity, we turn now to the sites of collective decision-making in the community depicted in *Remembering Babylon*. There are two and they are both informal. The men meet after work to talk, while the women gather at Ellen's to sew and also to discuss the concerns of the day (mostly Gemmy, after his arrival). While the men and women congregate separately, both have an active role in arriving at a community consensus on important issues.[6] While common interests result from the shared hardships of their lives, those who have the personal respect of their neighbours prevail. However, the fear engendered by

Gemmy's presence, especially after the appearance of his two black visitors, shifts the balance of power to less thoughtful and less tolerant contributors, such as Ben Corcoran or even the marginal Andy. The community is split or, more accurately, Jock and Ellen are isolated from the rest (103). As Jock muses, he has always been different in his thinking but his 'social self', his wanting to be well thought of, has concealed that difference even from himself (106). The rules and rituals of neighbourly interaction limit what can be said, or even thought. Nor is courage much in evidence, as the male members of the settlement terrorise Gemmy in a group and under cover of darkness.

Such incidents demonstrate that there is no coherent, ongoing political identity or political ideology in the community, its fragility being exposed by the effects of fear. This is not simply due to the lack of political institutions. Frazer's trip to Brisbane to try to help Gemmy demonstrates the distant and irrelevant nature of formal politics, as the activities of the governor and the premier are directed only to their own personal advancement and machinations back in England. Similarly, the incident that reunites Lachlan and Janet late in life will result in Lachlan's being ousted from his cabinet position by his own party in an act of expediency (191). Thus formal political relationships also may be fragile. This incident also parallels the main story involving Gemmy and his arrival in white society. Janet, an elderly nun by this time, has been in communication with a German scientist about raising bees. Janet's correspondence becomes connected to Lachlan's support for a German national in his constituency during World War I. The German's house is attacked, Janet's convent is attacked, and Lachlan will lose his ministry. This jingoism, as an extremely negative side of political identity, is linked to the treatment of Gemmy (and Jock) in the earlier and main part of the story as a politics of fear.

The apparent 'we', first of the outlying colonial settlement and later that of the state, then, is actually a contentious ground of meaning. In the early story most of the community found it obvious that the issue was what to do about the problem of Gemmy, while only the McIvors (and Mrs Hutchens, who provides sanctuary) see the issue as being whether or not there is a 'problem' at all. Later, during World War I, a single national interest is invoked and dissident voices are repressed. In both cases a kind of political identity emerges out of ignorance and fear of the unknown.

The Tax Inspector

Peter Carey's *The Tax Inspector* (1991),[7] like *Bliss* (1981) and many of Carey's early short stories, is set in the present rather than the past, so that the implications for the future that one might find in *Remembering Babylon* or, say, Carey's *Illywhacker* (1985) or *Oscar and Lucinda* (1988) have now arrived. There are other differences as well, so that Mackenzie's comments are not as useful here, although the inverse notion of identification based on differentiation from others does come into play. A more useful organising principle for examining political identity in *The Tax Inspector* is to view it as involving a confrontation between two different types of the political, in the sense of social institutionalisation. One type is based upon kinship and emotion, as represented by the Catchprice family in this novel. The other is based on rationality and differential institutions, as represented by Maria and the complex bureaucracy for which she works. And, as foreshadowed in my introduction, the predominance of what Almond and Verba called 'subject political culture' – focusing on the output functions of government rather than the participatory aspects – provides an additional perspective.

There are a few points about *The Tax Inspector* that are illuminated by Mackenzie's approach to political identity. One involves the notion that shared space leads to shared interests, which in turn contribute to political identity. The other involves the relationship between race and class, on the one hand, and political identity on the other. In all his fictions Carey questions general assumptions about the unity of language and national political culture in Australia, and he specifically questions these assumptions as they relate to shared space and to race and class (e.g. Fletcher 1994a, 1994b).

In *The Tax Inspector*, as in *Remembering Babylon*, the landscape is hostile. Nevertheless, while in *Remembering Babylon* this brings the settlers together, in *The Tax Inspector* it does not. The landscape is hostile, but of 'European' making, tamed but not civilised – ugly, polluted, and dangerous. People do not share the landscape but, rather, avoid being out in it, especially at night. And the fear that Carey depicts is ubiquitous, isolating individuals rather than bringing them together against perceived common enemies. This, of course, inhibits the development of community or political identity. In the contracted, shared space of households, there *are* shared interests and communication, but more predominantly there are intense conflicts, closeness itself causing people to hurt each other (162).

Race and class also divide people rather than bringing them together in shared political identity. Australia in this novel is multi-ethnic rather than divided into white settlers and Aborigines. The tax office crew include Sally Ho and Gia Katalanis as well as Maria Takis herself, and the other main characters (other than the Catchprice family) are Sarkis Alaverdian (the Armenian hairdresser) and Pavlovic the taxi-driver. The

rich and the poor are described as culturally alien to each other
(e.g. 251), again emphasising division rather than identity, and Jack and
Maria – synecdoche for these categories – find they live in different
worlds despite their attraction to each other. Concretely, Jack's beautiful
rainforest home contrasts sharply with the suburban wasteland described elsewhere in the book. As another isolating feature, all the main
characters have stereotyped occupations – car salesperson, property
developer, tax official, hairdresser and politician (and child-molester) –
a point that is overtly raised in the text.

From another perspective, more specifically political, *The Tax Inspector*
may be read as a confrontation between two basic kinds of social
institutionalisation, one based on kinship, the other on functionally
differentiated institutional structures. Superficially, at least, the former
emphasises private interests while the latter emphasises a public good;
incompatible desires versus common goals. This engagement is direct,
as Maria Takis and Jack Catchprice argue specifically about tax avoidance. Liberal political ideology and its endorsement of entrepreneur-
ship leads the rich to object to taxes (241) and provides justifications for
tax avoidance (243), which in turn is linked directly to the continuation
and exacerbation of poverty – the wealth of some is associated with the
poverty of others (249, 316) and taxation is sold by Maria as a public
good (124). At the same time, Jack also confronts Maria as a Catchprice, and his approach to her could be seen as similar to, if more
sophisticated than, his younger brother Benny's.

Both types of political institutionalisation are presented as having
strengths and weaknesses. The kinship system, as represented by the
Catchprice family, is suffocating and entrapping, and 'family values' are
undermined by excessive closeness in the form of Mort's sexual abuse
of Cathy and, particularly, Benny. At the same time, in Carey's fiction
virtually everyone suffers entrapment, and the incestuous relations are
not depicted entirely negatively. They involve a warmth between Mort
and Benny that may be the (Oedipal) reason why Benny's mother shot
at them (threatening Mort but hitting Benny), and why Benny's brother
John/Vish is jealous of their relationship. Xavier Pons (1991) has
argued that generation/filiation in Australian literature symbolises the
England–Australia relationship and that therefore incest denotes
repudiation of that relationship. If that is the case, however, then in *The
Tax Inspector*, insofar as it depicts a warm side to child sexual abuse, the
symbolism may involve the temptation for Australia to stay in the family
home and seek loving warmth there rather than face independence.

The institutional alternative is perhaps more 'functional', but it
excludes possibilities for personal intervention – once Catchprice
Motors is in the tax department computer files the investigation cannot

be stopped. There is bureaucratic output, but no effective input from those affected by the process. In addition, Jack Catchprice's personal connections work when formal legal institutions cannot protect Gia from the gangster, Wally Fischer. Nor is this type of institutionalisation without its affect side – Maria is punished by Sally Ho for her affair with Alistair, just as one might say she is punished by Benny for her independence and sexuality.

Not only is the institutionalised form of politics in conflict with a kinship-based system, it is only partial. In particular, people relate to formal government only as subjects, not as participants. They relate, at best, to output agencies of government rather than input structures. The suggestion that Freida had been a shire councillor (167) is so alien to the Catchprice ethos in the novelistic present that it reinforces this point rather than undermining it. Thus there is a division of agencies by function and a corresponding classification of 'clients' – tax, welfare, health, school authorities, milk and egg marketing boards – but no depiction of participation in community decision-making. Political identity, then, insofar as it is not familial, is subject rather than participant (compare Gemmy's initial [mis]statement to the McIvor children: 'I am a B–b–british object').

The bureaucracy–family confrontation is also reflected by other issues raised in the text. Although all the tax officials except one are women, there are nonetheless a gendered division of labour and a public/ private distinction pictured in the novel. Maria drives to her father's house every night to cook him dinner, even though he is perfectly healthy and she is many months pregnant and working full time. The message that women should get married is repeated, and not only by her father (58, 76). Language is generally shared, but Greek migrant women who do not know English cannot read newspaper job advertisements and end up in sweatshops. Men are valued and prevail. In the Catchprice family, 'Benny's mother' was forced out, and Freida's aspirations have been sacrificed. In the community, Maria is weak and relatively poor while Jack is wealthy and powerful even though (or because) she has official status and he is a stereotypical property developer and her activities are depicted as more useful to the community.

The Tax Inspector also raises questions about the kinds of issues that are appropriately considered political and public, as opposed to family and private. Should such issues as child abuse, wife-bashing and pornography, or of stalking and male violence towards females who reject them, remain private family matters or become public, political issues? The distinction between public and private parallels the distinction between participant political identification and subject identification, and these points lead on to Carey's attempt to expose corruption. Here again the public–private relationship is relevant because it is the Catch-prices' private vice that is exposed by the tax inspector's visit.

This allows Carey to make the feminist point that not only are women overwhelmingly associated with the private sphere, having a privatised political identity, but also that the family provides no sanctuary (cf. Pons 1991). That is, women and children are at risk in the home (contrast the McIvors in *Remembering Babylon*). As John Hartley (1993) has argued, despite perceptions to the contrary, the media in Australia do not depict enough violence, in the sense that they say little about child abuse and wife-bashing.

Creating the space to introduce these topics is costly, as it means that although the novel includes many references to widespread public corruption, the ultimate focus is on the Catchprice family secret and its consequences. Insofar as private vice is synecdoche for public corruption, it is depicted as 'systematic', Mort having been molested by his father, who inherited the practice from his father (155). As Robert Dixon (1992) argues, however, this deflects attention from public corruption to private vice, in a manner similar to the way in which the Australian media generally cover crime. Finally, however, this approach allows Carey to raise fundamental questions about liberalism. If liberalism justifies the pursuit of private interests to the point of including tax avoidance and, ultimately, violent abuse within the family as private matters, and individuals are isolated by fear, is effective political identification possible?

Conclusion

Malouf and Carey continue to challenge traditional stereotypes of Australian cultural and political identity. Reworking old themes, such as the implications of the hostile Australian landscape and Australian race (and ethnic) relations, they raise questions about courage and community, fear and isolation. By adding overtly (formal and informal) political dimensions to their fictions, they comment specifically on the problems and possibilities for Australian political identity. *Remembering Babylon* and *The Tax Inspector* are novels, not essays with a single and consistent argument about Australian politics. Nevertheless, they do explore political ideas, including notions of political identity, that reflect and perhaps inform political 'realities'. As novels they provide a variety of perspectives on relevant issues.

Malouf indicates how shared space, shared hardships and shared fear may lead to a shared political identity, but also how closing ranks against outsiders (and 'compromised' insiders) on the basis of fear and prejudice can distort community and undermine individual integrity. He demonstrates how language can contribute to political identity – and to divisiveness. And he challenges traditional assumptions by depicting how women not only may humanise settlements but also have their own political identities and decision-making role.

In *The Tax Inspector*, also, fear is ubiquitous, abetted by a (human-made) hostile landscape, isolating individuals and inhibiting a sense of public identity or public interest. Carey reminds us of the physical courage of women such as Maria Takis, and challenges distinctions between private and public in relation to such issues as sexual abuse and tax avoidance. He depicts the continuation of class conflict and sexual conflict in multicultural Australia as they relate to political identity, and he emphasises just how subject-oriented Australian political identity can be.

Notes

1. Willis (1993) has suggested that the lack of political independence in Australia has contributed to a predominant emphasis on cultural over political identity in this country. The absence of civics classes in the schools also is often cited.
2. Subsequent references to this text are indicated by page numbers only.
3. Exploration involved 'myths' because the Aborigines already knew about sites that the whites 'discovered' and often found only with the help of Aboriginal scouts (Brydon and Tiffin 1993: 46).
4. On 'pre-knowledge' generally, see Brydon and Tiffin (1993: 105).
5. Malouf's *An Imaginary Life* (1978) focuses on the theme of exile, which tends to inscribe the centre–periphery dichotomy; in *Remembering Babylon* it is, of course, explicitly Australia that is the site of exile. See also *An Imaginary Life* for Malouf's views on the centrality of language and the manner in which it affects ways of thinking.
6. Malouf explicitly explores the notion of women's distinctive type of power in *An Imaginary Life* (1978).
7. Subsequent references to this text are indicated by page number only.

CHAPTER 13

Australian Film and National Identity in the 1990s

Graeme Turner[1]

There was a time when to talk of the Australian film industry was implicitly to endorse something called 'national identity'. We had it, we needed to protect it, and Australian films would help: that's roughly how the discussion went. Things aren't quite so straightforward these days. Given the importance it has assumed in arguments for the establishment of the local industry and in criticism of the industry's early products, and given its brief revival in former Prime Minister Keating's *Creative Nation* policy statement (Australia 1994), as well as current Prime Minister John Howard's reference (1995b: 8) to the role of 'cultural vitality' in shaping national identity, it is worth revisiting the relationship between film and national identity. Is the issue still a relevant consideration, and if so, for whom?

Throughout the first decade of the revival, the Australian film industry was routinely assessed as a quasi-official system of representation. Its products were expected to tell 'our' stories to 'our' audiences, while also collaborating in the construction of the image of a culturally rich and diverse Australia for overseas consumption. At first, the discovery of a local audience and the occasional overseas critical success (e.g. *Picnic at Hanging Rock, Sunday Too Far Away, My Brilliant Career*) was enough to legitimate the establishment of the industry as a brave and progressive adventure in cultural policy. By the end of the first decade, however, the adventure seemed a little less brave and progressive; critics increasingly expressed their discomfort as the film industry seemed to have been incorporated, albeit imperfectly, into an official process of nation formation. Australian audiences, initially attracted by the novelty of seeing their own social conditions and physical locations on the screen, were worn down by the repetition of meandering period drama and tasteful art direction – what Dermody and Jacka called the 'AFC

[Australian Film Commission] genre'. Overseas, the reputation for visual exoticism remained, but the intimations of liveliness had dissipated; hence the often quoted putdown from Pauline Kael (in Hamilton and Mathews 1986: 21) who described our films as 'wholesome', the word 'Australian' serving a similar function to that of the 'Good Housekeeping Seal of Approval'. While the early 1980s provided some fresh (but not wholesome) material in such realist contemporary films as *Hard Knocks* and *Monkey Grip*, they belonged to a genre which could not attract large audiences. Despite being lured back sporadically by populist hits such as the *Mad Max* films, *The Man From Snowy River* and *Crocodile Dundee*, Australian audiences in the mid-1980s behaved in a way that suggested it was no longer enough simply to have access to 'daydreams of their own';[2] now they had definite preferences about which daydreams they were interested in seeing.

In conjunction with Australian audiences' mid-1980s disaffection with Australian films – a disaffection that is obscured, rather than reversed, by the success of *Crocodile Dundee* – the critical climate also changed. Critics who had tolerated their incorporation into what was, after all, an exercise in cultural nationalism began to remind their readers of the limitations and dangers inherent in any formation or deployment of nationalism. Elizabeth Jacka (1988) must have spoken for many when she asked if the whole idea of national cinema might not now be completely anachronistic. Her case was a powerful one: if, she argued, the prevailing movement within the film and media industries was towards globalisation, and if the appropriate countervailing force was that of localism, then Australia's dogged faith in the category of the nation was regressive.

In the year of the Bicentenary, when Jacka's piece was published, it would have been hard not to agree with the notion that the clearest product of government subsidies to the film industry was the revival of a dated and nostalgic version of Australian nationalism. True, among its products were such films as *Sunday Too Far Away*, *Newsfront* and *Breaker Morant*, but far more numerous were the dreary period dramas and politically regressive male ensemble movies (and I would include *Gallipoli* in both these categories) that dominated the first decade of the revival – from about 1973 to 1983. The prevailing definitions of 'Australianness' made explicit in the films of this decade (and many of these films *did* set out to make 'Australianness' explicit, one way or another), were entirely consonant with those constructed through the radical nationalist tradition (or, as it was called in literary studies, the 'Lawson–Furphy' tradition) through the 1940s to the 1960s.[3] Enthusiastically discredited within Australian history and literary studies, the social conditions which sustained it long since gone, the 'Australian

Legend' was revived in our movies, prolonging its mythological life well beyond probability. One of the great ironies is that the film industry embarked on this project at almost exactly the same time that another, contradictory, manoeuvre in the process of nation formation was initiated: the official ideology of multiculturalism which promoted toleration of cultural diversity. There seemed to be little relation between these two domains of cultural policy.

While no one would regard many films made during the first decade of the revival as attempting to construct a plurality of definitions of Australia, I think this would be a more plausible description of the products of the second decade of the revival – from about 1983 to the present. Since 1990 in particular, the relation between the Australian audience and Australian films has both revived and altered significantly, while the range of films being made and the definitions of the nation implicit within them has widened and multiplied.

One would not want to be too categoric about this, of course. It is possible to discover traces of 1970s representations of the typical Australian even in such apparently contemporary films as *Priscilla, Queen of the Desert*. I am thinking of, for instance, the map that enables the spectator to find Alice Springs, the *Walkabout*-style foregrounding of the exotic in the desert, and the invocation of the male bush worker as the national type against which the drag queens' outrageousness is positioned. More problematically still, *Priscilla, Queen of the Desert* could pass as an ocker film in drag with its vigorous misogyny, its racism, its dogged working of a simple vein of comedy, and its crude oppositions of city versus country, straight versus gay, love versus sex. *The Sum of Us* is a more unequivocally contemporary film which has as its central theme homosexuality and social acceptance. This film, too, has its resonances: its tendency towards being a 1990s variation on the male ensemble film is neatly emphasised by the casting of Jack Thompson as a main character.[4] For all its apparent lack of interest in issues of nationality, *The Sum of Us* has excited some interesting responses. When Peter Castaldi reviewed it for ABC-TV's *Review* he said it made him 'proud to be Australian'. One has to ask why one would say that about a film in which Australianness is not even an implicit issue. I can only guess that it has something to do with the film's charmingly plausible conflation of the categories of the SNAG (Sensitive New Age Guy), the gay and the ocker – as if they were all equally recognisable versions of the Australian male.

We are not looking at a complete break with earlier traditions when we consider such films as *The Sum of Us, Priscilla, Bad Boy Bubby, Spider and Rose, The Heartbreak Kid, Death in Brunswick, The Piano, Romper Stomper, The Big Steal* and so on. But these are fresh and unpredictable films. They may not (with the possible exception of *Bad Boy Bubby*) be avant-garde, but neither do they fit comfortably into already established genres. Furthermore, to address most of them for what they have to say about national identity would be to engage in a pretty arbitrary activity. As with so many Australian films over the last few years, the current crop are notable for their lack of self-consciousness about their national origins, their refusal of the official responsibilities of a culturally significant artform, their range of styles and subjects, their disrespect for the generic markers of 'art film', and their equally disrespectful indigenisation of mainstream commercial genres.

This last point is particularly important. While the debates do continue, the industry's embracing of transnational film genres that caused so much concern in the mid-1980s seems now to have stabilised so that the trappings of genre can be put to quite varied uses – uses which do not necessarily conflict with the principle of a national cinema. If *The Man from Snowy River* or *Crocodile Dundee* aroused arguments about the degree to which their cultural specificity was subordinated to the generic structure of their narratives and representational styles, there are other films equally indebted to Hollywood about which these arguments do not circulate. Steve Jodrell's *Shame*, generically dependent on the classic *Shane*, could hardly be regarded as a conservative or cynically commercial project. While *Romper Stomper*, a film about violent ethnic conflict in Australian suburbia, makes use of shooting and editing styles drawn from martial arts movies, few (other than perhaps the film critic David Stratton) would suggest that it does not take its core issues seriously and address its subject with a critical eye. Furthermore, in many films that make use of mainstream commercial genres, we also find a highly detailed representation of the local. The contradictions which have for so long dominated understandings of Australian films and genre films – between mainstream style and the cultural nationalist remit of the local industry – are reprocessed into a convincing, unselfconscious hybridity of structure and content.

It is probably fair to say that in most Australian films today national identity is simply not an issue. It is true that the link between film and national identity does remain – if with decreasing importance – as an explicit element within policy arguments for the continuation of support to the local industry. But something has happened to the way in which the nation is represented in our cinema, and this may be related to the fact that something has happened to the way in which arguments about the category of the nation are currently framed.

Of course, the idea of the nation is an ideological formation that operates within specific social and political contexts. Nationalism has no set content: it is a category available for capture, definition and mobilisation. And so any account of the link between nationalism and the film industry has to acknowledge the historical context. When the case for the film industry was being developed during the late 1960s and early 1970s, there was little expression of ideological discomfort with the category of the nation. Once the industry was established and its early successes celebrated, the ideological partnership between cinema and nationalism was exposed and the films' content did generate widespread critical anxiety.[5] As the industry began to prosper critically and commercially, but seemed likely to be captured by trans-national commercial interests, some Australian film critics found themselves occupying the contradictory position of supporting the nationalist case for the protection of the local industry while attacking the nationalism of its products. In the latter half of the 1980s, the idea of the nation was used in quite complicated ways: on the one hand, it was implicated in arguments for the protection of the local industry despite the limited definitions of the idea of the nation its products had so far constructed; on the other hand, within larger debates about globalisation, the economic and political union of the European nations predicted to occur in 1992 was hitched to an 'end of nationalism' narrative which made such things as national film industry subsidies look very old hat.

Once the European union failed to occur as predicted, and once events on the European continent demonstrated that nationalism – in both its negative and its positive formations – was far from dead, these arguments required revision. Some of the certainties that had marked critiques of nationalism, as well as some of the characteristics used to define the content and effect of different forms of nationalism, have recently undergone significant transformation. In particular, there is now a widespread renunciation of the traditional, European, notion of nationalism: as a social ideology built upon an expectation of cultural purity, of a people bound by a common religion, ethnicity, and cultural experience. A more standard definition of the nation now, even in countries where it would once have seemed anathema (Britain, for example), is as a political and cultural construction which must be more heterogeneous in its forms and practices.[6]

While none within cultural or media theory would argue for the nation-state (or, as Anthony Giddens (1993: 47) suggests we might call it now, 'state-nation') as an ideal category, it remains the prevailing form of political-social-economic organisation today. How that nation-state thinks of itself, however – precisely how its identity is defined – *is* undergoing significant change. For one thing, the term 'identity' is increasingly giving way to the plural: 'identities'. The surge of identity politics in Europe and the United States and the concerted efforts of indigenous or 'first' peoples in postcolonial countries, have exposed the fact that a group's inclusion within what is accepted as 'the national identity' is the outcome of a political battle – not a natural process. The prevailing definitions of national identity have been revealed as little more than the current standings in the competition for representation. Such a view converges with such critiques as those within post-modernism which want to undercut those ontological certainties still clinging to the idea of the nation, as well as with more materialist accounts which insist that the really important political categories are those which structure the workings and regulation of transnational capitalism. In a most crucial effect of the globalising economy, however, the west is confronting on an ever-widening scale the experience of diaspora. So, for instance, faced with the uncomfortable reality of the Empire moving back home, Britain is forced to confront what it calls 'the mongrelisation' of its national identity, the necessity of living with difference. Given that necessity, we find critics such as Stuart Hall (1993a) – long associated with a marxian rejection of the national – pointing out that there is still some potential to redefine what it is 'the nation' is expected to mean and do.[7]

What I describe does not, of course, amount to a total discrediting of the established orthodoxies, but it does offer some help as we seek (as we *must* seek) new ways of thinking about the nation which do not align us with regressive, nostalgic and exclusivist representations or their legitimating ideologies. It may now be possible to think of the national through the multiple signs of heterogeneity, rather than the singular sign of homogeneity; to redefine modern nations as inclusive political/symbolic entities rather than exclusive ethnic identities; to see 'the nation' as constituted through elaborated patterns of difference, as well as through constructions of unity.

What does this mean for Australian film? In my view, it helps us to locate and think about some of the versions of Australian identity that recent Australian films – films that one would not regard as especially active in constructing a national identity – have offered to us. For instance, *The Heartbreak Kid, Death in Brunswick, The Big Steal* and *Strictly Ballroom* have no interest in a singular version of Australian identity. What they offer their audiences is the opportunity of recognising, as Australian, representations of social experience which are defined by their hybridity. Christina, the schoolteacher heroine of *The Heartbreak Kid*, nicely exemplifies the hybridised Australian negotiating a cultural space for herself within a suburbia that is also negotiating its forms and meanings across grids of ethnic and cultural diversity. It is the territory opened up by those comedians of ethnic origins who draw upon and caricature ethnic experiences, Vince Sorrenti, 'Wogs out of Work', and Mary Coustas' 'Effie': here what we affectionately recognise as 'the local' is a hybrid – a Greek-Australian accent which signifies both 'national' locations *as well as* their unique combination in the Australian suburb.

It is tempting to hope that the Australian film industry may be abandoning the practice of periodically recycling nostalgic invocations of the 'Australian legend' for local and foreign consumption. Most successful contemporary Australian films are totally uninterested in that heritage and rely upon constructing images of a very different national context. If the future of nationalism in Australia lies in sorting through the limited repertoire of established national identities, discarding the regressive, and grafting the progressive onto more inclusive definitions for the future, then the film industry is well placed to participate in this process. It won't be participating in the way it did in the 1970s, however, looking backwards, validating Australian experience retrospectively. Nor will it be the aesthetically responsible 'safe' films of the 'national cinema' that will have most to offer us. It is possible to predict a progressive reinvention of Australian identities emerging from, for instance, 'youth' films like *The Heartbreak Kid*, 'feelgood' films like *Strictly Ballroom*, even confronting and highly idiosyncratic films like *Romper Stomper* and *Bad Boy Bubby*. The 'Australian legend' may survive in residual form in such films as *The Sum of Us*, but, if it does, this is still an indication of how far we have travelled since *Gallipoli*.

Like many other fields of conflict in the politics of identity, Australian films have begun to take account of the political requirement of the late twentieth century that we 'live with difference' (Hall 1993a: 361). The broad cultural challenge is to adopt and transform discourses of the national so that they deal better with our diverse social and historical circumstances. Australian films are leading the way in constructing a unifying discourse that transcends the regressive and exclusivist images of the past. This is one step towards developing a more radical kind of national discourse: one that accepts the multiplicities and contradictory natures of the various interests in whose name it speaks.

Notes

1. This is a revised version of a paper which first appeared in *Metro* 100, 1994.
2. The reference is to Tom Weir's piece 'No Daydreams of Our Own', reprinted in Moran and O'Regan (1985).
3. Conventionally, this concentrates on the romanticisation of the male bush-worker as the essential Australian. The fiction of Henry Lawson and Joseph Furphy are key locations of this nationalist tradition.
4. Jack Thompson has appeared as one version of the quintessential 'ocker' Australian male in numerous films.

5. Moran and O'Regan (1985) provide examples of this: Ian Hunter's review of *Picnic at Hanging Rock* (where Hunter calls it 'bloody awful', Paddy McGuinness calls it 'hauntingly beautiful'), and Sam Rhodie's denial of the idea of an Australian national cinema.
6. Something of a map of these arguments in the European context can be found in Schlesinger (1991); he spends some time dealing with problems of collective identity, and in particular 'collective identity in a changing Europe'.
7. A longer version of these arguments is developed in my *Making It National* (1994).

References

Abelove, H., M. Barale and D. Halperin, eds 1993. *The Lesbian and Gay Studies Reader*. New York: Routledge.

Abu-Lughod, J. 1989. *Before European Hegemony*. New York: Oxford University Press.

Allen, J. 1987. Mundane Men: Historians, Masculinity and Masculinism. *Historical Studies* 22(89): 617–28.

Allen, S. 1924. Newscutting. Rischbeith Papers, National Library of Australia [hereafter NLA] NLA 2004/4/302.

Almond, G. and S. Verba 1963. *The Civic Culture*. Princeton: Princeton University Press.

Alomes, S. 1988. *A Nation at Last? The Changing Character of Australian Nationalism 1880–1988*. Sydney: Angus & Robertson.

Altman, D. 1983. Interview with Gore Vidal. In M. Denneny, C. Ortleb and T. Steele, eds, *The Christopher Street Reader*. New York: Coward McCann, pp. 295–9.

Altman, D. 1987. The Creation of Sexual Politics in Australia. *Journal of Australian Studies* 20: 76–82.

Altman, D. 1992. The Most Political of Diseases. In E. Timewell et al., eds, *AIDS in Australia*. Sydney: Prentice Hall, pp. 55–72.

Altman, D. 1993. *Homosexual: Oppression & Liberation*, rev. edn. New York University Press.

Altman, D. 1994. Homosexuality. In Richard Nile, ed., *Australian Civilisation*. Melbourne: Oxford University Press, pp. 110–24.

Anderson, Benedict 1991. *Imagined Communities: Reflections on the Origin and Spread of Nationalism*, rev. edn. London: Verso.

Anderson, K. and R. Garnaut 1987. *Australian Protectionism: Extent, Causes and Effects*. Sydney: Allen & Unwin.

Anon. 1933. Letter to the *West Australian* from women's organisations re West Australian Royal Commission, 2 October. Rischbieth Papers, NLA 2004/12/56.

Anson, S. 1991. *Hawke: An Emotional Life*. Ringwood, Vic.: McPhee Gribble.

Appiganesi, L., ed. 1987. *ICA Documents 6: The Real Me: Postmodernism and the Question of Identity*. London: Institute of Contemporary Arts.

194   REFERENCES

Archer, J. 1990. But is it Australian Nationalism? *Australian Journal of Politics and History* 36(1): 84–93.

Archer, J. 1991. Ambiguity in Political Ideology: Aboriginality as Nationalism. *Australian Journal of Anthropology* 2(2): 161–70.

Archer, J. 1993. Australian National Identity. In S. Gamage, ed., *A Question of Power and Survival*. Armidale, NSW: UNE Symposium Group, pp. 110–15.

Ariss, R. 1988. Writing Black: The Construction of an Aboriginal Discourse. In Beckett, ed., *Past and Present*, pp. 131–46.

Arneson, R.J. and I. Shapiro 1996. Democratic Autonomy and Religious Liberty: A Critique of *Wisconsin v. Yoder*. In *NOMOS XXXVIII: Political Order*. New York: New York University Press, pp. 365–411.

Asia-Pacific Profiles 1994. Canberra: Australian National University.

Astbury, Leigh 1992. Death and Eroticism in the Anzac Legend. In Leon Paroissien and Dinah Dysart, eds, *Eroticism: Images of Sexuality in Australian Art*. Sydney: Craftsman House, pp. 67–73.

Atkinson, A. 1993. *The Muddle-Headed Republic*. Melbourne: Oxford University Press.

Atmore, Chris 1993. Feminism's Restless Undead: The Essential(ist) Activist. Paper presented to Feminist Cultural Studies Conference, Melbourne, 11 December.

Attwood, B. 1989. *The Making of the Aborigines*. Sydney: Allen & Unwin.

Attwood, B. 1992. Introduction. In Attwood and Arnold, eds, *Power, Knowledge and Aborigines*, pp. i–xvi.

Attwood, B. and J. Arnold, eds 1992. *Power, Knowledge and Aborigines*. Bundoora, Vic.: La Trobe University Press and National Centre for Australian Studies.

Augustine 1972 [1467]. *City of God*. Trans. Henry Bettenson. Harmondsworth: Penguin.

Australia, Asia & APEC: Supplement 1994. *Australian* 14 November: 1–8.

Australia, House of Representatives 1991. *Debates* 19 December.

Australia, Senate 1992. *Debates* 1 April.

Australia 1994. *Creative Nation: Commonwealth Cultural Policy*. Canberra: Department of Communications and the Arts.

Australian Dictionary of Biography, vol. 8: 1891–1939 [*ADB*] 1981. Melbourne: Melbourne University Press.

Australian Ethnic Affairs Council [AEAC] 1977. *Australia as a Multicultural Society*. Canberra: AGPS.

Ballard, John 1989. The Politics of AIDS. In H. Gardner, ed., *The Politics of Health: The Australian Experience*. Melbourne: Churchill Livingston, pp. 349–75.

Barbedette, G. 1982. A Conversation with Michel Foucault. Trans. Brendan Lemon. *Christopher Street* 64: 36–41.

Beaumont, J., ed. 1993. *Where To Now? Australia's Identity in the Nineties*. Sydney: Federation Press.

Beckett, J.R., ed. 1988. *Past and Present: The Construction of Aboriginality*. Canberra: Aboriginal Studies Press.

Bell, D. and T.N. Nelson 1989. Speaking About Rape is Everyone's Business. *Women's Studies International Forum* 14(5): 385–412.

Bell, P. 1992. *Multicultural Australia in the Media*. Canberra: Office of Multicultural Affairs.

Bennett, Mary 1932. Letter to Bessie Rischbieth, April. Rischbieth Papers, NLA 2004/12/23.

Bennett, Mary 1933a. The Aboriginal Mother in Western Australia in 1933. Rischbieth Papers NLA 2004/12/218.

Bennett, Mary 1933b. Letter to Bessie Rischbieth, 18 October. Rischbieth Papers, NLA 2004/12/57.

Bennett, Mary 1934. Letter to Bessie Rischbieth, 16 November. Rischbieth Papers, NLA 2004/12/64.

Bennett, T. et al., eds 1992. *Celebrating the Nation: A Critical Study of Australia's Bicentenary.* Sydney: Allen & Unwin.

Berry, C.J. 1986. *Human Nature.* Atlantic Highlands NJ: Humanities Press.

Bérubé, A. 1989. Marching to a Different Drummer: Lesbian and Gay GIs in World War II. In M.B. Dubermann et al., eds, *Hidden from History: Reclaiming the Gay and Lesbian Past.* Harmondsworth: Penguin, pp. 383–94.

Bhabha, Homi 1994. *The Location of Culture.* London: Routledge.

Birch, C. 1990. *On Purpose.* Kensington, NSW: University of New South Wales Press.

Bird, J. 1993. *The Changing Worlds of Geography.* Oxford: Clarendon.

Blackwell, Alice S. 1902. Entry in Autograph Book. Vida Goldstein Papers, 67 VG. Fawcett Library.

Blainey, G. 1984. *All for Australia.* Sydney: Methuen Haynes.

Blainey, G. 1985/86. Mr Hawke's Other Bicentennial Scandal. *Institute of Public Affairs Review* 39(3): 15–17.

Blainey, G. 1991. *Blainey – Eye on Australia.* Melbourne: Schwartz & Wilkinson.

Blaskett, B. and A. Smith, eds 1994. People's Sovereignty: Where To After Mabo? *Social Alternatives* 13(1), Special Issue.

Bottomley, G. 1991. Identity, Difference and Inequalities: Gender, Ethnicity and Class in Australia. In Price, ed., *Australian National Identity*, pp. 99–116.

Bottomley, G., M. de Lepervanche and J. Martin, eds 1991. *Intersexions: Gender, Class, Culture/Ethnicity.* Sydney: Allen & Unwin.

Bouma, G. 1993. Religious Identification in Australia: 1981 to 1991. *People and Place* 1(2): 13–17.

Bouma, G. 1994. *Mosques and Muslim Settlement in Australia.* Canberra: AGPS.

Bourdieu, P. 1989. Social Space and Symbolic Power. *Sociological Theory* 7(1): 14–25.

Bourke, E. 1994. On Being Aboriginal. In L. Dobrez, ed., *Identifying Australia in Postmodern Times.* Canberra: Bibliotech, pp. 131–6.

Boutros-Ghali, B. 1994. Address by the UN Secretary-General to Regional Conference of European United Nations Associations. Geneva, 7 November.

Bowen, A. 1981. *Empiricism and Geographic Thought: From Francis Bacon to Alexander von Humboldt.* Cambridge: Cambridge University Press.

Boyd, R. 1967. *Artificial Australia.* Sydney: Australian Broadcasting Commission.

Broinowski, A. 1992. *The Yellow Lady: Australian Impressions of Asia.* Melbourne: Oxford University Press.

Broinowski, A. 1993. An Australian Presence in Asia? An Australian Foundation? In Beaumont, ed., *Where To Now?* pp. 115–21.

Broinowski, A. 1994a. Asia-Literacy. In R. Trood and D. McNamara, eds, *The Asia–Australia Survey.* Melbourne: Macmillan, pp. 55–62.

Broinowski, A. 1994b. Can We Be Part of Asia? Only If Asians Want Us To Be. *Sydney Morning Herald* 2 March: 11.

Brunton, R. 1993. *Black Suffering, White Guilt?* Melbourne: Institute of Public Affairs.

Brydon, Diana and Helen Tiffin 1993. *Decolonising Fictions.* Sydney: Dangaroo Press.

Burger, A. 1979. *Neville Bonner.* Melbourne: Macmillan.

Burgmann, E. 1944. *The Education of an Australian.* Sydney: Angus & Robertson.

Burgmann, E. 1973 [1947]. Australia – A Part of Asia? In F.K. Crowley, ed., *Modern Australia in Documents, vol. 2: 1939–1970.* Melbourne: Wren, pp. 137–8.

Burgmann, V. and J. Lee, eds 1988a. Introduction. *Constructing a Culture.* Melbourne: McPhee Gribble/Penguin Books, pp. xi–xvi.

Burgmann, V. and J. Lee 1988b. *Staining the Wattle: A People's History of Australia Since 1788.* Melbourne: Penguin.

Butler, Judith 1991. Imitation and Gender Insubordination. In Diana Fuss, ed., *Inside/Out: Lesbian Theories, Gay Theories.* London and New York: Routledge, pp. 13–32.

Butler, Judith 1993. Critically Queer. *GLQ* 1(1): 17–32.

Caine, Barbara 1993. Vida Goldstein and the English Militant Campaign. *Women's History Review* 2(3): 363–76.

Calhoun, C., ed. 1994a. *Social Theory and the Politics of Identity.* Oxford: Blackwell.

Calhoun, C. 1994b. Social Theory and the Politics of Identity. In Calhoun, ed., *Social Theory and the Politics of Identity,* pp. 9–36.

Campbell, B. 1991. After Thatcher: A Class of her Own. *Marxism Today* January: 20–3.

Card, Claudia 1992. Lesbianism and Choice. *Journal of Homosexuality* 23(3): 39–51.

Carey, Peter 1981. *Bliss.* St Lucia: University of Queensland Press.

Carey, Peter 1985. *Illywhacker.* St Lucia: University of Queensland Press.

Carey, Peter 1988. *Oscar and Lucinda.* St Lucia: University of Queensland Press.

Carey, Peter 1991. *The Tax Inspector.* St Lucia: University of Queensland Press.

Carrigan, T., R. Connell and J. Lee 1985. Towards a New Sociology of Masculinity. *Theory and Society* 14: 551–601.

Carroll, J., ed. 1982. *Intruders in the Bush: The Australian Quest for National Identity.* Melbourne: Oxford University Press.

Carroll, J., ed. 1992. *Intruders in the Bush: The Australian Quest for Identity,* 2nd edn. Melbourne: Oxford University Press.

Carroll, J. and R. Manne, eds 1992. *Shutdown.* Melbourne: Text.

Carter, J.D. 1988. Am I Too Black To Go With You? In I. Keen, ed., *Being Black: Aboriginal Cultures in 'Settled' Australia.* Canberra: Aboriginal Studies Press, pp. 65–76.

Castles, S., M. Kalantzis, W. Cope and M. Morrissey 1988. *Mistaken Identity: Multiculturalism and the Demise of Nationalism in Australia.* Sydney: Pluto.

Chaudhuri, K.N. 1990. *Asia Before Europe.* Cambridge: Cambridge University Press.

Chipman, L. 1978. Multicultural Myth. *Quadrant* 22(3): 50–5.

Chipman, L. 1980. The Menace of Multi-Culturalism. *Quadrant* 24(10): 3–6.

Clark, C.M.H., ed. 1955. *Select Documents in Australian History 1851–1900.* Sydney: Angus & Robertson.

Clark, M. 1979. *The Quest for an Australian Identity.* James Duhig Memorial Lecture 1. St Lucia: University of Queensland Press.

Clarke, J. 1991. *New Times and Old Enemies.* London: Harper Collins.

Cochrane, H. 1987. What a Difference the Place Makes: The New Structuralism of Locality. *Antipode* 19: 354–63.

Cole, D. 1971. 'The Crimson Thread of Kinship': Ethnic Ideas in Australia, 1870–1914. *Historical Studies* 14(56): 511–25.

Collins, H. 1985. Political Ideology in Australia: The Distinctiveness of a Benthamite Society. In S.R. Graubard, ed., *Australia: The Daedalus Symposium.* Sydney: Angus & Robertson, pp. 147–69.

Collins, J. 1988. *Migrant Hands in Distant Lands.* Sydney: Pluto.

Cooray, L.J.M. 1986. Multiculturalism in Australia. *Quadrant* 30(4): 27–9.

Conference 1929. Conference of Representatives of Missions, Societies and Associations Interested in the Welfare of Aborigines, Minutes. Rischbieth Papers, NLA, 2004/12/506.

Connolly, W. 1988. *Political Theory and Modernity.* Oxford: Blackwell.

Connolly, W. 1991. *Identity/Difference: Democratic Negotiations of Political Paradox.* Ithaca and London: Cornell University Press.

Cowlinshaw, G. 1993. Introduction: Representing Racial Issues. *Oceania* 63(3): 183–94.

Crimp, Douglas 1993. Right On, Girlfriend! In Warner, ed., *Fear of a Queer Planet,* pp. 300–20.

Crowley, F. 1980. *A Documentary History of Australia, vol. 3: Colonial Australia, 1875–1900.* Melbourne: Nelson.

Dangler, C. 1993. *The Pacific Rim Region.* Lanham, MD: Madison.

Davidson, A. 1991. *The Invisible State: The Formation of the Australian State, 1788–1901.* Cambridge: Cambridge University Press.

Davidson, A. 1993. Understanding Citizenship in Australia. *Beyond the Headlines. Politics: Australia and the World.* Sydney: Public Affairs Research Centre, 1: 1–16.

Davidson, A. 1994. Citizenship, Sovereignty and the Identity of the Nation-State. In P. James, ed., *Critical Politics.* Melbourne: Arena, pp. 111–25.

Davis, J. 1974. Aborigines and White Society. *Identity* 2(10): 10–11, 18.

Day, D. 1992. Divided by Discredited Symbols. *Australian* 29 June: 9.

de Lauretis, Teresa 1991. Queer Theory: Lesbian and Gay Sexualities. *Differences* 3(2): iii–xviii.

de Lepervanche, M. 1992. Working for the Man: Migrant Women and Multiculturalism. In Saunders and Evans, eds, *Gender Relations in Australia,* pp. 82–96.

Department of Prime Minister and Cabinet 1994. Centenary of Federation 2001. Advertisement. *Campus Review* 24–30 March.

Derrida, J. 1978. *Writing and Difference.* Chicago: University of Chicago Press.

Dessaix, Robert 1994. *A Mother's Disgrace.* Sydney: Angus & Robertson.

Diaz, T. 1992. Forces Told: It's OK to be Gay. *Sydney Morning Herald* 24 November: 1.

Dixon, Robert 1992. Closing the Can of Worms: Enactments of Justice in *Bleak House, The Mystery of a Hansom Cab,* and *The Tax Inspector. Westerly* 37(4): 37–45.

Docker, J. 1993. The Feminist Legend: A New Historicism? In S. Magarey et al., eds, *Debutante Nation,* pp. 16–26.

Docker, J. 1994. Postnationalism. *Arena Magazine* 9: 40–1.

Docker, J. 1995. Postmodernism and Politics. *Arena Magazine* 15: 12–13.

Dodson, M. 1993. Introduction. In Australia. *Aboriginal and Torres Strait Islander Social Justice Commission, First Report.* Canberra: AGPS.

Dodson, M. 1994. The End in the Beginning: Re(de)finding Aboriginality. *Australian Aboriginal Studies* 1: 2–13.

Dowse, S. and P. Giles 1984. Australia: Women in a Warrior Society. In R. Morgan, ed., *Sisterhood is Global: The International Women's Movement Anthology.* Harmondsworth: Penguin, pp. 63–8.

Duggan, Lisa 1992. Making it Perfectly Queer. *Socialist Review* 22(1): 11–31.

Dumm, T.L. 1994. Strangers and Liberals. *Political Theory* 22(1): 167–75.

Dunn, J. 1985, *Rethinking Modern Political Theory*. Cambridge: Cambridge University Press.

du Preez, P. 1980. *The Politics of Identity: Ideology and the Human Image*. Oxford: Blackwell.

During, S. 1985. Postmodernism or Postcolonialism? *Landfall* 39(3): 366–80.

During, S. 1992. Postcolonialism and Globalization. *Meanjin* 51(2): 339–53.

During, S. 1995. [new] Discourse. *Arena Magazine* 15: 43–4.

Eagleton, T. 1980. Text, Ideology, Realism. In E.W. Said, ed., *Literature and Society*. Baltimore: Johns Hopkins University Press, pp. 149–73.

Edwards, Deborah 1991. Race, Death & Gender in the Anzac Memorial. *Art and Australia* 28(4): 476–81.

Enfranchised Women of Australia 1910. Open letter to Mrs Pankhurst, Christobel Pankhurst and Annie Kenney etc. Rischbieth Papers, NLA 2004/4/371.

Enloe, Cynthia 1989. *Bananas, Beaches and Bases: Making Feminist Sense of International Politics*. London: Pandora.

Entrikin, J.N. 1991. *The Betweenness of Place: Towards a Geography of Modernity*. Baltimore: Johns Hopkins University Press.

Epstein, Barbara 1992. Political Correctness and Identity Politics. In Patricia Aufderheide *Beyond PC: Toward a Politics of Understanding*. St Paul, MN: Graywolf Press, pp. 148–54.

Epstein, Steven. 1994. A Queer Encounter: Society and the Study of Sexuality. *Social Theory* 12(2): 188–202.

Erikson, E.H. 1951. *Childhood and Society*. New York: W.W. Norton.

Erikson, E.H. 1968. *Identity: Youth and Crisis*. London: Faber & Faber.

Ethnic Affairs Commission [EAC] of New South Wales 1978. *Participation*. Sydney: New South Wales Government Printer.

Featherstone, M. 1991. *Consumer Culture and Postmodernism*. London: Sage.

Fesl, E. 1990. How the English Language is Used to Put Us Kooris Down and Deny Us Our Rights. *Social Alternatives* 9(2): 35–7.

Fiske, J., B. Hodge and G. Turner. 1987. *Myths of Oz: Reading Australian Popular Culture*. Sydney: Allen & Unwin.

Fitzgerald, John 1995. Asian Studies and the National Interest. *Quadrant* 39(1–2): 53–6.

FitzGerald, S. 1988. *Immigration: A Commitment to Australia*. Canberra: AGPS.

FitzGerald, S. 1993a. Occasional Address, Honorary Doctorate of Letters. University of Tasmania, 24 April.

FitzGerald, S. 1993b. *Ethical Dimensions of Australia's Engagement With Asian Countries: Are There Any?* Sydney: St James Ethics Centre, Annual Lecture, 9 November.

FitzGerald, S. 1994. Don't Knock Oz's Moves Toward Asia. *Asian Business* 30(5): 3–5.

Fletcher, M.D. 1994a. Peter Carey's Post-Colonial Australia I: *Illywhacker*: Lies, Dependence, and Political History. In Stokes, ed., *Australian Political Ideas*, pp. 134–42.

Fletcher, M.D. 1994b. Peter Carey's Post-Colonial Australia II: *Oscar and Lucinda*: Misunderstanding, Victimisation, and Political History. In Stokes, ed., *Australian Political Ideas*, pp. 143–51.

Foley, G. 1988. Teaching Whites a Lesson. In Burgmann and Lee, eds, *Staining the Wattle*, pp. 198–207.

Foster, L. and D. Stockley, eds 1988. *Australian Multiculturalism: A Documentary History and Critique.* Clevedon, UK: Multilingual Matters.

Foucault, M. 1974. *The Archaeology of Knowledge.* Trans. A.M. Sheridan Smith. London: Tavistock.

Franklin, S. et al., eds 1991. *Off-Centre: Feminism and Cultural Studies.* London: Harper Collins.

Friedland, Sofja L. 1902. Entry in Autograph Book. 17 February, Vida Goldstein Papers, 67 VG, Fawcett Library.

Frow, J. 1985. Discourse and Power. *Economy and Society* 14(2): 193–214.

Frow, J. 1991. *What was Postmodernism?* Sydney: Local Consumption. Occasional Paper #11.

Fukuyama, F. 1992. *The End of History and the Last Man.* London: Hamish Hamilton.

Funabashi, Y. 1994. Asia's Great Awakening. *Weekend Australian* 15–16 January: 27.

Fuss, Diana J. 1989. *Essentially Speaking: Feminism, Nature and Difference.* New York and London: Routledge.

Gabay, A. 1992. *The Mystic Life of Alfred Deakin.* Cambridge: Cambridge University Press.

Galbally, F. 1978. *Migrant Services and Programs.* Canberra: AGPS.

Gardiner-Garden, J. 1993. *The Multiculturalism and Immigration Debate 1973–1993.* Canberra: Department of the Parliamentary Library.

Garnaut, R. 1989. *Australia and the Northeast Asian Ascendancy.* Canberra: AGPS.

Garnaut, R. 1992. Australia's Asia-Pacific Journey. *Australian Quarterly* 64(4): 359–77.

Garnaut, R. and P. Drysdale, eds 1994. *Asia Pacific Regionalism: Readings in International Economic Relations.* Sydney: Harper.

Garrison, Ellen W. 1902. Entry in Autograph Book. 18 April, Vida Goldstein Papers, 67 VG, Fawcett Library.

Gastin, D. 1994. Government Needs Strategy for APEC Now. *Australian* 21 November: 15.

Gellner, E. 1983. *Nations and Nationalism.* Oxford: Blackwell.

Gibb, D.M. 1973. *The Making of 'White Australia'.* Melbourne: Victoria Historical Association.

Giddens, A. 1991. *Modernity and Self-Identity: Self and Society in the Late Modern Age.* Cambridge: Polity.

Giddens, A. 1993. *The Consequences of Modernity.* Stanford: Stanford University Press.

Gilbert, K. 1971. My Countryman, My Country. *Identity* 1(1): 18, 23.

Gilbert, K. 1981. The Aboriginal Question. *Social Alternatives* 2(2): 34–5.

Gilbert, S. 1983. Soldier's Heart: Literary Men, Literary Women, and the Great War. *Signs* 8(3): 422–50.

Gilding, M. 1992. Men, Masculinity and Australian History. *Southern Review* 25(2): 60–8.

Gillen, K. 1993. Heritage and Identity: A Perspective from Ipswich. BA (Hons) thesis, Department of Anthropology and Sociology, University of Queensland.

Goh Chok Tong 1994. Strong Values the Backbone of Success. *Australian* 12 September: 11.

Goldstein, Vida 1902a. An Open Letter to the Women of the United States. *Woman's Sphere* 10 October: 218.

Goldstein, Vida 1902b. To America and Back, January–June 1902: A Lecture by
    Vida Goldstein. Manuscript. Vida Goldstein Papers, 67 VG, Fawcett Library.
Goldstein, Vida 1904. Miss Goldstein's Campaign. *Woman's Sphere* 15 January.
Goldstein, Vida 1930. Notes for a speech: 'Australia and National Righteousness'.
    Rischbieth Papers, NLA 2004/4/248.
Goodall, H. 1988. Crying Out for Land Rights. In Burgmann and Lee, eds,
    Staining the Wattle, pp. 181–98.
Goodall, H. 1994. Border Wars. Paper presented to Communal/Plural 2
    conference, University of Western Sydney, at the Australian Museum.
Goodall, H. 1995. New South Wales. In A. McGrath, ed., *Contested Ground:
    Australian Aborigines under the British Crown*. Sydney: Allen & Unwin,
    pp. 55–120.
Goodman, D., D.J. O'Hearn and C. Wallace-Crabbe, eds 1991. *Multicultural
    Australia: The Challenges of Change*. Newham, Vic: Scribe.
Goodwin, C.D. 1964. Evolution Theory in Australian Social Thought. *Journal of
    the History of Ideas* 25: 393–416.
Gordon, M. 1994. APEC The Next Challenge. *Weekend Australian* 19–20
    November: 26.
Gray, J.G. 1970. *The Warriors: Reflections on Men in Battle*. New York: Harper & Row.
Grassby, A.J. 1973. *A Multi-Cultural Society for the Future: Immigration Reference Paper*.
    Canberra: AGPS.
Green, T.H. 1941 [1879–80]. *Lectures on the Principles of Political Obligation*.
    London: Longmans, Green & Co.
Grimshaw, P. 1993. The 'Equals and Comrades of Men'?: *Tocsin* and 'the Woman
    Question'. In S. Magarey et al., eds, *Debutante Nation*, pp. 100–13.
Grosz, E. 1994. Identity and Difference: A Response. In P. James, ed., *Critical
    Politics*. Melbourne: Arena, pp. 29–33.
Guerin, B. 1886. The Development of National Character in Victoria. *Argus* 10
    July: 4.
Gunew, Sneja 1990. Denaturalizing Cultural Nationalisms: Multicultural Read-
    ings of Australia. In Homi K. Bhabha, ed., *Nation and Narration*. London:
    Routledge, pp. 99–120.
Gunnell, J.G. 1978. The Myth of Tradition. *American Political Science Review* 72:
    122–34.
Habermas, J. 1992. Citizenship and National Identity: Some Reflections on the
    Future of Europe. *Praxis International* 12(1): 1–19.
Hall, Catherine, Jane Lewis and Keith McClelland 1993. Introduction. *Gender
    and History: Special Issue on Gender, Nationalism and National Identity* 5(2):
    159–64.
Hall, S. 1987. Minimal Selves. In Appiganesi, ed., *Identity Documents* 6, pp. 44–6.
Hall, S. 1988a. *The Hard Road to Renewal*. London: Verso.
Hall, S. 1988b. The Toad in the Garden: Thatcherism Among the Theorists. In
    G. Nelson and L. Grossberg, eds, *Marxism and the Interpretation of Culture*.
    Houndmills: Macmillan, pp. 36–73.
Hall, S. 1989. The Meaning of New Times. In S. Hall and M. Jacques, eds, *New
    Times: The Changing Face of Politics in the 1990's*. London: Lawrence & Wishart,
    pp. 116–36.
Hall, S. 1990. Cultural Identity and Diaspora. In J. Rutherford, ed., *Identity:
    Community, Culture, Difference*. London: Lawrence & Wishart, pp. 222–37.
Hall, S. 1993a. Culture, Community, Nation. *Cultural Studies* 7(3): 349–63.
Hall, S. 1993b. Thatcherism Today. *New Statesman and Society* 26 November:
    14–16.

Hall, S. 1994. The Question of Cultural Identity. In *The Polity Reader in Cultural Theory*. Cambridge: Polity, pp. 119–25.

Hall, S. 1996. Introduction: Who Needs 'Identity'? In S. Hall and P. du Gay, eds, *Questions of Cultural Identity*. London: Sage, pp. 1–17.

Hall, S. and K-H. Chen 1996. The Formulation of a Diasporic Intellectual: An Interview with Stuart Hall by Kuan-Hsing Chen. In D. Morley and K-H. Chen, eds, *Critical Dialogues in Cultural Studies*. Routledge: London, pp. 484–503.

Hamilton, P. and S. Mathews, eds 1986. *American Dreams: Australian Movies*. Sydney: Currency.

Hancock, W. 1930. *Australia*. London: Edward Benn.

Hancock, W. 1961 [1930]. *Australia*. Brisbane: Jacaranda.

Harris, M. 1970. Again, The Great Australian Soul-search. *Australian* 7 November: 20.

Hartley, John 1993. *The Politics of Pictures*. London: Routledge.

Hartsock, N.C.M. 1982. The Barracks Community in Western Political Thought. *Women's Studies International Forum* 6(3/4): 283–86.

Hartsock, N.C.M. 1984. Prologue to a Feminist Critique of War and Politics. In J.H. Stiehm, ed., *Women's Views of the Political World of Men*. Dobbs Ferry, NY: Transnational, pp. 121–50.

Harvey, David 1990a. *The Condition of Postmodernity*. Oxford: Blackwell.

Harvey, David 1990b. Between Space and Time: Reflections on the Geographical Imagination. *Annals, Association of American Geographers* 80: 418–34.

Hegel, G. 1991 [1821]. *Elements of the Philosophy of Right*. Trans. H.B. Nisbet. Cambridge: Cambridge University Press.

Hill, R. 1994. Letter to the Editor. *Australian* 3 November: 8.

Hinder, Eleanor 1930. Letter to My Dear Friends in Many Continents, 12 February. Rischbieth Papers, NLA 2004/4/17.

Hirsch, G.C. and H. Hirsch 1990. Learning to Live Together: Political Socialization and the Formation of International Identity. *International Journal of Group Tensions* 20(4): 369–90.

Hirst, J. 1990. Australia's Absurd History: A Critique of Multiculturalism. *Overland* 117: 5–10.

Hirst, J. 1992. The Pioneer Legend. In Carroll, ed., *Intruders in the Bush*, 2nd edn, pp. 14–37.

Hobsbawm, E. and T. Ranger, eds 1983. *The Invention of Tradition*. Cambridge: Cambridge University Press.

Hocquenghem, G. 1993 [1978]. *Homosexual Desire*. Trans D. Dangoor. Durham, NC: Duke University Press.

Hogan, M. 1987. *The Sectarian Strand*. Melbourne: Penguin.

Hollinsworth, D. 1992. Discourses on Aboriginality and the Politics of Identity in Australia. *Oceania* 63(2): 137–55.

Hollis, M. 1977. *Models of Man*. Cambridge: Cambridge University Press.

Hollway, S. 1992. Multiculturalism as Public Administration: Myths, Challenges and Opportunities. *Australian Journal of Public Administration* 51(2): 248–54.

Honneth, A. 1995. *The Struggle for Recognition*. Cambridge: Polity Press.

hooks, bell 1990. *Yearning: Race, Gender and Cultural Politics*. Boston: South End Press.

Horne, D. ed. 1992. *The Trouble With Economic Rationalism*. Melbourne: Scribe.

Horne, D. 1994a. Identity Lies in Beliefs We Must All Uphold. *Australian* 8 February: 12.

Horne, D. 1994b. A Civic Identity – Not a National Identity. In M. Stephenson and C. Turner, eds, *Republic or Monarchy?* St Lucia: University of Queensland Press, pp. 34–49.

Horner, J. and M. Langton 1987. The Day of Mourning. In B. Gammage and P. Spearritt, eds, *Australians 1938.* Sydney: Fairfax Syme and Weldon, pp. 29–35.

Howard, J. 1995a. Yes, there was life before Whitlam. *Australian* 14 December: 9.

Howard, J. 1995b. Politics and Patriotism: A Reflection on the National Identity Debate. Address delivered at the Grand Hyatt Hotel, Melbourne, 13 December.

Howard, M. 1978. *War and the Liberal Conscience.* London: Temple Smith.

Howard, M.C., ed. 1982. *Aboriginal Power in Australian Society.* St Lucia: University of Queensland Press.

Hudson, W. 1991. Educational Policy and Geographic Romanticism. *Asian Studies Review* 15(1): 70–6.

Hughes, H. 1994. Centre Stage Will Be For Emperor Paul. Australia, Asia & APEC: Supplement. *Australian* 14 November: 6.

Hughes, W.M. 1970 [1910]. *The Case for Labor.* Sydney: Sydney University Press.

Humm, Maggie, ed. 1992. *Modern Feminisms.* New York: Columbia University Press.

Huston, N. 1982. Tales of War and Tears of Women. *Women's Studies International Forum* 6(3/4): 273–4.

Huston, N. 1986. The Matrix of War: Mothers and Heroes. In S.R. Suleiman, ed., *The Female Body in Western Culture: Contemporary Perspectives.* Cambridge MA: Harvard University Press, pp. 119–36.

Hutchinson, J. 1987. *The Dynamics of Cultural Nationalism.* London: Allen & Unwin.

Huttenback, R.A. 1976. *Racism and Empire: White Settlers and Colored Immigrants in the British Self-Governing Colonies 1830–1910.* Ithaca and London: Cornell University Press.

Inglis, K.S. 1991 [1988]. Multiculturalism and National Identity. In Price, ed., *Australian National Identity*, pp. 13–32.

Irigaray, L. 1985. Women on the Market. In *This Sex Which Is Not One.* Trans. Catherine Porter with Carolyn Burke. Ithaca: Cornell University Press, pp. 170–91.

Jacka, Elizabeth 1988. Australian Cinema: An Anachronism in the 1980s? In S. Dermody and E. Jacka, eds, *The Imaginary Industry: Australian Cinema in the 80s.* Sydney: Australian Film, Television and Radio School, pp. 117–30.

Jaensch, D. 1989. *The Hawke–Keating Hijack.* Sydney: Allen & Unwin.

Jakubowicz, A. 1984. State and Ethnicity: Multiculturalism as Ideology. In J. Jupp, ed., *Ethnic Politics in Australia.* Sydney: Allen & Unwin, pp. 14–28.

Jameson, F. 1991. *Postmodernism or the Cultural Logic of Late Capitalism.* London and New York: Verso.

Jenkins S. 1972. Letter to Forum. *Identity* 1(3): 11.

Jensen, H.I. 1909. *The Rising Tide.* Sydney: Workers Trustees.

Johnson, C. 1989. *The Labor Legacy.* Sydney: Allen & Unwin.

Johnson, C. 1990a. Labor Governments: Then and Now. *Current Affairs Bulletin* 67(5): 4–13.

Johnson, C. 1990b. Whose Consensus?: Women and the ALP. *Arena* 93: 85–104.

Johnson, C. 1993. Fightback and Masculine Identity: A Postscript on the 1993 Election. *Australian Feminist Studies* 17: 81–92.

Johnson, C. 1995. Women and Economic Citizenship: The Limits of Keating's Inclusive Social Democracy. *Just Policy* 2: 11–17.

Johnson, C. 1996. Shaping the Social: Keating's Integration of Social and Economic Policy. *Just Policy* 5: 9–16.

Johnston, Jill 1973. *Lesbian Nation: The Feminist Solution*. New York: Simon & Schuster.

Jones, D.J. and J. Hill-Burnett 1982. The Political Context of Ethnogenesis: An Australian Example. In Howard, ed., *Aboriginal Power in Australian Society*, pp. 214–46.

Jupp, J. 1986. *Don't Settle for Less*. Canberra: AGPS.

Jupp, J. ed. 1989. *The Challenge of Diversity: Policy Options for a Multicultural Australia*. Canberra: AGPS.

Jupp, J. 1991. Multicultural Public Policy. In Price, ed., *Australian National Identity*, pp. 139–54.

Jupp, J. 1993. The Ethnic Lobby and Immigration Policy. In J. Jupp and M. Kabala, eds, *The Politics of Australian Immigration*. Canberra: AGPS, pp. 204–21.

Jupp, J. 1994. Multiculturalism and Social Cohesion. Paper given to Australian Population Association, Annual Conference, September.

Kabarli, Marrangaroo 1966. Why Don't Aborigines Help Themselves? *Smoke Signals* 5(1): 19–21.

Kalantzis, Mary 1990. Ethnicity Meets Gender Meets Class in Australia. In S. Watson, ed., *Playing the State: Australian Feminist Interventions*. Sydney: Allen & Unwin, pp. 39–59.

Kamenka, E. 1993. 'Australia Made Me' ... But Which Australia Is Mine? *Quadrant* 37(10): 24–31.

Kantorowicz, E.H. 1957. *The King's Two Bodies: A Study in Mediæval Political Theology*. Princeton: Princeton University Press.

Kauffman, L.A. 1990. The Anti-Politics of Identity. *Socialist Review* 20(1): 5–11.

Keating, P. 1987. Traditions of Labor in Power: Whitlam and Hawke in the Continuum. In S. Loosley et al. *Traditions for Reform in New South Wales*. Sydney: Pluto, pp. 172–86.

Keating, P. 1992. Speech to the Federation of Ethnic Community Councils, Sydney, 12 August: 1–11.

Keating, P. 1993a. *Investing in the Nation*. Statement by the Prime Minister, The Honourable P.J. Keating, MP, 9 February.

Keating, P. 1993b. *Australian Labor Party Policy Speech, 1993 Federal Election*. Bankstown, 24 February.

Keating, P. 1993c. Only Option is to Become Master of Our Own Destiny. *Weekend Australian* 13–14 March: 34.

Keating, P. 1993d. Speech to His Personal Staff. Transcript in *Australian* 31 March: 9.

Keating, P. 1993e. Becoming a Republic Takes Courage. *Canberra Times* 29 April: 14.

Keating, P. 1994a. The Way Towards a Reshaped Future. *Australian* 24 February: 9.

Keating, P. 1994b. Spark For Creative Spirits. *Australian* 19 October: 13.

Keating, P. 1994c. Address to Asia–Australia Institute. Brisbane, 29 October.

Keating, P. 1995. Speech to National Social Policy Conference, University of New South Wales, Sydney, 7 July.

Keefe, K. 1988. Aboriginality: Resistance and Persistence. *Australian Aboriginal Studies* (1): 67–81.

Keene, I., ed. 1991. *Being Black: Aboriginal Culture in Settled Australia.* Canberra: Aboriginal Studies Press.

Keith, M. and S. Pile 1993. *Place and the Politics of Identity.* London: Routledge.

Kelly, P. 1992. *The End of Certainty: The Story of the 1980s.* Sydney: Allen & Unwin.

King, Edward 1993. *Safety in Numbers: Safer Sex and Gay Men.* London: Cassell.

Knopfelmacher, F. 1982. The Case Against Multi-culturalism. In R. Manne, ed., *The New Conservatism in Australia.* Melbourne: Oxford University Press, pp. 40–64.

Kolig, E. 1973/74. Progress and Preservation: An Aboriginal Perspective. *Anthropological Forum* 3(3): 264–79.

Kolig, E. 1982. An Obituary for Ritual Power. In Howard, ed., *Aboriginal Power in Australian Society*, pp. 14–31.

Kolig, E. 1989. *Dreamtime Politics: Religion, World View and Utopian Thought in Australian Aboriginal Society.* Berlin: Dietrich Reimer Verlag.

Krieger, J. 1991. Class, Consumption, and Collectivism: Perspectives on the Labour Party and Electoral Competition in Britain. In F. Fox Piven, ed., *Labour Parties in Postindustrial Societies.* Cambridge: Polity, pp. 47–70.

Kukathas, C. 1992. Are There Any Cultural Rights? *Political Theory* 20(1): 105–39.

Kukathas, C. 1993. Multiculturalism and the Idea of an Australian Identity. In C. Kukathas, ed., *Multicultural Citizens.* Sydney: Centre for Independent Studies, pp. 145–57.

Kymlicka, W. 1992. The Rights of Minority Cultures: Reply to Kukathas. *Political Theory* 20(1): 140–6.

Kymlicka, W. and W. Norman 1994. Return of the Citizen: A Survey of Recent Work on Citizenship Theory. *Ethics* 104: 352–81.

Lake, M. 1986a. The Politics of Respectability: Identifying the Masculinist Context. *Historical Studies* 22(86): 116–31.

Lake, M. 1986b. Socialism and Manhood: The Case of William Lane. *Labour History* 50: 54–62.

Lake, M. 1991. Socialism and Manhood: A Reply to Bruce Scates. *Labour History* 60: 114–20.

Lake, M. 1993. A Revolution in the Family: The Challenge and Contradictions of Maternal Citizenship. In S. Koven and S. Michel, eds, *Mothers of a New World: Maternalist Politics and Welfare States in Comparative Perspectives.* New York: Routledge, pp. 378–95.

Lane, W. 1980 [1892]. *The Workingman's Paradise.* Sydney: Sydney University Press.

Larbalestier, J. 1991. Through Their Own Eyes: An Interpretation of Aboriginal Women's Writing. In Bottomley et al., eds, *Intersexions*, pp. 75–91.

Lash, S. and J. Friedman, eds 1992a. *Modernity and Identity.* Oxford: Blackwell.

Lash, S. and J. Friedman 1992b. Introduction: Subjectivity and Modernity's Other. In Lash and Friedman, eds, *Modernity and Identity*, pp. 1–30.

Lattas, A. 1993. Essentialism, Memory and Resistance: Aboriginality and the Politics of Authenticity. *Oceania* 63(3): 240–67.

Lee Kuan Yew 1993. Is Democracy Necessary? *Weekend Australian* 24–25 April: 20.

Lee Kuan Yew 1994. Rich Resource Base a Poor Spur to Growth. *Australian* 19 April: 13.

Letters to the Editor 1991. *Women's Studies International Forum* 14(5): 403–16.

Liberal Party of Australia 1991. *Fightback! It's Your Australia: The Way to Rebuild and Reward Australia.* Canberra: Liberal Party of Australia.

Linnekin, J.S. and L. Poyer, eds 1990a. *Cultural Identity and Ethnicity in the Pacific.* Honolulu: University of Hawaii Press.

Linnekin, J.S. and L. Poyer 1990b. Introduction. In Linnekin and Poyer, eds, *Cultural Identity and Ethnicity in the Pacific*, pp. 1–16.

Loraux, N. 1981. Le lit, la guerre. *L'Homme* 20(1): 37–67.

Loraux, N. 1987. *Tragic Ways of Killing a Woman*. Trans. Anthony Forster. Cambridge MA: Harvard University Press.

Lyotard, J-F. 1984. *The Postmodern Condition: A Report on Knowledge*. Trans. G. Bennington and B. Massumi. Minneapolis: University of Minneapolis Press.

Mabo v Queensland (Mabo No. 2) 1992. 107 ALR 1.

McAllister, I. and R. Moore 1989. *Ethnic Prejudice in Australian Society: Patterns, Intensity and Explanations*. Canberra: Office of Multicultural Affairs.

McAuley, J. 1962. Literature and the Arts. In P. Coleman, ed., *Australian Civilization*. Sydney: F.W. Cheshire, pp. 122–33.

McClelland, K. 1991. Masculinity and the Representative Artisan. In Roper and Tosh, eds, *Manful Assertions*, pp. 74–91.

McConville, C. 1987. Rough Women, Respectable Men and Social Reform: A Response to Lake's 'Masculinism'. *Historical Studies* 22(88): 432–40.

McEachern, D. 1991. *Business Mates: The Power and Politics of the Hawke Era*. Sydney: Prentice Hall.

McGregor, R. 1993. Protest and Progress: Aboriginal Activism in the 1930s. *Australian Historical Studies* 25(101): 555–68.

McGregor, Richard 1994. Mahathir Attacks PM's Asian Trade Drive. *Australian* 25 October: 5.

McGrew, A.G. and P.G. Lewis 1992. *Global Politics: Globalisation and the Nation-State*. Cambridge: Polity.

McGuinness, P.P. 1993. A Confident Nation Has No Problems With Identity. *Weekend Australian* 2–3 October: 2.

Machiavelli, N. 1970 [1531]. *The Discourses*. Trans. Leslie J. Walker. Harmondsworth: Penguin.

McKenzie, S. 1994. Ignorance Responsible for Australia's Image Problem in Asia. *Weekend Australian* 13–14 August: 14.

MacKenzie, C. 1929. *Gallipoli Memories*. London: Cassell.

Mackenzie, W.J.M. 1978. *Political Identity*. New York: St Martin's Press.

Mackie, J. 1992. East and West: The Best of Both Worlds. *Australian* 15 December: 11.

McLeod, H. 1981. *Religion and the People of Western Europe*. Oxford: Oxford University Press.

McNamara, N. 1990. Australian Aborigines: A Question of Identity. In B. Hocking, ed., *Australia Towards 2000*. London: Macmillan, pp. 95–9.

McNeil, M. 1991a. Making and Not Making the Difference: The Gender Politics of Thatcherism. In Franklin et al., eds, *Off-Centre*, pp. 21–48.

McNeil, M. 1991b. Reflections on Eleven Years of Gender Politics. *Magazine of Cultural Studies* Spring: 12–17.

McQueen, H. 1970. *A New Britannia*. Melbourne: Penguin.

McQueen, H. 1978. *Social Sketches of Australia 1888–1975*. Melbourne: Penguin.

McQueen, H. 1986. *A New Britannia: An Argument Concerning the Social Origins of Australian Radicalism and Nationalism*, rev. edn. Melbourne: Penguin.

Maddox, G. 1989. *The Hawke Government and Labor Tradition*. Melbourne: Penguin.

Magarey, S., S. Rowley and S. Sheridan, eds 1993. *Debutante Nation: Feminism Contests the 1890s*. Sydney: Allen & Unwin.

Malouf, David 1978. *An Imaginary Life*. London: Chatto & Windus.

Malouf, David 1990. *The Great World*. London: Chatto & Windus.

Malouf, David 1993. *Remembering Babylon*. New York: Random House.

Mandle, W.F. 1980. *Going it Alone: Australia's National Identity in the Twentieth Century*. Melbourne: Penguin.

Manning, H. 1992. The ALP and the Union Movement: 'Catch-All' Party or Maintaining Tradition? *Australian Journal of Political Science* 27(1): 12–30.

Mansell, M. 1989. How the Bicentenary Helped the Aboriginal Nation Grow. *Social Alternatives* 8(1): 9–11.

Mansell, M. 1990. Provisional Future: Provisional Solution. *Weekend Australian* 30 June–1 July: 21.

Mansell, M. 1993. Australians and Aborigines and the Mabo Decision: Just Who Needs Whom the Most? In *Essays on the Mabo Decision*. Sydney: Law Book Company, pp. 48–57.

Mansfield, B.C. 1954. The Origins of 'White Australia'. *Australian Quarterly* 26(4): 61–8.

Markus, A. 1973. White Australia? Socialists and Anarchists. *Arena* 32/33: 80–9.

Markus, A. 1983. William Cooper and the 1937 Petition to the King. *Aboriginal History* 7(1): 46–60.

Markus, A. 1988. *Blood From a Stone: William Cooper and the Australian Aborigines' League*. Sydney: Allen & Unwin.

Martin, J. 1972. *Community and Identity*. Canberra: Australian National University Press.

Martin, J. 1981. *The Ethnic Dimension: Papers on Ethnicity and Pluralism*. Sydney: Allen & Unwin.

Martin, Jeannie 1991. Multiculturalism and Feminism. In Bottomley et al., eds, *Intersexions*, pp. 110–31.

Masefield, J. 1978 [1916]. *Gallipoli*. Adelaide: Rigby.

Matustik, M.J. 1993. Post-National Identity: Habermas, Kierkegaard and Havel. *Thesis Eleven* 34: 89–103.

Melleuish, G. 1985. Beneficent Providence and the Quest for Harmony: The Cultural Setting for Colonial Science in Sydney, 1850–1890. *Journal and Proceedings, Royal Society of New South Wales* 118: 167–80.

Melleuish, G. 1993. The Case for Civilisation: An Australian Perspective. *Thesis Eleven* 34: 156–64.

Melleuish, G. 1994. Utopians and Sceptics: Competing Images of Democracy in Australia. In Stokes, ed., *Australian Political Ideas*, pp. 114–33.

Melleuish, G. 1995. *Cultural Liberalism in Australia*. Cambridge: Cambridge University Press.

Mieli, Mario 1980. *Homosexuality and Liberation*. Trans. David Fernbach. London: Gay Men's Press.

Milburn, C. 1994. The Fraying of Multiculturalism. *Age* 19 March: 15.

Mishra, V. and G. Hodge 1993. What is Post(-)colonialism? In J. Frow and M. Morris, eds, *Australian Cultural Studies: A Reader*. Sydney: Allen & Unwin, pp. 30–46.

Mitchell, A. 1973. *Colonial Poets: Charles Harpur*. Melbourne: Sun Books.

Mohr, R.D. 1988. *Gays/Justice: A Study of Ethics, Society, and Law*. New York: Columbia University Press.

Moorehead, A. 1978. *Gallipoli*. London: Hamish Hamilton.

Moraga, C. and G. Anzaldua, eds 1984. *This Bridge Called My Back: Writings by Radical Women of Color*. Latham NY: Kitchen Table.

Moran, A. and T. O'Regan, eds 1985. *Australian Film Reader*. Sydney: Currency Press.

Morris, B. 1988a. The Politics of Identity: From Aborigines to the First Australian. In Beckett, ed., *Past and Present*, pp. 63–85.

Morris, B. 1988b. Dhan-gadi resistance to assimilation. In Keene, ed., *Being Black*, pp. 33–63.

Morris, B. 1989. *The Dhan-gadi Aborigines and the Australian State.* Oxford: Oxford University Press.

Morris, M. 1992. *Ecstasy and Economics: American Essays for John Forbes.* Sydney: Empress.

Morton, Donald 1993. The Politics of Queer Theory in the (Post)Modern Movement. *Genders* 17: 121–49.

Moss, I. 1993. *State of the Nation: Report on People of Non-English Speaking Backgrounds.* Sydney: Federal Race Discrimination Commissioner.

Mouffe, C. 1990. Radical Democracy or Liberal Democracy? *Socialist Review* 20(2): 57–67.

Muetzelfeldt, M., ed. 1992. *Society, State and Politics in Australia.* Sydney: Pluto.

Muller, Florence F. 1902. Entry in Autograph Book. Vida Goldstein Papers, 67 VG, Fawcett Library.

Munroe, C. 1992. *Inky Stephensen: Wild Man of Letters.* St Lucia: University of Queensland Press.

Murray, R. 1993. Menzies in Asia. *Australian* 7 January: 11.

Nason, D. 1994. Asia Trend Challenges Our Rights Policies. *Weekend Australian* 29–30 October: 2.

National Aboriginal Conference 1989. Aboriginal Ideology and Philosophy of the Land. In H. Reynolds, comp., *Dispossession.* Sydney: Allen & Unwin, pp. 88–92.

Nava, M. 1992. *Changing Cultures: Feminism, Youth and Consumerism.* London: Sage.

Newcomb, Harriet 1918. Letter to Bessie Rischbieth, 9 June. Rischbieth Papers, NLA 2004/4/7.

Newfong, J. 1972. The Aboriginal Embassy: Its Purpose and Aims. *Identity* 1(5): 4–6.

Norris, C. 1992. *Uncritical Theory: Postmodernism, Intellectuals and the Gulf War.* London: Lawrence & Wishart.

Northcott, C.H. 1918. *Australian National Development.* New York: Columbia University.

Nussbaum, Martha 1994. Patriotism and Cosmopolitanism. *Boston Review* XIX (5): 3–6.

Office of Multicultural Affairs [OMA] 1989a. *National Agenda for a Multicultural Australia.* Canberra: AGPS.

Office of Multicultural Affairs [OMA] 1989b. *Issues in Multicultural Australia, 1988: Frequency Tables.* Canberra: Social Science Data Archives.

Office of Multicultural Affairs [OMA] 1992. *Access and Equity Evaluation Report.* Canberra: AGPS.

O'Sullivan, N. 1993. Political Integration, the Limited State, and the Philosophy of Postmodernism. *Political Studies* XLI: 21–42.

Paisley, Fiona 1993. 'Don't Tell England': Women of Empire Campaign to Change Aboriginal Policy in Australia Between the Wars. *Lilith* 8 Summer: 139–52.

Palfreeman, A.C. 1971. The White Australia Policy. In F.S. Stevens, ed., *Racism: The Australian Experience*, vol. 1. Sydney: ANZ Book Co., pp. 136–44.

Palmer, V. 1954. *The Legend of the Nineties.* Melbourne: Melbourne University Press.

Partington, G. 1994. *The Australian Nation: Its British and Irish Roots*. Melbourne: Australian Scholarly Publishing.

Passmore, J. 1988. Australian Philosophy or Philosophy in Australia? *Age Monthly Review* 15–16 July and 17–19 August.

Passmore, J. 1992. Europe in the Pacific. *Quadrant* 26(9): 10–19.

Patten, J.T. and W. Ferguson 1938. *Aborigines Claim Citizen Rights!* Sydney: The Publicist.

Patton, Cindy 1993. Tremble, Hetero Swine! In Warner, ed., *Fear of a Queer Planet*, pp. 143–77.

Pearson, C.H. 1894. *National Life and Character: A Forecast*, 2nd edn. London: Macmillan.

Pearson, N. 1994a. Aboriginal Law and Colonial Law Since Mabo. In C. Fletcher, ed., *Aboriginal Self-Determination in Australia*. Canberra: Aboriginal Studies Press, pp. 155–9.

Pearson, N. 1994b. Mabo: Towards Respecting Equality and Difference. In Yunupingu et al., *Voices From the Land*, pp. 89–101.

Pearson, N. 1994c. A Troubling Inheritance. *Race & Class* 35(4): 1–9.

Penelhum, T. 1967. Personal Identity. In P. Edwards, ed., *The Encyclopedia of Philosophy*, vol. 6. New York: Macmillan, pp. 95–107.

Peressini, M. 1993. Identity – A Card With Two Faces. *UNESCO Courier* June: 14–18.

Perkins, C. 1968. Letter to Harold Holt. *Quadrant* January–February: 34–8.

Pettman, J. 1992. Gendered Knowledges: Aboriginal Women and the Politics of Feminism. In Attwood and Arnold, eds, *Power, Knowledge and Aborigines*, pp. 120–31.

Phillips, A.A. 1950. The Cultural Cringe. *Meanjin* 9(4): 299–302.

Phillips, A.A. 1988. Cultural Nationalism in the 1940s and 1950s: A Personal Account. In B. Head and J. Walter, eds, *Intellectual Movements and Australian Society*. Melbourne: Oxford University Press, pp. 129–44.

Plato 1989. *Symposium*. Trans. Alexander Nehamas and Paul Woodruff. Indianapolis: Hackett.

Plummer, K., ed. 1981. *The Making of the Modern Homosexual*. Totowa NJ: Barnes & Noble.

Pocock, J.G.A. 1992. The Idea of Citizenship Since Classical Times. *Queen's Quarterly* 99: 33–55.

Pons, Xavier 1991. Savage Paradise: History, Violence and the Family in Some Recent Australian Fiction. *Australian Literary Studies* 15(2): 72–82.

Poole, R. 1985. Structures of Identity: Gender and Nationalism. In P. Patton and R. Poole, eds, *War/Masculinity*. Sydney: Intervention, pp. 71–9.

Popper, K.R. 1966 [1945]. *The Open Society and Its Enemies*, 5th edn. 2 vols. London: Routledge.

Price, C.A., ed. 1991. *Australian National Identity*. Canberra: Academy of the Social Sciences in Australia.

Rabinow, P. 1984. *The Foucault Reader: An Introduction to Foucault's Thought*. London: Penguin.

Ramusack, B. 1992. Cultural Missionaries, Maternal Imperialists, Feminist Allies. In N. Chaudhuri and M. Strobel, eds, *Western Women and Imperialism*. Bloomington: Indiana University Press, pp. 119–36.

Rich, Adrienne 1980. Compulsory Heterosexuality and Lesbian Existence. *Signs* 5(4): 631–60.

Rimmer, S. 1988. *Fiscal Anarchy: The Public Funding of Multiculturalism*. Perth: Australian Institute for Public Policy.

Rintoul, S. 1993. *The Wailing: A National Black Oral History.* Melbourne: Heinemann.

Rischbieth, Bessie 1924. Letter to Carrie Chapman Catt, 24 November. Rischbieth Papers, NLA 2004/7/62.

Rischbieth, Bessie 1926. Letter to Carrie Chapman Catt, 22 July. Rischbieth Papers, NLA 2004/7/73.

Rischbieth, Bessie 1931. Letter to Senator G. Pearce, 24 March. Rischbieth Papers, NLA 2004/12/4.

Rischbieth, Bessie 1935. Notes for an address: 'Women's Work in the Empire'. Rischbieth Papers, NLA 2004/4/97.

Roe, J. 1986. *Beyond Belief: Theosophy in Australia 1879–1939.* Sydney: University of New South Wales Press.

Roper, M. and J. Tosh, eds 1991. *Manful Assertions: Masculinities in Britain Since 1800.* London: Routledge.

Rorty, Amelie O. 1994. The Hidden Politics of Multiculturalism. *Political Theory* 22(1): 152–66.

Rose, M.A. 1991. *The Post-modern and the Post-industrial: A Critical Analysis.* Cambridge: Cambridge University Press.

Roth, J. 1986. The Bust of the Emperor. In *Hotel Savoy.* Trans. J. Hoare. London: Picador Classics.

Rousseau, J-J. 1973 [1762]. *The Social Contract and Discourses.* Trans. G.D.H. Cole. London: Dent.

Rowse, T. 1978. *Australian Liberalism and National Character.* Malmsbury, Vic.: Kibble Books.

Rowse, T. 1985. On the Notion of Aboriginality: A Discussion. *Oceania* 15(1): 45–6.

Rowse, T. 1991. ATSIC's Heritage: The Problems of Leadership and Unity in Aboriginal Political Culture. *Current Affairs Bulletin* 67(8): 4–13.

Rowse, T. 1993. Rethinking Aboriginal 'Resistance': The Community Development Employment (CDEP) Program. *Oceania* 63(3): 268–86.

Rowse, T. 1994. The Principles of Aboriginal Pragmatism. In M. Goot and T. Rowse, eds, *Make a Better Offer.* Sydney: Pluto, pp. 185–93.

Rowse, T. 1994/95. Expert Testimony. *Arena Magazine* 14: 32–5.

Ruddick, S. 1983. Pacifying the Forces: Drafting Women in the Interests of Peace. *Signs* 8(3): 471–89.

Said, E.W. 1978. *Orientalism.* London: Routledge.

Sampson, Edward 1993. Identity Politics: Challenges to Psychology's Understanding. *American Psychologist* 48(12): 1219–30.

Sandel, M. 1982. *Liberalism and the Limits of Justice.* Cambridge: Cambridge University Press.

Sato, S. and Taylor, T., eds 1993. *Prospects for Global Order.* London: Royal Institute of International Affairs.

Saunders, K. and R. Evans, eds 1992. *Gender Relations in Australia: Domination and Negotiation.* Sydney: Harcourt Brace Jovanovich.

Sawer, M. 1990. *Public Perceptions of Multiculturalism.* Canberra: Centre for Immigration and Multicultural Studies.

Scates, B. 1990. Socialism, Feminism, and the Case of William Lane: A Reply to Marilyn Lake. *Labour History* 59: 45–59.

Schlesinger, Phillip 1991. *Media, State, and Nation.* London: Sage.

Scott, J. 1988. *Gender and the Politics of History.* New York: Columbia University Press.

Scott, Rose 1903. Letter to Vida Goldstein. In *Federal Senate Election: Miss Vida Goldstein's Candidature*. Rischbieth Papers, NLA 2004/4/311.

Sedgwick, E.K. 1985. *Between Men: English Literature and Male Homosocial Desire*. New York: Columbia University Press.

Segal, L. 1987. *Is the Future Female? Troubled Thoughts on Contemporary Feminism*. London: Virago.

Seidman, Steven 1993. Identity and Politics in a 'Postmodern' Gay Culture. In Warner, ed., *Fear of a Queer Planet*, pp. 105–42.

Serle, G. 1973. *From Deserts the Prophets Come: The Creative Spirit in Australia 1788–1972*. Melbourne: Heinemann.

Sestito, R. 1982. *The Politics of Multiculturalism*. Sydney: Centre for Independent Studies.

Shaffer, Kay 1988. *Women and the Bush: Forces of Desire in the Australian Cultural Tradition*. Cambridge: Cambridge University Press.

Shapiro, I. 1994. Three Ways to be a Democrat. *Political Theory* 22(1): 124–51.

Shapiro, Michael J. 1992. *Reading the Postmodern Polity: Political Theory as Textual Practice*. Minneapolis: University of Minnesota Press.

Shaw, G., ed. 1988a. *1988 and All That: New Views of Australia's Past*. St Lucia: University of Queensland Press.

Shaw, G. 1988b. Historical Context of Theological Thought in Australia. *St Mark's Review* 133: 14–21.

Sheridan, G. 1994a. The APEC Heretics. *Australian* 15 December: 25.

Sheridan, G. 1994b. Truth the First Victim in Keating's Foreign Policy Excess. *Australian* 21 December: 13.

Sheridan, G. 1995a. Howard's Big Regret. *Weekend Australian* 7–8 January: 19.

Sheridan, G. 1995b. Lure of the East. *Weekend Australian* 25–26 March: 24.

Shute, C. 1975. Heroines & Heroes: Sexual Mythology in Australia 1914–1918. *Hecate* 1(1): 7–22.

Smith, A.D. 1991a. *National Identity*. Harmondsworth: Penguin.

Smith, A.D. 1991b. The Nation: Invented, Imagined, Reconstructed? *Millennium* 20(3): 353–68.

Smolicz, J.J. 1991. Who is an Australian? In Price, ed., *Australian National Identity*, pp. 41–66.

Soja, E. 1989. *Postmodern Geographies: The Reassertion of Space in Critical Theory*. London: Verso.

Spain, D. 1992. *Gendered Spaces*. Chapel Hill: University of North Carolina Press.

Spence, W.G. 1909. *Australia's Awakening*. Sydney: Workers Trustees.

Spivak, G.C. 1990. *The Post-colonial Critic*. Edited by S. Harasym. New York and London: Routledge.

St Ledger, A. 1909. *Australian Socialism: An Historical Sketch of its Origins and Developments*. London: Macmillan.

Stacey, J. 1991. Promoting Normality: Section 28 and the Regulation of Sexuality. In S. Franklin et al., eds, *Off-Centre*, pp. 284–304.

Steedman, C. 1991. Living Historically Now. *Arena* 97: 48–64.

Steinberg, L. 1983. *The Sexuality of Christ in Renaissance Art and in Modern Oblivion*. New York: Pantheon.

Stilwell, F. 1993. Economic Rationalism: Sound Foundations for Policy? In S. Rees et al., eds, *Beyond the Market: Alternatives to Economic Rationalism*. Sydney: Pluto, pp. 27–37.

Stokes, G., ed. 1994a. *Australian Political Ideas*. Sydney: University of New South Wales Press.

Stokes, G. 1994b. Towards a National Trade Strategy. *Australian Quarterly* 66(1): 74–95.

Stokes, G. 1995. Politics, Epistemology and Method: Karl Popper's Conception of Human Nature. *Political Studies* 43(1): 105–23.

Stone, J. nd. *On Being An Australian*. np.

Stone, J. 1985. *De-regulate or Perish*. Perth: Institute of Public Affairs.

Stretton, P. and C. Finnimore 1993. Black Fellow Citizens: Aborigines and the Commonwealth Franchise. *Australian Historical Studies* 25(101): 521–35.

Strong, T.B. ed. 1992. Introduction: The Self and the Political Order. In T. B. Strong, ed., *The Self and the Political Order*. New York: New York University Press, pp. 1–21.

Suryakusuma, J. 1994. Can the Eagle and the Kangaroo Co-exist? *Special Review: Asians in Australia*. *Australian* 15 March: 3.

Tamamotu, M. 1994. The Ideology of Nothingness: A Meditation on Japanese National Identity. *World Policy Journal* 11(1): 89–99.

Tatz, C., ed. 1975. *Black Viewpoints*. Sydney: ANZ Book Co.

Taussig, M. 1987. An Australian Hero. *History Workshop* 24: 111–33.

Taylor, C. 1992. *Multiculturalism and 'The Politics of Recognition'*. Princeton: Princeton University Press.

Theweleit, K. 1987. *Male Fantasies*, vol. 1. Trans. Stephen Conway. Minneapolis: University of Minnesota Press.

Theweleit, K. 1989. *Male Fantasies*, vol. 2. Trans. Chris Turner and Erica Carter. Cambridge: Polity.

Thiele, S.J. 1984. Anti-Intellectualism and the 'Aboriginal Problem': Colin Tatz and the 'Self-Determination' Approach. *Mankind* 14(3): 165–78.

Thomas, J. 1993. Citizenship and Historical Sensibility. *Australian Historical Studies* 25(100): 383–93.

Thompson, E. 1994. *Fair Enough: Egalitarianism in Australia*. Sydney: University of New South Wales Press.

Thucydides 1972. *History of the Peloponnesian War*. Trans. Rex Warner. Harmondsworth: Penguin.

Tiffin, H. 1988. Post-colonialism, Postmodernism and the Rehabilitation of Post-colonial History. *Journal of Commonwealth Literature* 23(1): 169–81.

Tiffin, H. 1991. Introduction. In I. Adam and H. Tiffin, eds, *Past the Last Post: Theorizing Post-Colonialism and Post-Modernism*. Hemel Hempstead: Harvester/ Wheatsheaf, pp. vii–xvi.

Tilly, C. 1992. *Coercion, Capital and European States: AD 990–1992*. Cambridge MA: Blackwell.

Tomlinson, A. 1990. *Consumption, Identity and Style*. London: Routledge.

Tonkinson, M.E. 1990. Is It In the Blood? Australian Aboriginal Identity. In Linnekin and Poyer, eds, *Cultural Identity and Ethnicity in the Pacific*, pp. 191–218.

Touraine, A. 1991. What Does Democracy Mean Today? *International Social Science Journal* 128: 259–68.

Trood, R., ed. 1993. *The Future Pacific Order*. Brisbane: Centre for the Study of Australia–Asia Relations, Griffith University.

Truax, Alice 1993. The Wild Boy (review of *Remembering Babylon*). *New York Review of Books* XL(20): 13–15.

Turner, Graeme 1986. *National Fictions: Literature, Film, and the Construction of Australian Narrative*. Sydney: Allen & Unwin.

Turner, Graeme 1994. *Making It National: Nationalism and Australian Popular Culture*. Sydney: Allen & Unwin.

Unger, R.M. 1976. *Knowledge and Politics*. New York: Free Press.

Vance, Carole, ed. 1984. *Pleasure and Danger: Exploring Female Sexuality*. Boston: Routledge.

Walker, D. 1976. *Dream and Disillusion: A Search for Australian Cultural Identity*. Canberra: Australian National University Press.

Walker, D. 1994. A Brief History of the Future. *Australian Book Review* 158: 34–8.

Walker, J. 1994. Land Fund a Cause Divided. *Australian* 16 November: 15.

Wallace-Crabbe, C. 1990. Beyond the Cringe: Australian Cultural Over-confidence. *Age Monthly Review* 9(12): 5–8.

Ward, R. 1966. *The Australian Legend*, 2nd edn. Melbourne: Oxford University Press.

Ware, Vron 1992. *Beyond the Pale White Women: Racism and History*. London: Verso.

Warner, M. 1985. *Monuments and Maidens*. London: Picador.

Warner, M., ed. 1993. *Fear of a Queer Planet*. Minneapolis: University of Minnesota Press.

Warren, Patricia N. 1979. *The Beauty Queen*. New York: Bantam.

Watney, Simon 1989. *Policing Desire: Pornography, AIDS, and the Media*. Minneapolis: University of Minnesota Press.

Watson, S., ed. 1990. *Playing the State: Australian Feminist Interventions*. Sydney: Allen & Unwin.

Watts, R. 1990. Living Standards and the Hawke Government 1983–89. In I. Taylor, ed., *The Social Effects of Free Market Policies*. New York: Harvester/Wheatsheaf, pp. 143–74.

Weber, M. 1970 [1915]. The Political Sphere. In H.H. Gerth and C.W. Mills, eds, *From Max Weber: Essays in Sociology*. London: Routledge & Kegan Paul, pp. 333–40.

Weeks, Jeffrey 1991. *Against Nature: Essays on History, Sexuality and Identity*. London: Rivers Oram Press.

Weil, S. 1977 [1940]. The *Iliad*, Poem of Might. In G.A. Panichas, ed., *The Simone Weil Reader*. New York: David McKay, pp. 153–83.

Weil, S. 1978 [1949]. *The Need for Roots*. Trans. A.F. Wills. London: Routledge.

Wells, D. 1990. *In Defence of the Common Wealth*. Melbourne: Longman Cheshire.

West, D. 1994. Indigenous Media. In Yunupingu et al., *Voices from the Land*, pp. 12–29.

West, J. ['John Adams'] 1854. Letters on Australian Federation. *Sydney Morning Herald* 5 May.

Whelan, J. 1992. Homosexuality No Bar in Many Foreign Forces. *Sydney Morning Herald* 25 November: 6.

White, C. 1992a. Mastering Risk. In Carroll and Manne, eds, *Shutdown*, pp. 27–37.

White, C. 1992b. Australia and the Forgotten Economies of the Pacific Basin. Paper presented to conference on National Strategies for Australasian Countries in the Age of the Asian/Pacific Economy. 19–21 June, Surfers Paradise.

White, R. 1981. *Inventing Australia: Images and Identity 1688–1980*. Sydney: Allen & Unwin.

Whiteman, B. 1995. Australia Part of East Asia: Foreign Minister. *Insight* 4(4): 12.

Willard, M. 1923. *History of the White Australia Policy*. Melbourne: Melbourne University Press.

Willis, Anne-Marie 1993. *Illusions of Identity: The Arts of Nation*. Sydney: Hale & Iremonger.

Winant, Howard 1993. Amazing Race. *Socialist Review* 23(2): 161–83.

Wittig, Monique 1992. One Is Not Born a Woman. *Feminist Issues* 1(2): 47–54.

Wolin, S. 1960. *Politics and Vision: Continuity and Innovation in Western Political Thought.* Boston: Little Brown.

Women's Political Association, Victoria [WPA] 1903. Women's Suffrage, Roll of Honour. Rischbieth Papers, NLA 2004/4/98.

Wong, Loong 1992. Ethnicity, the State and the Public Agenda. In M. Muetzelfeldt, ed., *Society, State and Politics in Australia.* Sydney: Pluto, pp. 302–25.

Wood, D. 1992. *The Power of Maps.* New York: Guildford Press.

Woolcott, R. 1993. We Must Be the Odd Man In. *Weekend Australian* 17–18 April: 8.

Woolley, J. 1862. *Lectures Delivered in Australia.* London: Macmillan.

Wright, T. 1992. Cadets Fined Over Gay Games. *Sydney Morning Herald* 23 July: 3.

Wrigley, A. 1994. Pragmatist's Flattery Will Get Us Nowhere. *Australian* 30 August: 13.

Yarwood, A.T. 1962. The 'White Australia' Policy: A Re-interpretation of its Development in the Late Colonial Period. *Historical Studies* 10(39): 257–69.

Yarwood, A.T. 1968. *Attitudes to Non-European Immigration.* Melbourne: Cassell.

Yeatman, Anna 1984. Despotism and Civil Society: The Limits of Patriarchal Citizenship. In Judith Stiehm, ed., *Women's Views of the Political World of Men.* New York: Transnational Publishers, pp. 151–77.

Yeatman, Anna 1994. *Postmodern Revisionings of the Political.* New York and London: Routledge.

Yeatman, Anna 1995. Justice and the Sovereign Self. In M. Wilson and A. Yeatman, eds, *Justice and Identity: Antipodean Practices.* Sydney: Allen & Unwin, pp. 195–211.

Young, Iris M. 1990. *Justice and the Politics of Difference.* Princeton: Princeton University Press.

Yunupingu, M. et al. 1994. *Voices From the Land: 1993 Boyer Lectures.* Sydney: Australian Broadcasting Commission.

Zaretsky, E. 1994. Identity Theory, Identity Politics: Psychoanalysis, Marxism, Post-Structuralism. In Calhoun, ed., *Social Theory and the Politics of Identity,* pp. 198–215.

Zubrzycki, J. 1968. *The Questing Years.* Canberra: Citizenship Convention/ Department of Immigration.

Zubrzycki, J. 1982. *Multiculturalism for All Australians.* Canberra: AGPS.

Zubrzycki, J. 1991. The Evolution of Multiculturalism. In Price, ed., *Australian National Identity,* pp. 117–38.

Index

DATE DUE

DEC 0 9 2000		
FEB 1 8 2005		

Demco, Inc. 38-293